Modern Trinitarian Perspectives

Modern Trinitarian Perspectives

John Thompson

New York   Oxford
OXFORD UNIVERSITY PRESS
1994

Oxford University Press

Oxford   New York   Toronto
Delhi   Bombay   Calcutta   Madras   Karachi
Kuala Lumpur   Singapore   Hong Kong   Tokyo
Nairobi   Dar es Salaam   Cape Town
Melbourne   Auckland   Madrid

and associated companies in
Berlin   Ibadan

Copyright © 1994 by John Thompson

Published by Oxford University Press, Inc.
200 Madison Avenue, New York, New York 10016

Oxford is a registered trademark of Oxford University Press, Inc.

Library of Congress Cataloging-in-Publication Data
Thompson, John, 1922–
Modern trinitarian perspectives / John Thompson.
p. cm. Includes index.
ISBN 0-19-508898-0
ISBN 0-19-508899-9 (pbk.)
1. Trinity—History of doctrines—20th century.
I. Title.
BT109.T46   1994
231'.044'0904—dc20
93-37573

2 4 6 8 9 7 5 3 1

Printed in the United States of America
on acid-free paper

Preface

This book is an attempt to draw together much of the work that has been carried out in the field of trinitarian theology over the past twenty years. During that time the doctrine of the Trinity has emerged from relative obscurity to become the focus of renewed attention by theologians and to be seen as relevant to practical church life. One reason for this is the renewed interest in ecumenical dialogue between the Latin theology of the Western tradition represented mainly by Karl Barth and Karl Rahner, and Eastern Orthodox thought going back to the Cappadocian fathers. In fact Western contact with the East and the adoption of aspects of the latter's view has been a focal point in much of the modern debate.

Another reason for this renewed interest in the Trinity is the critique of scholasticism in favour of a new, dynamic understanding of the nature of the living God and the consequent theological task. This is particularly noticeable in the adoption of an approach by some Western theologians which is very close to a social view of the Trinity similar to that in the East. Several consequences flow from this. One means defining the Trinity as "being in relationship"; another is seeing it as the paradigm for the community of the church and its worship and also for social and political life. At the same time this approach has operated as a critique of what is regarded by some theologians as patriarchalism—a view of theology and the church which dominates and is oppressive rather than liberating. This is particularly seen in aspects of political, liberation, and feminist theologies.

A further factor in this renewed interest in the Trinity is the burden of suffering, poverty, and need in the world and the alienation of individuals and peoples. From this perspective theological reflection has focused on the suffering of Christ on the cross, and a new approach has developed which may be spoken of as a "trinitarian theology of the cross." Not only does the Son suffer by entering into our human situation but the Father is seen as accompanying him by the Holy Spirit in this work and lifting human beings up from this Godforsakenness to acceptance, reconciliation, and salvation. In other words, as several theologians have written, "the Trinity is the mystery of salvation."

This book sets out the views of various theologians on these and other themes, though it by no means claims to be exhaustive. It leans heavily on the European, particularly the German tradition, and gives both an exposition of a variety of writers and a critical evaluation of them. To this extent it is more an introduction to and summary of the current debate than an attempt at something original. However, the final chapter does make an attempt, in the light of the whole discussion, to show how we can speak of God as Father, Son, and Holy Spirit, and what is the best conceptuality to use in speaking of him as one "being" yet three "persons."

For those who read this book and are unacquainted with some of the names or the writings of the theologians surveyed, it may be of interest to know that they stem from at least seven Christian traditions. Their views interweave, coalesce, and diverge right across the ecclesiastical divides. Torrance, Moltmann, and Barth are from the Reformed tradition, Jüngel and Pannenberg are Lutherans, and Rahner, von Balthasar, Kasper, Congar, and Boff are Roman Catholics. R. P. C. and A. Hanson are Anglicans and Zizioulas and Lossky are Orthodox. Gunton and Newbigin are from the United Reformed Church in England and Geoffrey Wainwright is a Methodist. This rich variety, where there is much in common, is indicative of the interweaving of the theological perspectives today.

This book originated in a paper given to an ecumenical group in Ireland and was later published as an article in the *Scottish Journal of Theology*. At that time I was encouraged to develop the different sections of it into chapters of a book and am grateful for all those who did so. My particular thanks are due to all at Oxford University Press, New York, who saw the book through to print. Their encouragement and generous support is much appreciated.

My hope is that it will stimulate interest among students of theology and their mentors in this basic doctrine of the faith and in the lively, fruitful debate that continues on the implications it has for the life of the church and the world today.

Belfast, Northern Ireland   J. T.
January 1994

Contents

Modern Trinitarian Perspectives

1

Introduction

One of the most important developments in the field of theology in the last two decades has been a genuine revival of interest in the doctrine of the Trinity. "Its roots are hard to isolate, and the styles of theology within it vary widely, but the current trinitarian revival itself is unmistakable. . . . [V]irtually every serious theological movement of recent years has sought in its own terms to state and shape trinitarian doctrine."[1] Feminists, liberationists, process thinkers, and more traditionalist Catholic and Protestant theologians as well as Eastern Orthodox desire to free the Trinity from its isolation in traditional statements with the consequent lack of relation to practical Christian faith and life. The realization that in the economy of salvation we have to do with God as he is in himself has radically focused thought in a new way on the being and act of God as triune. Further, the emphasis on the liberation of human beings and the concomitant social and political thrust has undoubtedly been a contributing factor. This poses a question: Is God as triune not only the source of our salvation but also the ground and paradigm of true social life and liberation?

The double context of salvation and liberation in relation to the Trinity has been the prime reason for renewed interest in the doctrine today and in its practical implications. "Recent rejuvenation of the Trinity has owed much to the efforts and success of theologians in laying out a wide range of trinitarian implications. No doubt here, as elsewhere, Karl Barth is the great twentieth-century pioneer, resisting the unitarian, pietist, and nineteenth-century liberal convictions that the doctrine of the Trinity is practically sterile."[2] Barth's has been a massive and timely response to all who in theory and practice agreed with Kant's dictum that "absolutely nothing worthwhile for the practical life can be made out of the doctrine of the Trinity taken literally."[3] The modern trinitarian revival attempts to show exactly the opposite. It is as we properly understand God as triune that we will have a right view of the faith, of its doctrines, and of the relevance of all this for every sphere of human life and activity. It is in many ways remarkable that this insight, always latent in our traditions, has now, almost suddenly and unexpectedly, emerged as a (some might say *the*) central aspect of current theology. Whatever the varied reasons for this renewed interest, its concern to relate the Trinity to the life of the church and of the world is to be warmly welcomed.

The modern scene, however, exhibits a wide variety of opinion as far as this doctrine is concerned. The British Council of Churches has produced an important report[4] summarizing much of this fresh thinking and suggesting two main lines of approach. First, there are those critical elements in modern life and thought that make it difficult for many to envisage the reality and truth of such a doctrine. Second, there is the continuing fact that, from very early times in the Christian church, and certainly from the fifth century on, trinitarian belief has been a genuine and necessary aspect of the faith—in fact an affirmation of the Christian doctrine of God. However much this may have been rejected at various periods in the church's history, it still plays an important role in Christian faith and worship as well as forming the content and structure of accepted creedal and confessional statements.[5] It is in fact impossible to imagine the Christian church existing without this cardinal doctrine.[6]

Areas of Debate

We look briefly at some of the critical aspects which are said to make it difficult for some to envisage a realistic and relevant doctrine of the Trinity today.

Holy Scripture

It is widely accepted today that the doctrine cannot simply be read out of Holy Scripture by quoting biblical texts. Even as strong an exponent of the doctrine as Karl Barth states that trinitarian doctrine is not itself a direct statement of revelation but points to it.[7] While this is generally accepted, even Barth does expound scriptural passages in defense of the doctrine. Nor is it altogether true that the context and structure of biblical texts and passages do not lend credence to the doctrine or provide a basis for it. A. W. Wainwright has made a worthwhile attempt to prove the contrary.[8]

The British Council of Churches (B.C.C.) report,[9] however, indicates several developments that have left doubts in the modern mind about the validity of the doctrine in relation to Scripture. There is the critical and historical study of the biblical text influenced partly by humanist and Enlightenment thought. There is also the supposed paucity of explicitly trinitarian texts in the New Testament and the lateness of those we do have. In contrast to the unity which "biblical theology" was said to have discovered some decades ago, the modern emphasis is on diversity. Can a single doctrine such as the Trinity be found in or securely based on Holy Scripture?

There is, moreover, the uncertainty of some biblical texts and varied meanings applicable to them. The same can be said of titles applied to Jesus such as "Son of God" and "Son of Man" or even "Messiah." They may not necessarily imply divinity. All these critical areas raise questions about a view of Christ as divine, yet without this any trinitarian doctrine would be impossible. However, as we shall see later, this is only one and not necessarily the strongest side of the argument and debate on this issue.

While scholarly debate continues on all these issues, it would be quite wrong to suggest that the preceding assumptions are wholly valid or indeed accepted by a majority of biblical scholars today.[10]

The Shape of Theology

Western trinitarianism has come under increasing criticism lately as it stems from Augustine and was further shaped by Thomas Aquinas and Anselm.[11] The following are some of the main objections. The West begins with the unity of the being of God and then seeks to fit the three persons into that framework.[12] The oneness of God is, in this view, said to have an ontological priority over the persons and this makes it more difficult to conceive of them as distinct centers of consciousness, thought, and action. The Eastern view is now favored by many Western theologians, although they are not in full agreement with all its forms.[13] The three persons are, in this view, regarded as a community each of which is divine. This also gives a better basis for the social nature of the faith and is a paradigm for church and society.

If one follows this line of thinking it helps to overcome the view attributed to Augustine and more fully developed by Aquinas that the persons are simply relations.[14] But can a mere relation have personal characteristics such as those normally associated with the Father, the Son, and the Holy Spirit? It is further stated against the Western view that if the external works of the Trinity are indivisible, this undermines the distinctive roles the persons play in the work of the triune God.

Another objection is that too much has been read into the inner nature of God in himself so that one finds it hard to grasp; some have either abandoned it altogether or opted for a more economic view.[15]

It is one of the great merits of Karl Barth[16] and of Eastern theology that they start with revelation, understand the Trinity in this light, and seek to eschew all philosophical or other approaches prior to speaking and thinking of God as triune. That the objections to the Western view have some merit is unmistakable, though in turn the East is not without its difficulties in opting for a Trinity viewed primarily from the perspective of persons with the Father predominant. This has the danger of a form of hierarchy in God and possibly even of tritheistic tendencies. The B.C.C. report believes that the Cappadocian fathers are to be preferred to Augustine as coming closer to the biblical perspective on the nature of the triune God.[17] This, however, is a matter of opinion. At this point we simply state some of the problems in both traditions; they will be dealt with more fully later.

The Holy Spirit

Another reason advanced to explain why modern theology has shied away from the Trinity is the lack of adequate views of the Holy Spirit.[18] "The dominance of Christology over pneumatology in our interpretation of God's working in the world emerges . . . in what is often held to be a weakness of the theology of the Spirit in the West, where the Spirit sometimes appears to be little more than an appendage of Christ."[19] This is said to be a Barthian tradition and leads back to Augustine. It is assumed that the Spirit is scarcely recognized as a distinct divine person and unless this happens "his work in the world will not be discerned as truly that of God."[20]

This, however, is a highly dubious position and not a fair critique of Barth. For him the Holy Spirit is the One who creates faith in us, is known and experienced as our Lord, and so does not merely point us to Christ but has ontic reality at the same time. In other words the Spirit points away to Christ but at the same time is the Lord of our union with Christ, so that we know the Spirit too as personal Lord who is one with the Son and the Father.

Language and Meaning

It is a well-known fact in the history of trinitarian thought and debate that two main areas have proved extremely difficult of solution. The first is the fact that we are dealing with the mystery of God's very being and of his action in creation, revelation, and ultimate redemption. While the one God is known and worshiped as Father, Son, and Holy Spirit, this is beyond our rational understanding or grasp. This neither means a resigned acquiescence in a form of agnosticism, an inability to say anything about God as triune, nor does it leave us simply repeating biblical terms and language. Rather, all human language is here strained to the limit, proving by its inadequacy that everything runs out into mystery and that our human formulations (however true) always point beyond themselves to the truth of God as one, Father, Son, and Holy Spirit. Nonetheless, they do express truth as far as this can be stated and also speak and guard against error.

In the second place, since the meaning of language changes with the centuries, terms used in the past may convey another meaning today than originally intended. This is true in particular of the concept "person" applied to the three "persons" in the Trinity. If these are taken as three separate centers of consciousness in an individualistic way, as some modern thought seems to do, then one would end up with tritheism, a denial of the Trinity. Equally, one can overemphasize the unity of God to the detriment of the persons. Several suggestions have been made to assist us here. One is to revert to the Cappadocian use of "modes of being" for the persons favored by Barth[21] and a similar usage by Karl Rahner.[22] But this way of stating things has a certain impersonal sound though no connection with modalism, as some assert. Others favor beginning with the persons, seeing them in relational terms, and indicating that these relationships between persons have ontological significance pointing to the unity and being of God. The emphasis here is on a relational unity, a communion of mutual giving and receiving, indeed bordering on a social Trinity.[23]

This is also suggested by those philosophical theologians who think in terms of modern personalism.[24] A person exists only in relation and so the term as applied to the Trinity can be used only analogically. Here are several areas which call for our further thought and consideration.

Worship

On the more positive side the B.C.C. report[25] rightly underlines the fact that we stand today not only in the midst of critical problems in relation to scripture, philosophy, and language in the areas of trinitarian thought just noted, but we stand before the triune God himself as worshipers. It is argued that a quite different perception will be obtained if we see God in monotheistic or trinitarian terms. The former will result in unitarianism, a worship lacking a center in the person and work of Christ. The latter will allow access to the Father through the mediating work of Christ by the Holy Spirit. It will see Jesus as the true worshiper and come in and through him. Here is a central area of practical importance for our perception of what we do in relation to the triune God before whom we stand and a place for thinking out theologically what this relationship is.

Having surveyed briefly a few of the critical areas that are the concern of trinitarian perspectives today, we look now more fully at the basis of the Trinity in Holy Scripture and its confirmation in the writings of the Fathers of the fourth and fifth centuries.

The General Testimony of Scripture

R. P. C. Hanson in his massive volume on the patristics[26] states that all who believed in the doctrine of the Trinity—and indeed those also who held somewhat unorthodox views—sought to base these on Holy Scripture. It is true that philosophical concepts and the place and content of tradition also played a role, but the authoritative criterion of this and other doctrines was held to be Holy Scripture even if it did not express the doctrine in explicitly trinitarian terms. This did not create too many problems when Scripture was read largely uncritically as a unity. The modern age, however, as previously indicated, has altered this considerably and has seen the emergence of biblical criticism and sometimes of a merely historical reading of the Scriptures and the view that in them there is a variety of theologies and Christologies.

The question is how far modern trinitarian perspectives have been altered by these changes or, more radically, can one in their light have a Trinity at all? Modern biblical criticism is here to stay, but it requires continual re-examination lest it bring to bear on the Scriptures alien criteria, reading them in a light never intended by the original writers. There are good grounds for believing that the critical scholarship stemming from the Enlightenment brought certain alien categories to bear on the biblical data and came to largely wrong conclusions. The radical liberal approach of the last century often did this and argued that "the early christological and trinitarian formulae represented the Hellenization of christianity . . . distorted by the imposition upon it of foreign philosophical concepts."[27] This process and that of others read the Scriptures largely historically and left aside their basic theological thrust. The famous debate and disagreement between Adolf Harnack and Karl Barth in 1927[28] was not between historical criticism and its opposite but between a largely critical, historical reading of Scripture and one which, while accepting this, sought to penetrate more deeply into the meaning and message of Scripture—"The Strange New World within The Bible," as Barth called it.[29]

The B.C.C. report points out that historical critical studies "bear hard on the doctrine of the Trinity" for two reasons. First, there are in the New Testament very "few biblical texts which can be claimed to have an explicitly trinitarian significance." Second, "many of those passages which do appear to support the doctrine of the Trinity belong to later stages of the New Testament tradition,"[30] for example, Matthew 28:19. It is argued, though not necessarily correctly, that the earliest strata of tradition are the most reliable. The deity of Christ is not explicitly stated there and this is inextricably linked with the Trinity. But as the B.C.C. report underlines, even if these arguments have some validity—and not all scholars by any means agree that they have—this does not necessarily exclude a doctrine of the triune God. Moreover, that various Christologies are present in the New Testament does not mean that the church and its scholars have been wrong in having a clear faith in the divinity of Christ. Other even more important considerations must be taken into account. The faith of the early church had such a sense of the risen Christ and his saving acts, despite the variety of expression, such a relation to him in worship, that Christians found that in him they really met with God himself. This led inevitably to the question of the relation of Jesus Christ to God and to the formulation of views on the triune God.

The same applies (mutatis mutandis) to the Holy Spirit. The decisive element in this area also was not simply a matter of proof texts or results of critical scholarship. Rather it was the result both of these and of a Christian community's experience of salvation and reflection upon it. "It arose from the church's participation in the life of God, a participation granted by the Spirit and therefore requiring both the divinity of the Spirit and his distinction from the Father; and from her sending out into all the world, a mission deriving from the mission of the Son."[31] Thus the biblical texts are no mere historical records but testimony not only to faith and worship but to what God was doing in making himself known to people in the community of faith. The latter insight does not override the former critical one but includes and in a measure transcends it as the ultimate criterion.

> However much, therefore, we may be prepared to agree that a doctrine of the trinity cannot simply be read off the text of Scripture or based directly upon certain biblical texts, we can continue to affirm that the God who is made known in the Old and New Testaments is the triune God confessed in later worship and in the teaching of the Church. Nothing in modern historical criticism forces us to deny a true continuity between the way in which God is known in the Old Testament, is named in threefold form in the New Testament and is defined in trinitarian terms through the maturing of insights made possible by the ministry, death and resurrection of Jesus as well as by life in the Spirit in the Church.[32]

The Particular Testimony of Scripture

I want now to suggest that there are at least three possible ways of approaching an answer to the question of the Trinity as far as the Scriptures are concerned. The first is Criticism and Canon; the second, Unity and Plurality; and the third, Witness to Jesus Christ.

Criticism and Canon

As an example of this first area we consider Colin Gunton's critique of the Enlightenment.[33] His argument is not against critical studies but against the way in which the Enlightenment influenced these studies and brought an unacceptable preconception to bear on them. In this view the mind's function is given an excessive weight in imposing form and so it "makes it impossible to conceive adequately the mind's function and discernment, in rational apprehension of what is there beforehand."[34] Gunton quotes Brevard Childs and R. E. Clements, both Old Testament scholars, to the effect that historical and critical questions, while having a place, must be relative to a proper theological understanding. The Bible has a canonical shape, or what Barth has called a "biblical thought-form."[35] The historicity and humanity and the variety of the Scriptures are affirmed but there is a unity within this, an objectivity which we ignore at our peril. The danger of the Enlightenment and its modern critical followers is that it imposes an unnatural unity, often a merely historical one. The view of Childs and Clements, which Gunton follows, is that the Scriptures give us reason to believe that one can "discern a unity of *theological* form without imposing 'extrinsic' dogmatic categories."[36] To put it otherwise, "the *content* of the Bible is to be seen in terms of a unity underlying and supporting the variety of types of theology and literature"[37] found therein. Gunton is rightly against a canon within a canon or taking certain ideas like covenant or Christology as the unifying factors similar to Luther's idea of justification by faith. Rather, in the variety in Israel, in Christ, it is "the same God that is being described and referred to here."[38] This unity in variety leads us "to the very threshold of the doctrine of the Trinity."[39]

But why the Trinity? It could also be conceived as one God having many attributes. Gunton, despite previous denials, opts for a christological solution and views the person and work of Christ as the focal points around which the Scriptures revolve and in relation to which any trinitarian interpretation must be seen. "The root of the understanding of God's triunity . . . [is] in the life, death and resurrection of Jesus."[40] This approach, as Gunton freely admits, is clearly a pointer toward trinitarian theology but not an explanation of it. It is a counter to the accusation that to exalt God was to demean humanity. To think of God as triune is to point to the "power of the cross," to see God in Christ by the Spirit "in the very humanity and suffering of Jesus" showing us "what it is to be God-like."[41]

Gunton's work has therefore a dual role—to critique false Enlightenment views and to provide a basis on which he and others may build today a better doctrine of the Trinity than in the past. He is in effect saying that the Bible, properly understood and used, gives us the focus of an economic Trinity as the ground of future developments.

Unity and Plurality

If the doctrine of the Trinity is to be accepted and built on a biblical basis it must be that of the Bible as a whole. In the light of the fact that theology holds the Old and New Testaments to be a unity, it is inconceivable that one should omit the Old Testament in this respect. Gunton and the Old Testament scholars referred to were certainly not doing that. The New Testament lies hidden in the Old and the Old is made clear in the New. They form a unity. Yet it is clear that the Old Testament gives a basis for the Trinity in a much less obvious way than the New. If the Scriptures as a whole are relevant, how then can one see, however dimly, traces of the Trinity in the Old Testament? Several suggestions have been made which can be summed up as follows.[42] There is the role of the one and the many. God's personality, though one, is a corporate one which includes more than a barren unity.[43] The concept of plurality in the Godhead is not strange to the Jews. More specifically, Wainwright points to three conceptions which, while not explicitly personal in character or coinhering in God, point in this direction.[44] These are the Spirit, Wisdom, and the Word. There are also the ideas of the angel as a manifestation of God and the Shekinah, or Glory, which is shown to Israel as well as the name of God. Wainwright writes, "Post-exilic Jews had an idea of plurality within the Godhead. . . . It is conceivable that a trinitarian doctrine should have grown on Jewish soil."[45] All this can be affirmed while maintaining a strong belief in God as one.

What we are looking for in the Old Testament as uniquely bound up with the New is some foreshadowing of what was to come, since it was the same God manifest in both Testaments. It is therefore inconceivable that the Old

Testament should have a simple belief in a solitary monad as God, similar to Judaism or Islam, however much his unity and uniqueness were emphasized. Such a view would make a continuity of the Testaments impossible, would drive a wedge between them, would evacuate the New Testament of much of its content, and would make any kind of preparatory idea of the Trinity in the Old Testament impossible. In fact, it would end up with Marcionism. The Old Testament does, however, give ample evidence of such a prefiguration and has, as Schulte shows,[46] in this view a preliminary participation in the event of revelation.

Both Schulte and Courth[47] agree with Wainwright that the preceding concepts of word, spirit, wisdom, and the like, do indeed have a forward thrust and significance in the Old Testament and find fulfillment in Jesus Christ and the Holy Spirit in the New Testament. They add a further point that the Old Testament saw God both as wholly other than man yet coming close to him in saving action in Israel and in Jesus Christ. The Old Testament forms in which God comes are therefore ways by which he communicates and discloses his nature and will to his people and to creation and in these ways he is displaying a certain plurality in that nature.

These statements, neither singly nor together, are direct trinitarian statements. Rather, they are ways of mediation between God and his people which unite and do not divide. They can be regarded as almost hypostases of God and are taken up in the New Testament and applied directly to Christ and the Holy Spirit. It is in this way that they are significant, prefigure Christ, and point to more than a simple unity in God. "In the light of the full revelation in Christ these increasing personifications of the Old Testament mediation of God appear as the foretaste of the new covenant's unfolding of the 'more personal' fullness of being of the divine nature."[48] Or, as Schulte puts it, "in their unity they move towards the fullness of the New Testament revelation."[49]

The same obtains for the New Testament but centers now on the fact that the plurality is focused in Jesus Christ and the Holy Spirit and has a concrete form. Central to the Trinity is the deity of Christ affirmed and witnessed to in the New Testament revelation and redemption, in the worship ascribed to Jesus, in the attitudes adopted toward him by the early Christian community, and in the titles by which he was known. All of these set him on the side of God while maintaining his genuine humanity. The deity of the Spirit is likewise affirmed. The remarkable thing about the New Testament community was the way in which, without any embarrassment or great difficulty, mainly Palestinian Jews worshiped Christ and the Spirit and saw no contradiction between this and the worship of the God revealed through their fathers in the Old Testament. While no explicit doctrine was worked out, many threefold formulas are to be found in the New Testament and the beginnings of a more explicit doctrine are to be seen in the Fourth Gospel. Binding and coordinating all these different aspects is the fact that the New Testament community's experience of the revelation in these different forms at the same time affirmed the unity of God. Wainwright summarizes the biblical and particularly New Testament revelation in this way:

> The problem of the trinity was being raised and answered in the New Testament. It arose because of the development of Christian experience and thought. It was rooted in experience for men were conscious of the power of the Spirit and the presence of the Lordship of the risen Christ. It was rooted in worship, because men worshipped in the Spirit, offered their prayers to God the Father through Christ, and sometimes worshipped Christ Himself. It was rooted in thought, because the writers tackled first the Christological problem, and then at any rate in the fourth Gospel, the threefold problem. The whole matter was based on the life and resurrection of Jesus himself who received the Spirit during his earthly life and imparted the Spirit to others after his resurrection.[50]

Witness to Jesus Christ

In much theological writing on the Trinity in relation to the Old Testament little thought has been given to how the New Testament saw God as one yet diverse in character—how, in fact, Christ may be seen as really present to the people of God at that time. Several writers, however, have taken a line of thought that can be developed constructively in relation to the nature of God in the Old Testament.[51] A. T. Hanson probably goes further than any in this direction. He takes four areas of the New Testament where passages in the Old Testament are directly referred to Christ: Paul, Hebrews, John's Gospel, and the Catholic Epistles. Taking the Septuagint version of the Old Testament from which the New Testament quotes most frequently, he shows how in fact in each case Jesus is spoken of as present and active in the Old Testament, creating faith, showing grace, and exercising judgment. While some of the New Testament expositions of the presence and actions of Jesus in the Old Testament may seem strange or even bizarre, they are nonetheless in line with the close relationship and unity of the Old and New Testaments, as Wilhelm Vischer has shown.[52] It is right to interpret the Old Testament in its particular situation and time, and it is also right to see it in the light of the whole of Scripture and in particular what happens in the incarnation and atonement. In other words, a christological interpretation of the Old Testament, its main thrust as well as its individual passages, which the previously mentioned writers have carried out, is both legitimate and theologically requisite.

According to Hanson this is true of those passages which have Christ not merely as presence but envisaged as "speaker or as spoken to in Old Testament passages."[53] This is particularly the case in Pauline passages in Romans and Philippians and in the letter to the Hebrews. Hanson concludes that for the New Testament writers Jesus is in one sense identified with Kyrios and so with God, while in another sense he is distinguished from Adonai, Jehovah, the Ineffable One.[54] Hanson believes that there are two main ways in which Jesus is seen in the Old Testament, as "real presence of

Christ in Old Testament history"[55] and as speaker in prophecy. The latter "is not a mode of interpretation that casts everything necessarily into the future."[56] It often tells us as much about the relation of the preexistent Son to the Father as about what was to take place in the Messianic era.

If one accepts that the New Testament writers did interpret the Old Testament passages correctly, and that Hanson's own exegesis is a possible one, then one can see here too definite foreshadowing of the nature of God as triune or at any rate pointing to a twofold aspect. For a further trinitarian perspective a similar interpretation and exposition of the Spirit in the Old and New Testaments would be necessary, and Hanson does not undertake this.

What in fact is being said here is that the interpretation which the New Testament gives to Old Testament passages implies that Jesus Christ the Son of God was not absent from the Old Testament understanding even though the writers only realized this dimly. At this point Old Testament scholars are more cautious and nuanced. They see and affirm clearly the interrelationship between the Old and New Testaments in their view of God. Gerhard von Rad, for example, shows how the Old Testament traditions were both affirmed and transcended in later times and situations by prophets and others under the impact of the word and spirit of God.[57] Similarly, the New Testament apostles and evangels took up the Scriptures of the Old Testament and in the light of Christ gave them a new and fuller interpretation. At the same time the Christ event went beyond anything envisaged or realized in ancient Israel. Von Rad writes,

> Thus a new name was once again proclaimed over the ancient tradition of Israel: like one who enters into an ancient heritage, Christ the Kyrios claimed the ancient writings for himself. A characteristic feature of this appropriation is the transfer to the new Kyrios of those sayings in the LXX where Jahweh is called Kyrios, with the result that the old statements were at once given a new theological frame of reference.[58]

The nature of the Old Testament was such that it was self-transcending, had a sense of present incompleteness, and so had an openness to future fulfillment. Stories and events therefore had a predisposition to reinterpretation in the light of what was to come. This is precisely what happened in the New Testament and in the history of the church and Christian doctrine. It is therefore to the whole of Scripture in its varied relationships and mutual conditioning that one must look for a witness to Christ, to the Spirit, and to the Father and so for a basis for trinitarian doctrine.

In line with the modern emphasis on interpreting the totality of Scripture as testimony to divine revelation, it is helpful to follow Karl Barth and Thomas F. Torrance at this point. For them it is not so much in individual passages (though these are, as Hanson shows, relevant) that we have the real prefiguring and indeed presence of him who was to come. Rather, the Old Testament as a whole is the context of the New, the background and framework of God's coming in Christ and of the humiliation of Christ on the cross. Barth sees this prefiguration in a threefold way in the Old Testament:

1. In God's election of a small people he humbles himself, comes and acts in Israel, calls his people his Son.
2. In Israel's faithlessness and rebellion against God and his identification with this people we see foreshadowed the alien way the Son of God went and God's faithfulness to his promises.
3. In the wrath, curse, and judgment of God that fell on Israel we see in outline Christ's bearing God's judgment on our sin in this alien territory of the far country.[59]

In one sense Israel's history is but a prophecy and foreshadowing of the presence and sufferings of Christ and so a pointer to the Trinity. But in another, as Barth points out, the Son of God was present in Israel as the One who was to come just as he is present with his people now as the One who has come. Barth puts the two together in this way. Jesus Christ is "the fulfillment, the superabundant fulfilment of the will revealed in the Old Testament of the God who even there was the One who manifested himself in this one man Jesus of Nazareth—the gracious God who as such is able and ready to condescend to the lowly and to undertake their case at his own cost."[60] There is therefore, according to this view, this otherness in God not just in relation to his creatures, but in relation to Israel as a whole, which reflects what he is in himself. It is in these ways in the Old Testament history as a whole that God was present and active already by his word and spirit, yet his reality and truth were not fully manifested in history until the birth of Jesus Christ. Torrance calls Israel the womb or matrix of the incarnation,[61] and if it was such it already (in the way we have seen) not only foreshadowed but contained the One who was to come. Barth puts it this way. If genuine expectation of revelation is really in the Old Testament, "we cannot ultimately and in principle point to any other authority than to the revelation itself—that is to Jesus Christ himself. . . . Jesus Christ is manifest in the Old Testament as the *coming* expected one."[62]

In this way God's speech and action in Israel in the Old Testament cannot be apart from but through the One who was to come. It is in this way too and perhaps best of all that we can see the Old Testament not only as pointing to the Son of God, but as knowing him already present in the prehistory of the people of Israel. The *vestigia trinitatis* are not only in the humanity of the incarnate one but in God's action in Israel in preparing for the full coming of the One who was to be incarnate.

Modern Patristic Studies

In the area of patristic scholarship negative and critical approaches to the doctrine of the Trinity can be seen in the attempt to reinstate some aspects of Arian teaching.[63] However, two magisterial volumes[64] indicate that the early Christian writers were right to oppose Arius since he raised the crucial question of the person of Christ and gave the answer that there was a time when he was not. Arius saw Jesus as created before time, less than fully divine and not wholly human. This was found to be unacceptable to the church as a whole both then and now. In his lengthy and careful study R. P. C. Hanson has shown that in the trials and errors of the early centuries and the search for the Christian doctrine of God the Patristics as a whole, though not entirely, affirmed the "traditional and catholic doctrine of the Holy Trinity."[65] He states that an attempt was being made to show that the doctrine was founded on Holy Scripture. With Athanasius he believed that in affirming the trinity the Fathers were "grasping the intention (dianoia) and the drift (skopos) of scripture."[66] While in one sense countering error and affirming truth they were developing dogma, but in another sense "this was rather a return to scripture than development of dogma."[67] Modern attempts to reinstate Arius founder on this fact, not that they are too radical but that they are not radical and revolutionary enough. The doctrine of the Trinity of the early church is in fact a reformulation and rethinking of previous inadequate thoughts about God. By contrast, "the Arians failed just because they were so inflexible, too conservative, not ready to look at new ideas."[68] In other words, Hanson is stating that certain views held by Arius and his supporters were inadequate when measured by the full weight of Scripture and that no real attempt to reformulate them was made in the light of better scriptural knowledge. They also "failed to see what were the basic elements of christianity itself"[69] and they remained fixed in a dualistic ontology and metaphysics whereby God in his impassable nature could not have any direct dealings with the world. "Athanasius produced the decisive doctrine which the Cappadocians later elaborated."[70] This was the view that God was triune, three in one and one in three.

Basic to this whole decision and debate is the affirmation of the *homoousion*, that Jesus Christ is of the very nature of God. This has been linked to the incarnation in a particularly clear way by Torrance in his exposition of the trinitarian faith and of the Nicene Creed.[71] With Hanson he sees the nature of Jesus Christ as within the sphere of essential Godhead; the *homoousion* is an affirmation of the oneness of being between Father and Son in a dynamic, living relationship while at the same time pointing to the distinction between them. For Torrance, following Nicaea, the relation of oneness of Father and Son is the heart and substance of the christian faith[72] and that upon which "the very substance of the Christian gospel depends."[73] Moreover, the debates that centered around this dealt with the very essence of salvation and were neither esoteric nor impractical speculations. Everything was in jeopardy if this were not true. The linking of the being and action of Jesus Christ in his oneness with the Father and the reality of our salvation are the key to the doctrine of the Trinity in the early church and at Nicaea in particular.

According to Torrance, Arius and his followers, while seeking to base their teaching on certain aspects of Scripture, at the same time worked also with certain philosophical and theological tools. Basic to this was the idea of the platonic or philonic separation between the sensible and the intelligible world. This, combined with Jewish transcendentalism, left a disjunction between God and the world and had the effect of "shutting God out of the world of empirical reality in space and time."[74] This made a real incarnation impossible and led the Arians to see Jesus Christ as belonging "to the creaturely side of the disjunction. . . . [T]he Logos is thus to be regarded as detached from the being of God."[75] To speak therefore of the Son as divine as the Father is and of one being with him was impossible for the Arians, as it is for all who accept a dualistic philosophical framework.

Torrance believes that this radical dichotomy is manifest in modern times in Schleiermacher and Bultmann (in different ways), who call in question the fundamental truth that "in Jesus Christ we have none other than the being of God himself in our human existence in space and time."[76] The twin truths of the incarnation and the Trinity are at stake in this whole debate.

This truth of the *homoousios* was especially associated, as Hanson also indicates, with Athanasius and was the linchpin on which all else was based. It led Athanasius to think more fully not only about the nature and person of Christ but about that of the Holy Spirit also and to affirm that the Spirit too was of the divine nature. Athanasius' approach to the doctrine of the Trinity, Torrance states, "was entirely in line with his approach to the doctrine of the Son or Logos."[77] Because of his relationship to the Son, the Spirit could not be a creature but must be one in being with both Father and Son. Athanasius moves from the Father–Son relationship to the divinity of the Spirit. How otherwise could we know God (and that savingly) as Father and Son were the Spirit, who makes this knowledge possible, less than divine? On the basis of the Nicene and Athanasian teaching Torrance shows how God is not only Father, Son, and Holy Spirit but that we by the Holy Spirit are caught up into and participate by faith in the divine self-knowledge, that is, in the very life of the triune God.[78]

In other words, patristic theology as outlined by both Hanson and Torrance—however different their approaches—is clearly right in underlining the Trinity as basic to our knowledge of God and as the mystery of our salvation. This doctrine affects and determines the whole of life, faith, worship, and theology within the Christian church. Arian or semi-Arian views, ancient or modern, fail here and leave us with a quite different concept of God and all that follows upon such belief. The tendencies of modern Christology as outlined in *The Myth of God Incarnate* are contrary to the trinitarian view and so to the essence of the faith. These critical views can be countered only by a better statement in line with the ancient creeds of Nicaea and Chalcedon.

Notes

1. Ronald J. Feenstra and Cornelius Plantinga, Jr., eds., *Trinity, Incarnation and Atonement. Philosophical and Theological Essays* (Notre Dame, Ind.: University of Notre Dame Press, 1989), p. 3.

2. Ibid., p. 4.

3. Immanuel Kant, *Der Streit der Fakultäten*, A 50, 57, quoted in Jürgen Moltmann, *The Trinity and the Kingdom of God*, tr. Margaret Kohl (London: S.C.M. Press, 1981), p. 6.

4. *The Forgotten Trinity. The Report of the B.C.C. Study Commission on Trinitarian Doctrine Today* (London: British Council of Churches, Inter-Church House, 1989), vol. 1, (hereafter cited as *B.C.C. Report*).

5. See the Apostles' and the Nicene creeds.

6. Cf. R. P. C. Hanson, *The Search for the Christian Doctrine of God* (Edinburgh: T. & T. Clark, 1988), who states that the dispute in the early church which culminated in the clear affirmation of the Trinity "concerned the basic elements of Christianity itself . . . it was about the Christian doctrine of God" (p. 875).

7. Karl Barth, *Church Dogmatics*, I/1, p. 375 (hereafter cited as *C.D.*).

8. Arthur W. Wainwright, *The Trinity in the New Testament* (London: S.P.C.K., 1962).

9. *B.C.C. Report*, vol. 1, p. 31f.

10. Cf., for example, the positive statements of C. F. D. Moule, *The Origin of Christology* (London: Cambridge University Press, 1977). Moule believes the later developments to a high Christology are implicit in the early strata of tradition. For two contrasting and opposite views see Michael Goulder, ed., *Incarnation and Myth* (London: S.C.M. Press, 1979). This follows John Hick, ed., *The Myth of God Incarnate* (London: S.C.M. Press, 1977).

11. Cf. Colin Gunton, "Augustine, the Trinity and the Theological Crisis of the West," *Scottish Journal of Theology* (hereafter cited as *S.J.T.*) vol. 43, no. 19, pp 33–58, for a summary of the chief objections. Werner Löser, "Trinitätstheologie Heute: Ansätze und Entwürfe," in *Trinität: Aktuelle Perspektiven der Theologie*, Wilhelm Breuning, ed, (Freiburg: Herder, 1984) speaks of the need for correction in trinitarian thought in the light of salvation history (p. 20). *B.C.C. Report*, vol. 1, pp. 11, 32.

12. Gunton, pp. 34–35.

13. Jürgen Moltmann, *The Trinity and the Kingdom of God*, tr. Margaret Kohl (London: S.C.M. Press, 1981) begins, as does the East, with the persons rather than the unity of God, though differing in many respects from the Easterners. What Moltmann proposes to offer is "a social doctrine of the Trinity" (p. 19).

14. Gunton, p. 41f. Thomas Aquinas, *Summa Theologica*, I, q. 28, A.2.C.

15. *B.C.C. Report*, vol. 1, p. 14.

16. Ibid., p. 15.

17. Ibid., pp. 21–22.

18. Ibid., p. 27.

19. Ibid., p. 31.

20. Ibid.

21. *C.D.*, I/1, pp. 349ff.

22. Karl Rahner, *The Trinity*, tr. Joseph Donceel (London: Burns and Oates, 1970), pp. 103ff.

23. Cf. T. F. Torrance, *The Mediation of Christ* (Exeter, Eng: Paternoster Press, 1983), p. 59. He says that "the relations which persons have with one another are onto-relations, for they are person-constituting relations."

24. David Brown, "Trinitarian Personhood and Individuality," in *Trinity, Incarnation and Atonement: Philosophical and Theological Essays*, Ronald J.

Feenstra and Cornelius Plantinga, Jr., eds. (Notre Dame, Ind.: University of Notre Dame, 1989).

25. *B.C.C. Report*, vol. 1, p. 3.

26. Hanson, p. 825.

27. *B.C.C. Report*, vol. 1, p. 7.

28. H. Martin Rumscheidt, *Revelation and Theology: An Analysis of the Barth–Harnack Correspondence* (London: Cambridge University Press, 1972).

29. Karl Barth, "The Strange New World within the Bible," in *The Word of God and the Word of Man*, tr. Douglas Horton (London: Hodder and Stoughton, 1928), pp. 28–50.

30. *B.C.C. Report*, vol. 1, p. 7.

31. Ibid., p. 9.

32. Ibid.

33. Colin Gunton, *Enlightenment and Alienation: An Essay towards a Trinitarian Theology*, (London: Marshall Morgan and Scott, 1985), pp. 133ff.

34. Ibid., p. 133.

35. See Wolfhart Schlichting, *Biblische Denkform in der Dogmatik: Die Vorbildlichkeit des biblischen Denkens für die Methode der "Kirchlicher Dogmatik" Karl Barths* (Zurich: Theologischer Verlag, 1972).

36. Gunton, *Enlightenment and Alienation*, p. 128.

37. Ibid., p. 140.

38. Ibid., quoting Clements.

39. Ibid.

40. Ibid., p. 142.

41. Ibid., p. 154.

42. Walter Kasper, *The God of Jesus Christ*, tr. Matthew J. O'Connell (New York: Crossroad, 1989), pp. 241–243.

43. Aubrey R. Johnston, *The One and the Many in the Israelite Conception of God* (Cardiff: University of Wales Press, 1942).

44. Wainwright, pp. 29–37.

45. Ibid., p. 37.

46. R. Schulte, "Die Vorbereitung der Trinitätsoffenburung," *Mysterium Salutis*, vol. 11, 1967, pp. 49ff. esp. pp. 55ff.

47. Ibid., pp. 63–71. Franz Courth, "Trinität in der Schrift und Patristik," in *Handbuch der Dogmengeschichte*, vol. 2, Michael Schmaus, Alois Grillmeier, Leo Scheffczyk, and Michael Scybold, eds. (Freiburg: Herder, 1988), pp. 11–13.

48. Courth, p. 13.

49. Schulte, p. 60.

50. Wainwright, pp. 266–67.

51. A. T. Hanson, *Jesus Christ in the Old Testament* (London: S.P.C.K., 1965). Wilhelm Vischer, *The Witness of the Old Testament to Christ*, vol. 1, tr. A. B. Crabtree, 2 vols. (London: Lutterworth Press, 1949).

52. Vischer, vol. 1, pp. 7–34.

53. Hanson, *Jesus Christ*, p. 139.

54. Ibid., p. 161f.

55. Ibid., p. 176.

56. Ibid.

57. Gerhard von Rad, *Old Testament Theology*, vol. 2, tr. D. M. G. Stalker (Edinburgh: Oliver and Boyd, 1965), p. 327.

58. Ibid.

59. *C.D.*, IV/1, pp. 167–74. For a summary of and commentary on this see Berthold Klappert, *Die Auferweckung des Gekreuzigkten: Der Ansatz der Christologie Karl Barths im Zusammenhang der Christologie der Gegenwart*, (Neukirchener: Neukirchener Verlag, 1971), pp. 164–72. John Thompson, *Christ in Perspective in the Theology of Karl Barth* (Edinburgh: Saint Andrew Press, 1978), pp. 53–55.

60. *C.D.*, IV/1, p. 170.

61. Torrance, pp. 18, 28, 42. Torrance provides a profound interpretation of the role of Israel as a whole in God's revelation and reconciliation (Chaps. 1 and 2).

62. *C.D.*, I/2, p. 72.

63. See especially Maurice Wiles, *Working Papers in Doctrine* (London: S.C.M. Press, 1979), pp. 28–38; *The Making of Christian Doctrine: A Study in the Principles of Early Christian Development* (Cambridge: Cambridge University Press, 1987); "In Defense of Arius," *Journal of Theological Studies*, vol. 13, 1962, pp. 339–47. Wiles does not defend Arius in any respect but regards his teaching as more worthy of consideration than simply to be labeled heresy.

64. Hanson, *The Search for the Christian Doctrine.* T. F. Torrance, *The Trinitarian Faith: The Evangelical Theology of the Ancient Catholic Church* (Edinburgh: T. & T. Clark, 1988).

65. Hanson, *The Search for Christian Doctrine*, p. 870.

66. Ibid., p. 875.

67. Ibid.

68. Ibid., p. 873.

69. Ibid., p. 874.

70. Ibid.

71. Torrance, *The Trinitarian Faith*, passim, esp. p. 125.

72. Ibid., pp. 5, 9ff.

73. Torrance, *The Mediation of Christ*, p. 64.

74. Torrance, *The Trinitarian Faith*, p. 47.

75. T. F. Torrance, "The Logic and Analogic of Biblical and Theological Statements in the Greek Fathers," in *Theology in Reconstruction* (London: S.C.M Press, 1965), pp. 30–45.

76. Torrance, "A New Reformation?" in *Theology in Reconstruction*, p. 263.

77. Torrance, "Athanasius: A Study in the Foundation of Classical Theology," in *Theology in Reconstruction*, p. 231; *Trinitarian Faith*, p. 232.

78. Torrance, *Trinitarian Faith*, p. 111.

2

The Trinity: The Mystery
of Salvation

God as One and God as Triune

We have seen that the doctrine of the Trinity has its basis in God's self-revelation in Israel and in Jesus Christ his Son by the Holy Spirit. In other words, it is to be found exclusively in this revelation as the Scriptures bear witness to it. This positive affirmation carries a negative within it. Since the unity of God is a unity in trinity no other conceived or supposedly proven unity of God is a Christian conception of the true God. Traditional doctrine has sometimes been at fault here. It brought a division into the whole conception of God beginning with a general doctrine of the one God and his attributes on the basis of some biblical material or philosophical proofs and then went on to speak of God as triune.[1] This clearly has various dangers which are being recognized today. It could lead to the Trinity being subordinated to an already preconceived idea of God with a consequent weakening and undermining of its true nature in a modalistic way. Again, it could be seen as a creator God as Father being largely divorced from Son and Holy Spirit so that the Father was known otherwise than by faith, whereas Jesus Christ and the Holy Spirit were the true objects of our belief and worship. This could bring a serious division into our conception of the Trinity, endangering the equality and nature of the persons and misunderstanding their mutual relationships.[2] This dichotomy in the doctrine of God meant a real difficulty too in relating it to Christian life, faith, and worship.

Karl Barth has continually pointed out that the doctrine of the one God, as indeed that of God as Father and Creator treated separately, brings just such a division into our conception of the being of God. Who God is as Father as well as Son and Holy Spirit has proper meaning and significance not as a general truth of reason, religion, or philosophy but only as an affirmation of God's revelation in Jesus Christ. Barth writes,

> The first article of faith in God the Father and his work is not a sort of "forecourt" of the Gentiles, a realm in which Christians and Jews and Gentiles, believers and unbelievers are beside one another and to some extent stand together in the presence of a reality concerning which there might be some measure of agreement, in describing it as the work of God the Creator. . . . It is not the case that the truth about God the Creator is directly accessible to us and that only the truth of the second article needs a revelation. But in the same sense in both cases we are faced with the mystery of God and his work and the approach to it can only be one and the same."[3]

In other words, we can know God as Creator, as Father, only in the way we know Jesus Christ and the Holy Spirit through revelation received by faith. Otherwise we gain a false conception of God. T. F. Torrance comments, "It was this basic split in the conception of God which troubled Karl Barth and prompted him to attack the division of theology into natural theology and revealed theology, when natural theology is taken to be the ground of the doctrine of the one God and revealed theology is taken to be the ground of the doctrine of the triune God . . . that would posit a schizoid state of affairs in the very foundations of theology."[4] Otto Weber comes to a similar conclusion and shows how a general view of God means that Christ and the Holy Spirit must conform to this idea.[5] This would also apply, as we have seen, to God the Father. In other words, taken literally and carried out logically it leads to a form of subordinationism or modalism or both. Fortunately, as often happens, a proper trinitarian theology sometimes triumphs over false starts and premises. This in no way excuses such a division or precludes its serious human weaknesses and dangers.

There can be little doubt that views like these encourage the perception of many in the pews that the Christian faith means a vague general belief in God which is little focused on and determined by Christ and the Holy Spirit. The loss of a proper trinitarian basis in revelation has often led to a minimal place given to the Trinity in faith and worship.

In modern Catholic theology Karl Rahner has sought to counter similar tendencies which have inhibited and been detrimental to proper trinitarian doctrine. He points out that the two separate treatises *De Deo Uno* and *De Deo Trino* brought the same kind of division into our understanding of God.[6] This either separated the unity from its true locus in tri-unity or later tried to show how the one and the triune could be integrated. It also led to a quite abstract philosophical approach to the whole enterprise of trinitarian theology and as a result "refers hardly at all to salvation history."[7] "Thus the treatise of the trinity locks itself in even more splendid isolation, with the ensuing danger that the religious mind finds it devoid of interest."[8]

Two results followed from this approach.[9] First, the Trinity became relatively self-enclosed and the doctrine *De Deo Trino* was influenced by a conception of God's unchangeableness, to a great extent developed in the context of Greek metaphysics. Second, it had only a minimal connection with the treatise *De Verbo Incarnato*. In other words, Christology and the Trinity were virtually divorced. It was both stated and assumed that any one of the three persons could become incarnate. The Son was designated such by "appropriation" only so that he could be described without any real reference to the history of Jesus Christ. His life, work, and history thus stood relatively outside the triune God. There was thus only an accidental relation between the economy of revelation and redemption and the eternal triune being of God.

Walter Kasper sums up well the foregoing and the proper place for a trinitarian confession:

> This trinitarian confession is not, however, a specific difference that is added as a Christian characteristic, or perhaps oddity, to a general religious conception of God of one kind or another; rather, it is the Christian form of speaking about God. . . . [I]t is the objective and even objectively necessary and binding formulation of the eschatological revelation God has given of himself in Jesus Christ through the working of the Holy Spirit.[10]

One can add here that the philosophical approaches of the West to the doctrine of God were strongly eschewed by Easterners, whose basis was more in worship and doxology. This is probably an additional reason, as well as the *Filioque*, why East and West were for so long estranged theologically. The merit of the modern approach to the Trinity and of the revival of trinitarian theology is that it seeks to put the church and its theology on a better basis and to project from its center in the incarnation, cross, and resurrection the meaning and saving import of our common faith in the one God, Father, Son, and Holy Spirit.

The Trinity as Mystery

The chief way today in which modern writers seek to find a proper basis for and give a more adequate doctrine of the Trinity is to say with Karl Rahner: "The Trinity is the mystery of *salvation*."[11] This gives it a particular relation to Christian faith and practice which is one of the main emphases of the whole of the modern approach. Older, more traditional scholastic approaches also emphasize the Trinity as mystery which had to be believed, if one were to be saved.[12] The Trinity is a mystery in the sense of being knowledge obtained exclusively by God's self-disclosure (Matt. 11:27). According to Kasper, it was contrasted to rationalism, which sought to prove it by reason, and semirationalism, which accepted it as one of our revealed doctrines "but then goes on to assert that once [it has] been revealed we are able to understand [it]."[13] The scholastic approach also saw revelation as largely propositional rather than as personal communication.

Modern perspectives see the mystery of the Trinity in terms of the history of salvation. It is not an obscure theologoumenon, an esoteric dogma mystifying like a riddle and unrelated to us. It is a mystery because it is how God *is* and how he has made himself known to us in Jesus Christ by the Holy Spirit. It is a mystery because it is known and apprehended only in the event of revelation. Even in this event it is and remains a mystery. Kasper writes, "The revelation given in the history of salvation does not therefore explain the mystery of God to us but rather leads us deeper into this mystery; in this history, the mystery of God is revealed to us as mystery."[14]

The mystery is thus another way of saying, with Barth,[15] that the God revealed and concealed is the same God—the *Deus Revelatus* remains even as such the *Deus Absconditus.* God remains veiled in the flesh of the incarnate Son and, while entering into intimate personal and corporate communion with us, never gives himself over into our control. In so speaking we are affirming his sovereignty. The fact that the Trinity is God's mystery is thus a truth of revelation received by faith. While it is correct to say that the Trinity is the mystery of our salvation, Kasper includes creation and redemption within this one comprehensive event.[16] It is right that it should be so since it is not salvation in the more limited sense that alone is the work of the triune God but the whole drama and panorama of his actions *ad extra* in creation, redemption, and consummation.

In agreement with Rahner, Kasper not only sees mystery applied to God as triune but believes "it can be shown from philosophy and anthropology that, because of the self-transcendence proper to their spirit, human beings are beings of ineradicable mystery."[17] This view embraces the all-inclusive totality of human existence as it is the image and likeness of God. This is, however, a thesis that squares ill with a proper trinitarian view which understands our humanity christologically in relation to the humanity of Jesus Christ. In this respect it runs counter to what Kasper and Rahner both say so well elsewhere about the Trinity as the mystery of salvation. It is here also that it disagrees with Barth and his modern followers.

Revelation and the Trinity

We have seen that modern theology finds the basis of the Trinity in the whole content of revelation witnessed to in the Scriptures of the Old and New Testaments. This emphasis owes more to Karl Barth[18] than to any other theologian in modern times but has been taken up by Rahner, Kasper, and the B.C.C. report and earlier by Claude Welch.[19] Welch points out that there are roughly three attitudes toward the Trinity in the recent debates in this century.

The Trinity as Defensive Doctrine

In this view the Trinity sets out the parameters within which one must remain in order to defend orthodox teaching against heresy. Typical representatives of this way of thinking are Emil Brunner and Helmut Thielicke.[20]

The weakness of this approach is specifically its defensive character and its failure to relate the economic Trinity adequately to the eternal background of God's immanent being.

The Trinity as Synthesis

In this view one begins with a particular form of Christian experience based on Holy Scripture, but instead of having a controlling concept around which one thinks, there is a variety. These could be, for example, monotheism, incarnation, and the Holy Spirit; when brought together they give us a necessary trinitarian faith and conception of God. "The doctrine of the Trinity is thus interpreted as the completion of a doctrinal system, as the keystone which brings together in a unity the various aspects of the faith and which is therefore of great importance as the ultimate and necessary safeguard of the doctrinal system."[21]

The Trinity as Implicate of Revelation

This third aspect is regarded by Welch as the most acceptable view since it expresses who God is and what he does in the economy of salvation as testified in Holy Scripture. Instead, therefore, of being the combination of various aspects of the faith, the Trinity is "an arche, a *first* principle of all Christian thought and life."[22] In this way it points to and expresses the basic mystery of the faith, and so is to be set at the forefront of theology as determinative of the whole of its content and as the hermeneutical principle by which we interpret the nature of our faith. Its understanding and interpretation imply that God who is and acts is the triune God.[23]

This is the view which has most profoundly affected the theological scene today and has in large measure been adopted by a great many theologians, including Rahner,[24] Kasper,[25] and Torrance.[26] In contrast to the other views, it has a single basis, is positive rather than defensive in its meaning and significance, and has a concrete, relevant character. It means God himself speaking to us, addressing us in his freedom as sovereign, as Lord, in the event of his self-revelation. This is the root and basis of the doctrine of the Trinity. In this view revelation is the self-interpretation of God.[27] Barth sees the biblical testimony making known God who reveals himself as Lord—a sovereignty manifest in three forms, as Revealer, Revelation, and Revealedness. It points to an origin in God, to his self-disclosure in time, in reconciliation, to his giving us knowledge of this in our lives personally and communally.[28]

The doctrine of the Trinity is thus not directly identical with revelation since it is a work of the church with both positive and negative significance. But when this task is undertaken and this analysis made the implication of revelation is the doctrine of the Trinity. The Trinity, therefore, cannot be directly identical with revelation but only indirectly so. In other words, the witness of Scripture is to God's revelation, which leads in faith and life and by analysis of its content to the doctrine of the Trinity.

Economic and Immanent Trinity

When we say that God has revealed himself to us in Jesus Christ by the Holy Spirit we are speaking of the divine economy (*oikonomia*). "The term *economic* was the patristic expression for the orderly way in which God communicates himself to us within the structures of space and time, in which he remains what he is eternally in himself while communicating himself to us really and truly and without reserve in Jesus Christ and in his Spirit."[29] This is identical with revelation. The economy of salvation, while having a single basis, has a structured form and relationship manifested in God's actions for us. Torrance calls this the *theological level* when we speak of God, Christ, and Spirit.[30] The economic, however, points us to and conveys a higher level where in faith and thought we move to the being and act of God in himself as Father, Son, and Holy Spirit—the immanent Trinity. What God is in the economy of salvation he is antecedently and eternally in his own divine life. Torrance calls this the *higher theological and scientific level,* where "we discern the trinitarian relations immanent in God himself which lie behind, and are the ground of the relations of, the economic Trinity."[31] Modern theology has rightly emphasized that our analysis of the economic Trinity leading us to posit God as he is eternally in himself is no mere academic exercise, however rigorous our thought about it must be. Inspiration and content are and must always be the fellowship of faith, what Torrance calls the *evangelical and doxological level* of the Gospel and worship.[32] As the B.C.C. report reminds us, we are set not only before the task of analysis of revelation but before the being of the living God himself, *coram Deo.*[33]

The question now arises: How do we see economic and immanent Trinity related? They are, in our view, to be seen both in their *unity* with and *distinction* from each other. Both speak about one and the selfsame God. What the unity is meant to affirm is that it is really God himself in the fullness and wholeness of his being who is present and active in the economy of salvation. There are not two trinities, but the one eternal triune God in his own being and action is present with us and for us in the history of salvation. What the distinction is meant to underline is the priority of the immanent Trinity, that God is in himself Father, Son, and Holy Spirit eternally before time and creation were. "The immanent and economic trinity could not be identified or confused but *distinguished* and *united* in a way analogous to the Incarnate Logos."[34] Just as the incarnate word is the unity of two natures, divine and human in one person, so this being in the flesh is one with the eternal Word within the divine life. At the same time the Word comes into our humanity and as such, though one with it, is distinguished from the humanity assumed. So the economic Trinity as the coming of God in time and space is not confused or simply identified with these temporal events. This christological unity and distinction is the key to the trinitarian one since the unity of the Word or Son with the Father, the *homoousios,* is the key to the Trinity as such. Molnar expresses this correctly when he writes, "The immanent trinity is the indispensable premise of the economic trinitarian action *ad extra* but cannot be simply identified with these historical events."[35] To do so would be to draw up creaturely aspects into the deity and blur the very real distinction between creator and creature, the infinite qualitative distinction between God and humanity. Yet it is precisely this error that, in reaction to a barren scholasticism, much modern trinitarian theology is in danger of committing or actually does commit.

Karl Rahner

The strengths and some of the weaknesses of modern trinitarian perspectives may best be illustrated by their response to the thesis of Karl Rahner: "The 'economic' trinity is the 'immanent' trinity and the 'immanent' trinity is the 'economic' trinity."[36] Rahner's is basically a one-sided programmatic statement intended to focus attention on the reality of the triune nature of God in relation to his saving acts in time and space. In identifying the economic and immanent Trinity and vice versa Rahner is concerned to do two things. First, he seeks to link the being of the triune God (immanent) with the mystery of the free grace of God to us and our world (economic). Second, he wishes to emphasize that it is God who communicates himself to us. When we speak of God for us by the Son and in the Spirit we are speaking of God as he is, Father, Son, and Holy Spirit and not of some being other than God. Economic and immanent are one and the same.[37] Rahner writes, "In the trinity, in the economy and history of salvation and revelation we have already experienced the immanent trinity as it is in itself . . . because its free and supernatural manifestation to us in grace manifests its innermost life."[38]

This manifestation has a threefold form but the use of the term "persons" to indicate this could easily be misunderstood since person in modern parlance normally denotes an individual center of consciousness and freedom. This is not what was originally understood by the term. Rahner proposes that instead of three "persons" we should speak of three "distinct ways of subsisting."[39] This way of speaking suits better the unique oneness of the triune God.[40] Rahner is in fact saying that there is one nature and consciousness in God but there are three distinct ways in which God is as he communicates himself to us. This has strong support in the Western tradition, in dogma as well as in metaphysics.[41]

Further, Rahner is against these distinctions being seen as mere "appropriations" as in much traditional Catholic theology. The incarnation is central and crucial here. Since God has come in the incarnate Logos, this means that the manner of his communicating himself to us and being known is through the second person of the Trinity. Rahner states this clearly: "We cling to the truth that the logos is really as he appears in revelation, that he is *the one* who reveals to us (not merely *one* of those who might have revealed to us) the triune God, on account of the personal being which belongs exclusively to him, the Father's logos."[42] The Logos is the Father's word, his self-expression in eternity and time. Thus "we can assert, in the full meaning of the words: here the logos with God and the logos with us, the immanent and the economic logos are strictly the same."[43] So, too, analogous to this is the immanent and economic Trinity.

Again, Rahner sees the divine "processions" (Son from Father and Spirit from Father and Son) as the same as the "missions" of the three persons (their work in the world). "The communication bestowed on the creature in gratuitous grace can, *if* occurring in freedom, occur only in the intra-divine manner of the two communications of the divine essence by the Father to the Son and the Spirit."[44] God's self-relations are the same as his relations to us; his processions are his missions.

General Responses to Karl Rahner. Rahner has clearly succeeded in several ways: in showing that the triune God we know in revelation is God eternally without reserve; and in turning attention away from abstract and general theories that God could become man in any one of the three persons. He clearly affirms that the Logos and not simply God in general is incarnate even though this involves participation of the Father and the Spirit with the Son in this act of incarnation. The obvious inference is also that the immanent and economic Trinity are one since the one Logos leads us to the Father and the Holy Spirit. This is true as far as it goes, and Rahner is clearly to be supported in so underlining and emphasizing the unity of immanent and economic Trinity.

However, his position fails to make any real kind of distinction, which is equally necessary. Rahner has also largely failed to distinguish between the free mystery of grace in the economy and the *necessary* mystery of the Trinity per se. This risks making God's actions *ad extra* a necessity of his being rather than a freely willed decision. Neither an inner necessity of being nor an outward compulsion, but only his will to be our God, obliges God to act. Yves Congar writes: "As the fathers who combated Arianism said, even if God's creatures did not exist God would still be a trinity of Father, Son and Holy Spirit since creation is an act of free will."[45] One might add here too that salvation is an act of the same gracious will. What God wills must obviously correspond to and not contradict his divine nature but the two are nevertheless to be distinguished. The truth and the reality of God's triune nature as immanent are alluded to only tangentially by Rahner himself. "Distinction and mediation show us God *as he is in himself.*"[46] Molnar, countering the position of Rahner, states clearly the freedom of God in the incarnation: "Thus the incarnation can neither be seen nor described as *essential* to God; what is here revealed can neither be deduced from a general theory of incarnation, nor from the intra-trinitarian life,"[47] namely, the being of the triune God.

A similar point is seen in Rahner's tendency to identify the "processions" and the "missions," or "sendings" as they were called. The eternal generation of the Son by the Father belongs to the reality of the being of God. "The procession of the persons takes place in accordance with nature, *kata phusin.*"[48] Congar quotes Athanasius as saying, "Even if God had decided not to create, he would nevertheless have had his Son."[49] The mission of the Son is, as noted, an act of God's purpose in salvation. Rahner calls the generation, self-possession, and missions "self-expression."[50] But, as DiNoia states, such tight identification of processions and missions "can suggest that the trinity really would not be fully itself independently of the orders of creation and redemption."[51] To make the immanent Trinity, God in fact, depend on or be identical with his creaturely acts in the economy, though understood from this perspective, is surely a misplaced judgment and a real reversal of roles.

A further criticism has been offered by DiNoia. Rahner, following a Greek tradition, identifies the Father with God. In this way he attempts to overcome the dichotomy between the unity and trinity of God. The Father in that case is true God and one who gives his deity to Son and Spirit. The danger here is that the Son and Spirit are treated in a way that could easily lead to subordinationism, to a hierarchy in God. "Lurking in this approach is the danger of subordinationism which can only be overcome by a vigorous subsequent defense of the substantial divinity of the Son and the Spirit against the suggestion that they are only derivatively divine."[52] This is followed by the controversial remark by DiNoia which runs counter to much current thinking about the Trinity: "In any case, it is not clear that a creative recovery of Greek patristic trinitarian theology would necessarily facilitate a spiritual and pastoral retrieval of what might be called trinitarian realism."[53] DiNoia goes on to support Augustine and Aquinas, as in one sense he must. The Cappadocians, however, following Athanasius, "were champions of the homoousios both of the Son . . . and of the Spirit"[54] and cannot justly be accused of subordinationism.

The final and most serious criticism of Rahner's thesis, though not necessarily of his intention, is that while the economic Trinity is one with the immanent (though distinguished from it), to say that the immanent is the economic may be a serious error. The danger lies in collapsing the immanent Trinity into the economic and making God dependent on his historical manifestation. In this view God is the triune God only in the economy of salvation. But as Thielicke says, "The economic trinity becomes a heretical alternative only when it integrates and completely absorbs the being of God into the event of revelation."[55] If, therefore, our knowledge of God is limited to the economy, there is then no ontic background to the historical revelation and no knowledge of an ontological nature of God in himself; in fact no such God exists.

In this view we usually find a Christology where Jesus is merely human, is an adopted son, and where Father, Jesus, and Spirit have a being only in the history of Jesus by the Spirit in time. Alternatively, the triune being of God can come to full existence only as it takes up into itself the history with which it is involved. Again, God may be said to have no fullness or perfection of life in himself but needs the other, the world and human beings, to be in some sense triune. Here one can easily end up with a philosophical concept of Trinity or with one where, as Thielicke puts it, "The three persons of the trinity become masks in a phenomenal drama."[56] The most obvious example of this type of thinking is the work of Schoonenberg,[57] where any idea of an immanent Trinity disappears and God is known as triune only in his relation to us and the world. This means not only the evaporation of the immanent Trinity but of the real economic as well since one cannot have an economy of salvation without the reality of the eternal triune God. "Such a course only deprives the economic trinity of all meaning and significance. For it has meaning and significance only if God is present in the history of salvation as the one who he is from all eternity; more accurately, if God does not simply *show* himself to us as Father, Son and Spirit in the history of salvation, but *is* in fact Father, Son and Spirit from all eternity."[58] In Schoonenberg's view the trinity of God is dissipated by being radically historicized though not explicitly denied.

Walter Kasper clearly sees what is necessary here and states it simply by showing how Rahner's thesis can be better interpreted. He writes,

> We may therefore rephrase Rahner's basic axiom as follows: in the economic self-communication the intra-trinitarian self-communication is present in the world in a new way, namely under the veil of historical works, signs and actions, and ultimately in the figure of the man Jesus of Nazareth. The need is to maintain not only the kenotic character of the economic trinity but also its character of graciousness and freedom in relation to the immanent trinity and thus to do justice to the immanent mystery of God in (not behind) his self-revelation.[59]

This clearly is correct and must be understood in the light of Kasper's own clear view. God is eternally Father, Son, and Holy Spirit and knowledge of this comes through the gracious revelation of God in Christ by the Spirit in the economy of salvation.

Ecumenical Reponses to Karl Rahner. There have been two main ecumenical responses to Rahner's thesis. First is a colloquium held in Switzerland from 18 to 21 March 1975, whose findings are summarized and interpreted by Thomas F. Torrance.[60] The other is a series of essays edited by Wilhelm Breuning published in 1984.[61]

In the first colloquium Torrance believes Rahner's treatise points in the direction of a theological consensus in three ways: (1) between a systematic theology of the Trinity and biblical teaching; (2) between East and West in relating it to worship and church; and (3) between Roman Catholic and Evangelical theology, especially that of Karl Barth, who bases his doctrine on revelation and gives the Trinity a normative role in dogmatics.[62] Yet while Torrance believes Barth and Rahner have many points in common, he also believes that Rahner never quite frees himself from the abstractions of Scholasticism, even though he moves in the direction of a more biblical, Eastern conception of the Trinity. Rahner's use of terms like truth and love, replacing intelligence and love of Augustine, to describe the relation of Son and Spirit leads to abstraction, as does the use of the Anselmic view of personal distinctions as the "opposition of relation." "He is misled by a rational analysis of merely inter-human connections and this allows connections of that kind to dictate what can and cannot be within the interpersonal relations of God."[63] Here a logical scholastic framework applied by analogy to the divine persons has not been fully broken through to a theology of revelation and the economy; as a consequence, the doctrine of relations is inadequately stated.

A further critical point similar to this one is made by Werner Löser[64] in relation to the unity of God. He asks: Is there not in Rahner's understanding and expression of unity traces of Western thinking as seen in the philosophy of being and spirit which understands unity to mean identity, consciousness, and absence of plurality? This is clearly not Rahner's intention but he does have a particular, indeed classical, metaphysic, a certain understanding of being which colors his views of God's nature and his self-disclosure. If, as at times seems the case, he reads the latter in light of the former there is a tension between this and how the New Testament speaks of the interrelationship of Father, Son, and Holy Spirit. This is never quite overcome in Rahner's thinking.

The Swiss colloquium, while rejecting a purely individualistic concept of person, expressed its dissatisfaction with Rahner's alternative proposals of a change to "distinct manner of subsisting." The phrase as such is not really objectionable but is close to Barth's "mode of being," going back as far as the _modi entis_ of the Cappadocians. Rahner, however, contrary to his identification of economic and immanent Trinity, inconsistently uses "person" to speak of God's relation to us in our Christian life and worship but "distinct manner of subsisting" to speak of God as such.

Thus, conscious of tritheistic tendencies, Rahner does not speak of the "persons" of Father, Son, and Holy Spirit as experiencing mutual relationships of love and so does less than justice to the biblical witness which clearly speaks of such interrelationships. Torrance sees this as a weakness and proposes instead that "while Father, Son and Holy Spirit constitute one indivisible God they do so as three conscious subjects in mutual love and life and activity."[65] This depends very much on how one defines person, whether it has ontological connotations per se or whether persons are distinctive personal relationships within an existing ontological reality. Here East and West still divide, and Torrance's suggestion of three subjects does not lead us wholly away from divided views to an ecumenical consensus.

Eberhard Jüngel

Jüngel[66] takes up Rahner's axiom and agrees with it but interprets it in the context of his own theology. His is a theology of the cross which shows us the selfless love of God and defines God as one who identifies himself in his Son with the death of the man Jesus. That love displays both a self-related aspect—one who is loved—and a self-giving aspect. In speaking of the trinitarian nature of the divine love, he maintains that there is "a 'still greater selflessness in the midst of a very great and justifiably great self-relatedness.'" This

> is nothing other than a self-relationship which in freedom goes beyond itself, overflows itself, and gives itself away. It is pure overflow, overflowing being for the sake of another and only then for the sake of itself. That is love. And that is the God who is love: the one who always heightens and expands his own being in such great self-relatedness still more selfless and *thus* overflowing. Based on that insight, Karl Rahner's thesis should be given unqualified agreement. . . . This statement is correct because God himself takes place in Jesus' God-forsakenness and death (Mark 15 34–37). What the Passion story narrates is the actual conceptualization of the doctrine of the Trinity."[67]

Jüngel makes four statements here which are of the essence of his trinitarian thinking and which distance him somewhat from his mentor Karl Barth and bring him closer to Rahner. First, as Father, Son, and Holy Spirit, God is self-related in love. Second, the very nature of this love is its utter selflessness seen on the cross where the Father gives the Son to death by the Holy Spirit. Third, this love by its very nature surpasses God's inner relationships with himself. Since it is free and selfless it overflows and expands in giving itself away to humanity and creation. Fourth, in this act of God's identification with the death of the man Jesus, God himself as triune has his being and life. In the selfless death of Jesus God is manifest not only as love but also as *victorious* life.

One could summarize Jüngel's position in this way by saying that it is only as God is for us in the Son Jesus that he is for himself as Father, Son, and Holy Spirit. For this reason "it is unnecessary to safeguard divine aseity by positing an essence of God behind his loving *pro nobis*; for his aseity takes form as loving self-renunciation. . . . The God who is love is thus neither master nor victim. His self-love is not the antithesis of his self-gift, but its ultimate ground: in giving himself away, he does not lose but becomes himself."[68]

Jüngel acknowledges only a very minor rational distinction between economic and immanent Trinity. Their unity must not be thought of as tautological but as an expression of the free, undeserved grace of God present in the act of his self-communication. This *distinctio rationis* points to the Trinity as mystery.[69]

Evaluation and Critique

Jüngel is in line with much modern thought on the Trinity in linking it to the cross as the cost of our salvation. He is critical of Rahner centering his thesis on the incarnation and lacking a proper soteriological interpretation where Jesus is seen as the accursed one judged for our sin.[70] Löser is critical of both Rahner and Jüngel in that Rahner reaches back too much to classical metaphysics, which accepts being as spirit and identity, whereas

Jüngel rejects this and also natural theology and theism in line with Karl Barth. Löser pleads for a middle way, an alternative metaphysic of love based on book 3 of Richard of St. Victor's *De Trinitate.*[71]

Several critical points must, however, be made in relationship to Jüngel's own work. First, there is a certain ambivalence in the use of the term love. Is it, as is generally understood, a predicate of God known in his self-revelation, or does a general view of love in some sense condition our understanding of God's love? Jüngel, as Molnar states,[72] appears to follow Barth's method when he writes, "obviously the being of the triune God is not to be deduced from the logic of the essence of love."[73] Yet, for all his wish to follow this, Jüngel" cannot hold this position consistently,"[74] since he believes "even the understanding of the trinitarian history as the history of love presupposes a pre-understanding of love."[75] Even thinking within a christological context Jüngel can say that he believes he can provide help for a "better understanding when we first ask generally what love is."[76] Here the general (love) and the particular (God's love in Christ) are set side by side and seem to some extent to condition one another. Jüngel thus does not, as is his intention, allow Christ alone to interpret the meaning of God's love.

Second, Jüngel comes perilously near making the incarnation and the cross a necessity for God. His idea is that God almost automatically overflows in creation and redemption so that this becomes not free grace but a natural expression of the being of the triune God. Further, involved in this is the dubious idea of "a heightening and expansion . . . of the divine being."[77] Does this not imply that God becomes "ever more" (to use von Balthasar's phrase) in his self-giving on the cross to his creation than in his eternal life?

Third, Jüngel's affirmation is that God "takes place" in Jesus' God-forsakenness and death on the cross. If one means by this that God reveals his very self, this is clearly correct. However, the ambiguity in the phrase could also point to the fact that on the cross God becomes himself; the cross thus becomes constitutive of God— immanent and economic are one. This is again scarcely Jüngel's intention but it is the logic of his position. There is thus a weakness here which fails to speak of the eternal Son and Spirit as from the Father before all ages or of God being truly God without the creation of the world.

What in fact seems to be happening here is that Jüngel takes Barth's view of the humanity of God and presses it further than its original meaning and significance. This view is that in his eternal election God wills to be and is our God, "ours in advance," so that there is no *Logos Asarkos* but only a *Logos Ensarkos.* Jüngel writes, "God aims in his divine eternal becoming towards the incarnation of man."[78] There are places in this same section where Jüngel seems to understand this, as Barth does, as a distinction between immanent and economic since he qualifies it by saying that though "God is adequate to himself,"[79] he is overflowing being and this is an expression of his grace. But if, as we have seen, overflowing being is something which is in the very nature of God, is it not a necessity of that nature?

Here there is continuing lack of clarity, an ambiguity which is at best obscuring and at worst misleading. Jüngel's subtle argument would be better served by greater emphasis on the distinction between the immanent and economic trinity.

Trinity and Eschatology

The theme of eschatology has also dominated the modern scene and plays its part in the debate on the Trinity, especially in the writings of Jürgen Moltmann[80] and Wolfhart Pannenberg.[81] We look at each briefly in turn to see how they react to Rahner's thesis.

Jürgen Moltmann

In his earlier writing Moltmann accepted Rahner's thesis but related it to the cross and the relation of Father and Son rather than the incarnation.[82] Later he developed his own distinctive position which could no longer maintain an identity between the economic and immanent Trinity.[83] His teaching can be usefully summed up in the following sentences. "The Trinity in the Sending is, from its eternal origin, open to the world and to men. For with this the history of God's seeking love is begun. The trinity in the glorification is, from its eschatological goal, open for the gathering and uniting of men and the whole creation with God and in God."[84]

There are three significant elements in this process or trinitarian movement. First, the Trinity in the origin is prior to the economic form, is its source and basis. "Now . . . Moltmann allows the validity and Barthian inference back from economic trinity to an immanent trinity."[85] This form is scarcely in line with the traditional teaching on the immanent Trinity since later this takes another form which is manifest at the end of time. Second, the Trinity in the origin is open for its own sending, for man and all creation. This is equivalent to the economic Trinity. Here God has a history with the world. He allows what happens to him in the world in time and on the cross to act back and influence him and so change him. "Moltmann still wishes to maintain an important element of historical becoming in God in his history with man."[86] Third, this becoming in God points forward to a Trinity at the end in glorification. God's history with the world "points beyond itself to the goal of the trinitarian history of God's dealings with the world."[87] "The glory of God is only completed (Rom. 11.36) when 'the creation at the beginning' is consummated by 'the new creation at the end.'"[88] The Father reaches out by the Son and, through his experience in and with the world by the Holy Spirit, gathers humanity and all creation into unity with and in himself. Only then will God be all in all. Bauckham remarks, "This history is for God not only an experience of the world, but also an experience of himself in that the events between the persons of the trinity cannot leave the relationships between the persons absolutely the same as before."[89] God's earlier experiences to and on the cross are those of suffering, death, and hell. From the resurrection to the end they are experiences of joy in the creation of history. "As a consequence the trinity in glorification has the predominance and prominence before the trinity in the Sending."[90]

Bauckham points out that for Moltmann "the economic trinity could be seen as open both behind and in front to an immanent trinity."[91] But how can one have two conceptions of the immanent Trinity which are manifestly different? Is not the eschatological Trinity in Moltmann's terms the real and only permanent, immanent Trinity? That it is so is due to his continued overemphasis on eschatology and the Hegelian structure, if not content, of his doctrine. This involves a "becoming" in God in time, on the cross, in humanity and creation which is inconsistent with an immanent Trinity where God is eternally Father, Son, and Holy Spirit—a being in eternal becoming, as Jüngel interprets Barth. God, in Moltmann's terms, is not truly God without his history with humanity and creation and his suffering on the cross. For Moltmann, "The cross as the key to the doctrine of God, not only reveals God as the kind of love which is willing to suffer, but in the sense that the actual sufferings of the cross are essential to who God is. This attempt to take God's temporal experience as seriously as possible ends up by eternalising it."[92] This is the same as saying that Moltmann confuses economic and immanent Trinity since he fails to make a proper distinction between creator and creature, the redeemer and the redeemed. Does he not also end up with a form of universalism at one with his panentheism?

Wolfhart Pannenberg

Pannenberg's theology, like Moltmann's, is determined throughout by its eschatological dimension. Two main aspects of it are relevant for our present discussion and these are based on Old Testament prophecies and biblical Apocalyptic writings, which, according to Pannenberg, give the future of God priority in determining his nature.[93]

Pannenberg begins with a Christology from "below."[94] The history of Jesus is seen as that of one who calls God his father and preaches the coming kingdom of God. The resurrection works retroactively and shows that, whether Jesus claimed and knew it or not, he was the Son of God and so one with the Father. This is equivalent to God's self-revelation[95] and already shows the beginnings of a trinitarian outline. Pannenberg sums this up in these words:

> The foundation of the doctrine of the trinity must derive from the *content* of the revelation of God in Jesus Christ, from the relationship of Jesus to the Father as this finds expression in the context of the news of God's rule. . . . The relationship of [Jesus'] message and work to the Father forms the basis for the confession of the christian community of the sonship of Jesus in the light of the divine confirmation by the Easter event.[96]

The resurrection is central for another reason: it gives access to a proper understanding of the role of the Spirit.[97] The Spirit comes from the risen Christ, is given to believers, and is seen as drawn into the fellowship of the Son with the Father.

Second, the resurrection of Jesus is the prolepsis of the final manifestation of God as he will be and so is.[98] This eschatological perspective anticipated in Jesus but not yet fulfilled is determinative for our understanding of the persons and relationships of the triune God. Further confirming factors are the general view of universal history implicit in all human experience, the understanding of all reality as historical, following Hegel, and the perception of its universal scope gained from the Christian revelation. "This view of history . . . from which the unity of history can be conceived is anticipated in the destiny of Jesus of Nazareth."[99]

Pannenberg clearly affirms the unity of being of Father and Son and with them of the Holy Spirit. He believes, however, that the eschatological dimension both gives us a better conception of the persons of the Trinity and their interrelationship than past doctrine and also offers a valid critique of some aspects of traditional teaching both East and West.[100] The Son receives not only his being from the Father but all power in heaven and on earth (Matt. 28:18). But in the eschatological perspective the Son will return the power to the Father and the rule of God will be complete (1 Cor. 15:28).[101] This means that the latter act is an aspect of the inner trinitarian relationships. At the same time it is a critique of the older view of a distinction between the "generation" of the Son in the immanent Trinity and the "sending" in the economic. What happens at the end in the climax of God's rule in history by Jesus belongs to the nature of the triune God. Pannenberg sees this as, with Rahner, identifying the immanent and economic Trinity. He believes, with Moltmann, that this end fulfillment is doxological. "The glorification of the Son and the Father by the Spirit . . . is to be evaluated as an inner trinitarian relationship because it is not directed outwards but to the Son and Father."[102] In contrast to Moltmann, however, Pannenberg denies that this means God becomes triune at the end. His view envisages a mutual giving and receiving between the persons, which constitutes their triune identity at the last and provides an aspect of dynamic and mutuality lacking in traditional teaching. His answer to the problem this eschatological perspective poses is to say that just as the Easter event gives us knowledge that Jesus is the eternal Son, so it is retroactively decided and confirmed from the end that the triune God is such eternally. Pannenberg writes, "The eschatological future of the fulfilment of history in the kingdom of God is given a very special function as a foundation for faith in the triune God. Based on this event the being of God has been decided from eternity to eternity, that is before the foundation of the world."[103]

The twin models Pannenberg uses—Jesus-resurrection and resurrection-eschaton—have their proper place in New Testament teaching. In this respect Pannenberg has many illuminating insights and a more cohesive systematic doctrine of the Trinity than Moltmann. Yet it must be questioned if these models are used correctly. In the first the cross is little mentioned and the ephapax (once-for-allness) of revelation and reconciliation as a completed event making known at the center of history the full reality of the triune God is scarcely touched upon. This latter view, if accepted, gives a quite different conception of the final consummation than the one Pannenberg envisages. Is it not also reading too much into one text in 1 Corinthians 15:28 to give it such overall significance for the doctrine of the Trinity? And is a reading back of an eternal Trinity from the end constituted by the rule of God through Jesus and the Spirit in the world a valid approach to the immanent Trinity? It does unite the immanent and economic Trinity but does it not at the same time make the rule of God in history in some measure constitutive of his being? Pannenberg wants to avoid this but also seems to want to have it both ways and say that the Trinity so constituted is God's being from and to all eternity. Yet he enters so fully and subtly into the relationships and nature of the triune God that the identity and union of economic and immanent Trinity cannot be fully maintained even on his interpretation of the Scriptures. He writes, "The affirmation of a *trinity of revelation* implies . . . an *ontological trinity*, a trinitarian fellowship of Father, Son and Holy Spirit from and to all eternity."[104] Here it would seem that a proper distinction as well as union is being hinted at by Pannenberg, though his intention was earlier clearly only identity. Thus, despite Pannenberg's eschatology, there eventually emerges not only the union of immanent and economic Trinity but a distinction as well between the being and action of God in himself and that toward the world.

Trinity: Unity and Distinction

I have taken the position in this chapter that, while there is a union between the economic Trinity and the immanent Trinity, there is good reason also to distinguish them. Some of the arguments against this view have been examined and found wanting since they largely fail to give proper place to the freedom and grace of God or, as it is sometimes put, they confuse the creator and his creation.[105] Two writers, though different in many ways, who have given detailed analysis of this question and basically agree with the foregoing thesis are Karl Barth and Han Urs von Balthasar. Their views are outlined briefly in conclusion.

Karl Barth

Barth's earlier trinitarian theology was written from the perspective of the revelation of God as Lord. Revelation is centered in Christ but has a threefold form indicative of a trinitarian conception of God. God is as he is revealed. The economy of salvation is the key to the nature of God in his eternal, immanent life. Barth writes,

"We have consistently followed the rule, which we regard as basic, that statements about the divine modes of being antecedently in themselves cannot
be different in content from those that are being made about their reality in
revelation. All our statements concerning what is called the immanent trinity have been reached simply as confirmations or underlinings or, materially,
as the indispensable premises of the economic trinity. . . . The reality of God
which encounters us in his revelation is his reality in all the depths of eternity.[106]

God as antecedently in himself what he is in revelation underlines the
unity. But the fact that he is God without us indicates the distinction when
Barth writes, "He is this loving God without us as Father, Son and Holy
Spirit, in the freedom of the Lord who has life from himself."[107] The economic is, however, the *Erkenntnisgrund*, the basis of our knowledge that
God has a life in himself. Our knowledge of the immanent Trinity is thus
indirect but true knowledge. The distinction is meant to establish God's
sovereign Lordship, the unity to avoid any dichotomy between God in himself and God revealed.

Barth makes several significant and original contributions to this debate.
First, he interprets God in the light of his election of himself and of Jesus
Christ his Son to be the God of humanity and humanity to be with God.
This is seen in the economy of salvation. God cannot be known apart from
this election and the relationship to humanity it involves. This relationship
"once made . . . belongs definitively to God himself, *not in his being in himself* [but] in his being within this relationship."[108] Jesus Christ is thus no
Logos Asarkos but *Logos Ensarkos*, one whose will is to become man. This
means no divinizing of our humanity but affirms that the Logos in God
has such a nature and will that makes it possible in his freedom to be one
with us; the immanent has a thrust toward the economic. God is "ours in
advance."[109]

Second, Barth's doctrine of reconciliation works this out in practice with
a trinitarian theology of cross and resurrection.[110] The high and holy God
who has life in himself is known only in the humility, obedience, and contradiction of the cross of Jesus Christ the Son. The resurrection reveals that
death as life and victory; the Holy Spirit brings us the benefits of this passion, death and triumph. The high and holy one who inhabits eternity (immanent) is not identical with humility as such but nonetheless has this ability
to be himself *sub contrario in cruce* (economic). "It is in the light of the
fact of his humiliation . . . that all the predicates of his Godhead, which is
the true Godhead, must be filled out and interpreted."[111] Barth here both
speaks against false conceptions of God and shows at the same time the
greatest possible unity between God as he is in himself and the crucified
God. To this extent the immanent and economic are one. Yet Barth never
forgets that there is also a distinction to be made between the two—the
eternal creator and his involvement in the created temporal order.

It is in the light of the preceding views of the humanity of God, as Barth
calls it, in Jesus Christ that we may interpret passages where, Molnar feels,

Barth "occasionally appears to have blurred the distinction" between economic and immanent Trinity.[112] There are undoubtedly such passages and ambiguities in Barth, but they do not go against the prevailing evidence that Barth maintained to the end in his *Church Dogmatics* a proper balance between the immanent and economic Trinity.

Third, an important further piece of evidence here is Barth's teaching on analogy, which, together with his christological concentration, forms one of the most prominent features of his writing. Revelation or the economy of salvation has "its basis and prototype in his [God's] own essence, in his own being as God."[113] Jüngel, interpreting Barth, writes, "God's being *ad extra corresponds* essentially to his being *ad intra* in which it has its basis and prototype. God's *self*-interpretation [revelation] is interpretation as 'correspondence.'"[114] Or, as Jüngel puts it epigrammatically, "God corresponds to himself."[115] It is, however, a correspondence which is not a synthesis or simple identity but a relationship of union and distinction. Here in a clear way the economic Trinity is God himself present with us interpreting himself analogically as the one he really is (immanent). Barth in his own original ways is fully in line with those who see God's trinitarian life interpreted from the perspective of the cross and resurrection but also related to the incarnation. More, however, than many modern interpreters he gives the latter its full place within this context.

Hans Urs von Balthasar

Werner Löser is correct when he states that von Balthasar's "whole theological work has trinitarian contours."[116] Balthasar explicitly deals with Rahner's thesis. He states clearly his opposition to both Rahner and Moltmann. O'Hanlon writes,

> This drama of the immanent trinity, revealed in the economic, can be appreciated properly only if one avoids an incorrect notion of the relationship between the immanent and economic trinity. It will not do, like Rahner, to identify too closely the two emphasising the economic trinity excessively and formalising the immanent. Nor may one, like Moltmann, propose a Hegelian-type identification in which the cross is seen as the fulfilment of the trinity in a Process Theology-like way which has no difficulty in directly ascribing change and suffering to God, and which ends up with a mythological, tragic image of God. . . . [T]he economic does not constitute the immanent trinity.[117]

The two perceptions of the Trinity clearly belong together and say two things: the economic is the place from which one knows the immanent, but they are not simply to be identified else God could be equated with or absorbed into a world process.

Balthasar puts it in this way: "We know the Father, Son and Holy Spirit as divine persons only from the manner and behaviour of Jesus Christ. The basic formula much used in our day that we know the immanent trinity only from the knowledge of the economic and can venture statements about it is to be accepted."[118] In this he is close to Rahner but immediately qualifies this statement:

> From the Christian perspective the economic trinity is to be seen as the exposition of the immanent but the latter is the basis which sustains the former and may not be identified with it. For in that case the immanent and eternal trinity of God threatens to disappear in the economic or, more clearly expressed, God will be interwoven with the world process and only through this come to himself. In the trinity opened up to us in Jesus Christ both are known together—that God as Father, Son and Holy Spirit is involved with the world for its salvation. The dogma of the Trinity has profound soteriological meaning. However it is as God who is love that he is involved with it. He does not first become love because he has the world as his counterpart and partner but because in himself, exalted over the world, he is love itself.[119]

This could scarcely be put more clearly and succinctly. Molnar, who strongly supports Barth's position and thus also that of Balthasar, summarizes: "The immanent trinity (God's antecedent existence as Father, Son and Spirit) can neither be identified with, separated from nor synthesized with each other or with the sphere of history (the economy)."[120] Both Barth and Balthasar thereby understand God's transcendence and freedom in relation to creation. Both state that God's Godness can be preserved only if a distinction is made between his eternal being and life on the one hand and his action in the drama of the world and its salvation on the other. Barth, however, more closely than Balthasar draws into this relationship of God with himself as triune by election, by reconciliation, and by the *Logos Ensarkos* the element of our humanity.

Notes

1. Karl Rahner, *The Trinity*, tr. Joseph Donceel (London: Burns and Oates, 1970), pp. 15–20, for a Catholic critique of these views. Traditional Protestant Dogmatics were equally at fault. Cf. Heinrich Heppe, *Reformed Dogmatics. Set Out and Illustrated from the Sources*, foreword by Karl Barth, rev. and ed. Ernst Bizer, tr. G. T. Thomson (Grand Rapids, Mich.: Baker Book House, 1978). Chapters 4 and 5 speak of "The Existence and Notion of God" and "The Attributes of God" (pp. 47–104), before coming in Chapter 6 to "The Holy Trinity" (pp. 105ff). Similarly, Heinrich Schmid, *Doctrinal Theology of the Evangelical Lutheran Church*, 3d ed., tr. Charles A. Hay and Henry E. Jacobs (Minneapolis: Augsburg Publishing House, 1961) has a chapter entitled "Of God" (pp. 104–29) preceding "Of the Holy Trinity" (pp. 129ff).

2. Karl Barth, *Church Dogmatics*, II/1, pp. 79ff. (hereafter cited as *C.D.*). Herbert Hartwell, *The Theology of Karl Barth: An Introduction* (London: Duckworth, 1964), writes of Barth's position: "We know God exclusively as one who acts upon us as the triune God . . . since he is the living God, it is not possible to abstract his real work and action in favour of a being of God in general. Holy Scripture does not allow us 'this splitting up of the concept of God'" (p. 50).

3. Karl Barth, *Dogmatics in Outline*, tr. G. T. Thomson (London: S.C.M. Press, 1949), p. 50.

4. T. F. Torrance, *The Ground and Grammar of Theology* (Belfast: Christian Journals, 1980), pp. 147–48.

5. Otto Weber, *Foundations of Dogmatics*, vol. 1, tr. Darrell L. Guder (Grand Rapids, Mich: William B. Eerdmans, 1981), p. 351.

6. Rahner, pp. 15–20.

7. Ibid., pp. 17–18.

8. Ibid., p. 17.

9. Werner Löser, "Trinitätstheologie Heute: Ansätze und Entwürfe," in *Trinität: Aktuelle Perspektiven der Theologie*, Wilhelm Breuning, ed. (Freiburg: Herder, 1984), p. 22.

10. Walter Kasper, *The God of Jesus Christ*, tr. Matthew J. O'Connell (New York: Crossroad, 1989), p. 233.

11. Rahner, p. 21.

12. See Heppe, p. 105.

13. Kasper, p. 268.

14. Ibid.

15. *C.D.*, I/1, pp. 321, 330.

16. Kasper, p. 271.

17. Ibid., p. 270.

18. *C.D.*, I/1, pp. 304ff.

19. Claude Welch, *The Trinity in Contemporary Theology* (London: S.C.M. Press, 1953), pp. 161ff., 226ff.

20. Ibid., pp. 65ff. It should be pointed out, however, that Welch also sets out a great variety of trinitarian statements other than these. See Helmut Thielicke, *The Evangelical Faith*, vol. 2, tr. Geoffrey W. Bromiley (Edinburgh: T. & T. Clark, 1977), pp. 137–57.

21. Welch, p. 47. See also pp. 125–60.

22. Ibid., p. 48; also see exposition of Karl Barth's position (pp. 161–216). Welch, while following this, has some critical reservations about Barth's views, especially on natural theology.

23. Welch, p. 45.

24. Rahner, pp. 83ff.

25. Kasper, pp. 238–48.

26. T. F. Torrance, *The Mediation of Christ* (Exeter: Paternoster Press, 1983), pp. 11ff., and in most of Torrance's other writings.

27. *C.D.*, I/1, p. 311. Cf. Eberhard Jüngel, *The Doctrine of the Trinity*, tr. Horton Harris (Edinburgh: Scottish Academic Press, 1976), p. 15.

28. *C.D.*, I/1, pp. 295ff.

29. Torrance, *Ground and Grammar*, p. 157.

30. Ibid.

31. Ibid., p. 158.

32. Ibid., p. 156.

33. *The Forgotten Trinity. The Report of the B.C.C. Study Commission on Trinitarian Doctrine Today* (London: British Council of Churches, Inter-Church House, 1989), vol. 1, p. 3 (hereafter cited as *B.C.C. Report*).

34. Paul D. Molnar, "The Function of the Immanent Trinity in the Theology of Karl Barth: Implications for Today," *Scottish Journal of Theology*, vol. 42, no. 3, 1989, pp. 369–70 (italics added). Molnar here is interpreting Barth.

35. Ibid., p. 373.

36. Rahner, p. 22.

37. Ibid., pp. 21ff.

38. Karl Rahner, *Foundations of Christian Faith: An Introduction to the Idea of Christianity*, tr. William V. Dych (London: Darton, Longman & Todd, 1978), p. 137.

39. Ibid. Also Rahner, *The Trinity*, pp. 103ff. esp. p. 110f.

40. Rahner, *Foundations*, pp. 134–5.

41. Löser, p. 26.

42. Rahner, *The Trinity*, p. 30.

43. Ibid., p. 33.

44. Ibid., p. 36.

45. Yves Congar, *I Believe in the Holy Spirit*, vol. 3, *The River of Life Flows in the East and in the West*, tr. David Smith (London: Geoffrey Chapman, 1983), p. 13.

46. Rahner, *The Trinity*, p. 36 n. 4.

47. Molnar, p. 381. Cf. Löser, who asks if Rahner can really think of God's freedom given his presuppositions. Does not the close association or identification of economic and immanent Trinity undermine the free grace of God in his revelation? (p. 30).

48. Congar, p. 13.

49. Ibid., p. 18 n. 7. Athanasius, *Contra Arianos*, I, 18.

50. See J. I. DiNoia, "Karl Rahner," in *The Modern Theologians: An Introduction to Christian Theology in the Twentieth Century*, vol. 1, David Ford, ed. (Oxford: Basil Blackwell, 1989), p. 197.

51. Ibid., pp. 197–98.

52. Ibid., p. 196. John Zizioulas, at a conference on the Trinity at King's College, London, September 1990, admitted in answer to questions that this is a possible interpretation and danger of Eastern thought on the Trinity.

53. Ibid., pp. 196–97.

54. J. N. D. Kelly, *Early Christian Doctrines*, 5th ed. (London: Adam & Charles Black), p. 264.

55. Thielicke, p. 181.

56. Ibid.

57. Cf. P. Schoonenberg, "Trinität—der vollendete Bund. Thesen zur Lehre vom dreipersönlichen Gott," in *Orientierung* (Zurich, 1973), pp. 115–17. Also Hans Küng, *Does God Exist? An Answer for Today*, tr. E. Quinn (New York: Doubleday, 1980), p. 499. On similar lines Hendrikus Berkhof, *Christian Faith: An Introduction to a Study of the Faith*, tr. Sierd Woudstra (Grand Rapids, Mich.: William B. Eerdmans, 1979) sees the terms Father, Son, and Spirit as "the summarizing description of the covenantal event" (p. 336) and not as a description of God as triune.

58. Kasper, p. 276 (italics added).

59. Ibid.

60. T. F. Torrance, "Towards an Ecumenical Consensus on the Trinity," *Theologische Zeitschrift*, vol. 31, no. 6, 1975, pp. 337–50.

61. Wilhelm Breuning, ed., *Trinität: Aktuelle Perspektiven der Theologie*, (Freiburg: Herder, 1984).

62. Torrance, "Ecumenical Consensus," p. 337.

63. Ibid., p. 344.

64. Löser, pp. 29–30.
65. Torrance, "Ecumenical Consensus," p. 347.
66. Eberhard Jüngel, *God as the Mystery of the World*, tr. Darrell L. Guder (Edinburgh: T. & T. Clark, 1983).
67. Ibid., pp. 369–70.
68. John Webster, *Eberhard Jüngel: An Introduction to His Theology* (London: Cambridge University Press, 1986), p. 72.
69. E. Jüngel, "Das Verhältnis von 'ökonomischer' und 'immanenter' Trinität," in *Entsprechungen, Gott-Wahrheit-Mensch* (Munich: Ch. Kaiser, 1980), p. 275.
70. Ibid., p. 273.
71. Löser, p. 35.
72. Molnar, p. 391.
73. Jüngel, *Mystery*, p. 316.
74. Molnar, p. 391.
75. Jüngel, *Mystery*, p. 316.
76. Ibid., p. 317.
77. Ibid., p. 368.
78. Ibid., p. 384.
79. Ibid.
80. Jürgen Moltmann, *The Crucified God*, tr. R. A. Wilson and John Bowden (London: S.C.M. Press, 1976), pp. 235ff.: *The Church in the Power of the Spirit*, tr. Margaret Kohl, (London: S.C.M. Press, 1977); *The Trinity and the Kingdom of God*, tr. Margaret Kohl (London: S.C.M. Press, 1981), pp. 158ff.
81. Wolfhart Pannenberg, *Systematische Theologie*, vol. 1 (Göttingen: Vandenhoeck and Ruprecht, 1988), pp. 285–364.
82. Cf. Moltmann, *The Crucified God*, pp. 235ff.
83. Moltmann, *The Church in the Power of the Spirit*, pp. 50ff.; *The Trinity and the Kingdom of God*, pp. 108ff.
84. Moltmann, *The Church in the Power of the Spirit*, p. 60.
85. Richard Bauckham, "Jürgen Moltmann," in *One God in Trinity*, Peter Toon and James D. Spiceland, eds. (London: Samuel Bagster, 1980), p. 126.
86. Ibid., p. 127.
87. Moltmann, *The Church in the Power of the Spirit*, p. 59.
88. Ibid., pp. 59–60.
89. Bauckham, p. 128.
90. Moltmann, "The Trinitarian History of God," *Theology*, vol. 78, 1975, p. 645.
91. Richard Bauckham, *Moltmann: Messianic Theology in the Making* (London: Marshall Pickering, 1987), p. 108.
92. Ibid., p. 109.
93. Pannenberg, pp. 211ff., 289. Wolfhart Pannenberg, *Jesus—God and Man*, tr. L. Wilkens and Duane A. Priebe (London: S.C.M. Press, 1968), pp. 81ff.
94. Pannenberg, *Systematische Theologie*, p. 287f.; *Jesus—God and Man*, pp. 53f., 135–38.
95. Pannenberg, *Systematische Theologie*, p. 326.
96. Ibid., p. 331.
97. Ibid., pp. 342–47; Pannenberg, *Jesus—God and Man*, pp. 170–83.
98. Pannenberg, *Systematische Theologie*, p. 273; *Jesus—God and Man*, p. 157.
99. Christoph Schwöbel, "Wolfhart Pannenberg," in *The Modern Theologians: An Introduction to Christian Theology in the Twentieth Century*, David Ford, ed.

(Oxford: Basil Blackwell, 1989), vol. 1, p. 265. Pannenberg, *Systematische Theologie*, pp. 251ff.

100. Pannenberg, *Systematische Theologie*, p. 340. Schwöbel, p. 275.

101. Pannenberg, *Systematische Theologie*, p. 340.

102. Ibid., p. 358.

103. Ibid., p. 359.

104. Ibid., p. 360 (italics added). Roger E. Olsen, "Wolfhart Pannenberg's Doctrine of the Trinity," *Scottish Journal of Theology*, vol. 43, no. 2, 1990, concurs (p. 196f.). Olsen is critical of Pannenberg on two counts: his tendency toward tritheism and (as in my view) his assertion that God's rule in history, consummated at the end, is determinative of his eternal, triune being.

105. For good summaries of Barth see the following: Molnar, pp. 367–99; Welch, pp. 182ff.; Jüngel, *The Doctrine of the Trinity*, pp. 23ff.; and Robert Theis, "Die Lehre von der Dreieinigkeit Gottes bei Karl Barth," *Freiburger Zeitschrift für Philosophie und Theologie*, vol. 24, nos. I/2, 1977, pp. 270ff.

106. *C.D.*, I/1, p. 479.

107. *C.D.*, II/1, p. 257.

108. *C.D.*, II/2, pp. 6–7.

109. *C.D.*, I/1, p. 383.

110. *C.D.*, IV/1, pp. 157ff. See J. Thompson, "On the Trinity," in *Theology beyond Christendom: Essays on the Centenary of the Birth of Karl Barth May 10, 1886*, John Thompson, ed. (Allison Park, Pa.: Pickwick Publications, 1986), pp. 13-32. See also Berthold Klappert, *Die Auferweckung des Gekreuzigten: Der Ansatz der Christologie Karl Barths im Zusammenhang der Christologie der Gegenwart* (Neukirchen: Neukirchener Verlag, 1971).

111. *C.D.*, IV/1, p. 130.

112. Molnar, p. 371.

113. *C.D.*, I/1, p. 383.

114. Jüngel, *The Doctrine of the Trinity*, p. 23.

115. Ibid., p. 24.

116. Löser, p. 39. See Hans Urs von Balthasar, *Theodramatik IV: Das Endspiel* (Einsiedeln: Johannes Verlag, 1983). See also G. F. O'Hanlon, *The Immutability of God in the Theology of Hans Urs von Balthasar* (London: Cambridge University Press, 1990), pp. 37–40, 66–68.

117. O'Hanlon, pp. 37–38.

118. Von Balthasar, *Theodramatik II/2: Die Personen in Christus* (Einsiedeln: Johannes Verlag, 1978), p. 466, as quoted in Löser, p. 40.

119. Ibid.

120. Molnar, p. 372.

3

A Trinitarian Theology of Cross and Resurrection

The previous chapters have shown us in general terms that God is revealed in Jesus Christ by the Holy Spirit as the triune God. To stop there, however, could leave us open to the valid criticism that all we have in revelation is an epiphany, an appearance of God in our space and time. This, while true, would fail to plumb the depth of the reality of God's nature, his coming and appearing in the form of man. For he comes in Jesus Christ right into the midst of our human opposition and alienation, our sin and the opposing forces of the universe, frees us from their bondage, and reconciles us with himself. Revelation in our actual situation can take place only as reconciliation or atonement. God was in Christ reconciling the world to himself and has given us this knowledge by the Holy Spirit. What we are therefore discussing in this chapter is the Trinity and reconciliation—the mystery of salvation in Jesus Christ. For it is not in word only but also in act that God is and comes to us.

Put succinctly, I have argued that the center of our knowledge of the triune God is in Jesus Christ the Word incarnate. Further, the whole being, life, and activity of Jesus Christ is consummated and crowned on the cross and confirmed by the resurrection and the Holy Spirit. What I now propose to expound is a trinitarian theology of cross and resurrection. This in no way queries the importance of the incarnation. Modern perspectives, however, see the focal points of Christ's life and work more in the cross and resurrection and interpret the incarnation in that light.[1]

This raises several main issues which are being hotly debated in modern theology: first, the question of the humility and obedience of the Son; second, the question of the abandonment of the Son by the Father on the cross; and third, the place of suffering in relation to the nature of God in the light of the cross. We look at these in turn but first give the background and context in the cross and resurrection.

A Trinitarian Theology of Reconciliation

The Cross

If, as so many modern theologians state,[2] the Trinity is the mystery of salvation and salvation comes through Christ and his cross, we have here the key to the understanding of the nature and action of the triune God. Paul Fiddes states that a formulation of the Trinity from the event of the cross builds upon the pioneering work of Karl Barth.[3] Barth points out that while the cross is clearly, from one point of view, the contradiction of all that God is, a concealing of his deity *sub contrario in cruce*, at the same time it is the place where the mystery of the deity of Christ is revealed.[4] The concealment is not simply in our humanity but in our sinful humanity. When the New Testament speaks of majesty, glory, lordship, and deity it speaks at the same time of Jesus obedient in humility, condescension, suffering, and death on the cross. Barth shows that although this was validated and confirmed only in the resurrection, it was the truth of his life as a whole concealed in the cross.[5] "This is the decisive testimony to the deity of Christ—Jesus in ignominy and suffering and so under the wrath and judgment of God—Jesus Christ the crucified."[6] Klappert points out the indirectness of Barth's method developing his christological understanding in the mirror of Jesus' humanity, in his obedience, suffering, and death. Klappert concludes, "Barth reaches his basic thesis: the character of the whole history of Jesus Christ as the history of humiliation on the cross is the centre from which he interprets the early Christian confession of the deity of Jesus."[7] The cross reveals Jesus as the One he is—exalted in humility, crowned as king on the cross. To human perception all this might seem a contradiction of what we believe God to be. In fact, to faith it reveals most profoundly and surely who God is. "In *him* we discern the true features of this God and discover that he does not terrify us by his distant and infinite majesty and pure absoluteness but that he is near us in the 'powerlessness' of humiliation on the cross."[8] What is being said here is that if Jesus on the cross reveals the true nature of God, there is in the divine life, in the relation of Son to Father, an obedience, a lowliness, which are his eternally and are in the economy manifest in this way. He can and does act thus because this corresponds to the very nature and life of God and forms the basis of his saving action on the cross.

Resurrection and the Holy Spirit

For a proper interpretation of the whole New Testament witness and through it for a real trinitarian theology of the cross two further acts of God are recorded for us. The first is the new act of God in raising his Son Jesus

Christ from the dead, thereby both vindicating all that Jesus said and did and showing his whole life as revealing the work of God—a confirmation of his deity.[9] The New Testament, in contrast to later creeds, rarely speaks of Jesus as rising from the dead by his own volition and power as divine Son, although in John's gospel this is not excluded. Rather it is the Father (sometimes less frequently the Holy Spirit) who acts. In the crucifixion the Son went obediently to death, actively, willingly carrying out the Father's will. In the raising from the dead the Son is basically passive, is raised and confirmed as Son.

The cross and resurrection together as the acts of Father and Son give a certain shape to the Trinity and the intradivine relationships. They show God as Father majestic, gracious in loving relationship with the Son, with him in his coming, passion, and death. They show the Son as obedient in humility unto death, triumphant in it, overcoming it and all God's enemies. There is here, as Klappert points out,[10] a differentiated relationship of cross and resurrection which reflects the very nature of God as Father and Son.

The second aspect of the Christ event which makes a trinitarian faith and theology possible is the Holy Spirit.[11] If God reveals himself as Father of the Son in the cross and resurrection and thereby reconciles us to himself, opening up for us a way back to the Father, this cannot be possible except by the Holy Spirit. It is he who makes what Father and Son are and have done real to us. One could put the relationship of the Holy Spirit to the Trinity, incarnation, and reconciliation in this way. The Holy Spirit awakens faith in us so that we are incorporated into the life of God through the living community of his people on earth. The Holy Spirit is the bond of union who binds us to Christ and his reconciliation. At the same time the Holy Spirit is the means of union between God and man in Jesus Christ. He is the Spirit of union and fellowship, and, since he comes to us as the divine Lord, he is also the bond of union of Father and Son in the divine life. Without the Holy Spirit there would be no Trinity—in fact, no true God.

Another way of stating the same truth is to say that in the Holy Spirit we are dealing with God present to us as humans and to our world. It is the Holy Spirit who opens up the meaning of Jesus Christ to us as the truth of God, just as Christ as Son leads us to the Father. It is the Holy Spirit who opens up our lives to God and brings about a meeting between God and us which enables us effectively to enter into the significance of Christ's reconciliation. The Spirit acts in sovereign power, coming from the resurrection of Christ, exalting us to be "in Christ." He is the Lord and giver of life and as such is one with the Father and the Son, together with them to be worshiped and glorified.[12] He is the Holy Spirit as the Spirit of Christ given to us by the crucified and risen Lord, testifying to him as the *parakletos*, one (almost identical) with Christ yet distinguished from him. The Spirit as Lord is truly divine, not simply a relation of Father and Son as it is sometimes put,[13] but as the author of eternal life, one in being with Father and Son, the open door into the divine life and out of it to us at the same time.

All this comes from a trinitarian theology of cross and resurrection bringing us into the very heart of God to share in his intimate life of relationships of holy love. It also brings the triune God right into the heart of our lives for our salvation.

I will now try to show, from the example of Karl Barth and other writers, how the nature of God's reconciliation in his Son on the cross points to the relationships within the triune God. We do this by using four terms which together in many ways sum up the significance of a modern trinitarian doctrine based on the cross and resurrection. These four are the humility, obedience, abandonment, and suffering of Jesus on the cross revealing the nature of God.

Humility and Obedience

Humility

Karl Barth restructured traditional evangelical Christology and the doctrine of atonement to enable us to see them as one in the unity of the working person and the personal work of Jesus Christ.[14] He is the Son of God humbled to reconcile and humanity exalted as Lord in this one movement. As such he is our reconciliation with God. The humiliation that takes place is in the contradiction and lowliness of the cross. This is to be understood neither as a giving up of some aspects of the deity, as in nineteenth-century kenotic theories, nor as a contradiction in God or opposition between God in himself and in his action for us. Such views minimize the true deity of Christ and so make a real reconciliation impossible.

For Barth, rather, this humiliation exhibits a divinely chosen way—a way that is effective for us and for the whole world—the Son going, as Barth puts it, into the far country and giving himself for all.[15] This conception questions the view that God is high and majestic only in remote isolation from us or in a way that has dualistic tendencies. Nor can it be a metaphysical conception of God where he is so unchangeable that it makes an incarnation and a humiliation almost impossible. Here, by contrast, God in his Son enters into our greatest lowliness, contradiction, and sin and by his sacrifice there shows his exalted nature. This action manifests the true divinity of the Son. "The true God shows his majesty in humility and thus contradicts what we generally know of God, all our general concepts."[16] Barth shows how God is the true majestic, almighty Lord in the form of One who is lowly, weak, temporal, and given up to death.

If this is how the eternal Son appears in the economy of salvation and reconciliation, what does this say about God in his triune nature? It indicates a self-differentiation of God as Father and Son within the divine life in which, without any loss of his deity—rather, in supreme affirmation of it—there is movement and relationship in God of Father to Son. This is the basis and possibility of his action *ad extra*. "In this humiliation God is supremely God . . . in this death he is supremely alive . . . he has maintained and revealed his deity in the passion of this man as his eternal Son."[17] One can characterize this as reflecting a self-giving in God of Father to Son and Son to Father which is manifest in God's election and decision to come in humiliation to us in the Son in reconciling love. Thus we have no immobile, passionless God exalted above us and far from us, but a God of love, life, movement, and action in his Son in the very depth of our humanity *for us*. This whole conception of the triune God shows him as one who, in love and movement within himself, is *our* God, one who in his humiliation contradicts any conception of God as apathetic without the possibility and reality of coming to us and suffering with and for us. It also reveals One who by the eternal Spirit offered himself on the cross to the Father (Heb. 9:14).

Obedience

This can be summed up in the phrases "obedient unto death" and "obedient in humility." The two are in one sense synonymous; in another it is the obedience of the Son to the Father that enables the humiliation to take place. The obedience of the incarnate Son reflects that of the Son in the eternal life of God. Were this not so, the obedience in the incarnate life up to and including the cross would not be possible. In going this lowly way of obedience to death Jesus is not following a capricious or arbitrary way but one which God the Father has chosen for him and which has its basis in the very being of God in the relation of Son to Father.

The idea of an obedience in God himself, of Son to Father, conjures up two pictures to many today and this is reflected in much current theology. These are of a patriarchal, authoritarian conception of God[18] and of a subordination of the Son which implies inferiority of being or status. How can either conception tally with a trinitarian view of God and what practical consequences flow from these? Two theologians—Karl Barth and P. T. Forsyth, who have both supported the idea of obedience in God—answer the charges of inferiority and authoritarianism in one. Forsyth points out that the self-emptying of the Son to become incarnate and to go to the cross involves a form of sonship which includes both subordination and acceptance of the servanthood of the cross.[19] The glory of the Godhead was possessed by the Son, "but it was the godlike glory of subordination. There is place and order in the Godhead, and he kept it."[20] Forsyth goes on to show that "subordination is *not* inferiority, and it *is* Godlike. The principle is imbedded in the very cohesion of the eternal trinity and it is inseparable from the unity, fraternity and true equality of men. It is not a mark of inferiority to be subordinate, to have an authority, to obey. It is divine."[21]

It is worth quoting Forsyth's "The Matter of Subordination," where he points out that our moral principles as Christian must flow far less from precepts than from the revealed nature of the Christian God. He goes on:

> Now the nature of that God is Father, and Son, and Holy Spirit. Father and Son co-exist, co-equal in the Spirit of holiness, i.e. of perfection. But Father and Son is a relation inconceivable except the Son be obedient to the Father. The perfection of the Son and the perfecting of his holy work lay, not in his suffering but in his obedience. And, as he was eternal Son, it meant an eternal obedience; for the supreme work of Christ, so completely identified with his person, could not be done by anything which was not as eternal as his person.
>
> But obedience is not conceivable without some form of subordination. Yet in his very obedience the Son was co-equal with the Father; the Son's yielding will was no less divine than the Father's exigent will. Therefore, in the very nature of God, subordination implies no inferiority. It is as divine as rule, for it is self-subordination on an infinite scale; it is not enforced. It is sacrifice, it is not mere resignation. It is no slavery, but willing service.[22]

Forsyth draws out the practical implications when he writes, "If man is to be holy as he [God] is holy, our self-subordination to each other is not necessarily inferiority, nor need obedience be slavery. There is an obedience bound up with the supreme dignity of christian love, so that where most love is, there also is most obedience."[23]

Significantly, Forsyth sees the trinitarian dimension and eternal basis intimately related to the Son's holy, obedient work on the cross for our salvation. Barth makes the same type of comment in relation to the doctrine of reconciliation. He points out that while the outer form of Christ's work on the cross is humiliation, its inner nature is not merely the human obedience of the incarnate Lord. This but reflects an eternal obedience, a relationship in God which the cross reveals. Barth adds an important point to Forsyth's views: the Son as obedient eternally to the Father is not simply compliant to the Father's will. It is an active passivity, one in which he shares the power, disposing, and majesty of the Father by the Holy Spirit. Barth writes, "In his humility and compliance as the Son he has a supreme part in the majesty and disposing of the Father."[24] Barth points out that "the one who rules and commands in majesty and the one who obeys in humility" is the one God. What God does *pro nobis* in reconciliation in his life consummated on the cross has "its basis in his own being, in his own inner life,"[25] in his holy, loving obedience of Son to Father. But this eternal relationship is possible only by the Holy Spirit, which is in relationship to Father and Son as "their free but also necessary fellowship of love."[26] One can sum this up by saying that "one must not, therefore, see obedience in the Son as indicating an inferiority to the Father, but rather as the expression—the essential expression—of this relationship. These distinctions indicate that the Father is primarily majestic in commanding love and the Son primarily obedient to the Father, but each shares in the being and work of the other. It is in this way that God is God and triune, in this differentiated relationship he is Father, Son and Holy Spirit, one God."[27]

The Question of Abandonment

Jürgen Moltmann

Much modern theology regards the God-forsakenness and abandonment of the Son by the Father as a crucial aspect of a trinitarian theology of the cross. One of the most radical but oft-criticized views is that of Jürgen Moltmann.[28] Beginning with the human history of Jesus, who calls God Father and understands himself as Son, this history culminates on the cross, which is the key to the mystery of the Trinity.[29] What happens on the cross is that Jesus the Son is abandoned by the Father and knows the deep pain of God's forsakenness—witness the cry of dereliction on the cross. The traditional idea that the divine nature cannot suffer—only the human can do so—is here replaced by a dichotomy between Father and Son, a stasis in God. The cross is at the heart of God separating Father and Son, the Father delivering up the Son in love and likewise the Son surrendering himself to this dereliction and to the Father's will.

In this God is against God, yet at the same time Father and Son are one in purpose and will. Moltmann sees this unity made possible in two ways. The first is by the resurrection. "The resurrection of the Son abandoned by the Father unites God with God in the most intimate fellowship."[30] The other is by the Holy Spirit. By the Spirit the cross as the gulf between Father and Son is also their most intimate union in love. By including this gulf of abandonment and death within itself the trinitarian being of God reaches out to all abandoned, sinful, suffering people. The purpose of this suffering abandonment is that the godless may not be God-forsaken. In this way the cross is a dialectical trinitarian event in which all that opposes God is taken up into the divine life and ultimately overcome, reconciled, and transformed.

Moltmann further states:

> A trinitarian theology of the cross perceives God in the negative element and therefore the negative element in God, and in this dialectical way is panentheistic. For in the hidden mode of humiliation to the point of the cross, all being and all that annihilates has already been taken up in God and God begins to become "all in all". To recognise God in the cross of Christ, conversely, means to recognise the cross, inextricable suffering, death and hopeless rejection in God.[31]

This view of God, therefore, is a call for a "revolution in the concept of God."[32] As Bauckham says, "If God reveals himself in the God-forsakenness of Jesus on the cross, then all other concepts of God must be given up and the attempt be made to understand the christian God completely from the cross."[33] The cross so understood is Moltmann's hermeneutical principle which guides his main thinking on the triune God and is related both to suffering and to abandonment.

Moltmann's view can be evaluated in the following ways. First, because the starting point for understanding the relation of Father and Son is on the cross, the resulting cleft or gulf in the being of God is never adequately bridged. For Moltmann it is the separation of God-forsakenness which is treated almost in isolation from other aspects of the passion narratives. Should one not begin with the unity of Father and Son in the act of reconciling the world to God and interpret the God-forsakenness of Jesus Christ in this light? There can, therefore, be no ultimate separation, despite the clear evidence that in Christ God himself comes to our side and bears the judgment of his own holiness. In this sense God is against God in atonement. But this is not how Moltmann sees it. A desideratum in this whole debate and in Moltmann's doctrine in particular is a more specific relationship of the abandonment of the Son by the Father to his saving work in atonement. Barth does this in his massive doctrine of reconciliation[34] and Balthasar by his emphasis on the atonement as Christ in Hades bears the utter judgment of the Father on our sin.[35] When Father and Son are one in the event of reconciliation by the Holy Spirit the problem of a separation in God is not set aside but overcome in a greater, indissoluble unity.

Second, Moltmann's way of attempting to solve this problem is to say that the Father and Son, while separated on the cross, are also most at one here. This union is the work of the Holy Spirit and therefore a trinitarian view of God is necessary. However, this seems more a communion of will than an actual definition of union. Moltmann's view of the unity of God, however, is to be understood primarily not as that of will but as that of three divine "persons" or "subjects" united perichoretically.[36] The emphasis is so much on the three persons as subjects that the unity is underemphasized, or, to put it differently, there is a serious lack of an ontological dimension in his trinitarian formulations. This also borders on tritheism. Regina Radlbeck has given a penetrating critique of Moltmann's views on "person" and "subject" at this point and their relation to the question of the unity of God.[37] She concludes that he has not reconciled what are two different concepts. Moreover, he has failed to show how, in the light of this, one can properly speak of a unity in the triune God.

Third, Moltmann's trinitarian view—Father, Son, and Holy Spirit opening out to take into the trinitarian event the whole God-forsakenness of the cross, of the evil and suffering of the world, and so at the same time overcoming and transforming it—is questionable. It is doubtful whether Moltmann sees evil, as some suggest, as a necessary step on the road to the final understanding of the triune God.[38] But there is no doubt that the Trinity in his view is an evolving event between three divine subjects and the world and that the triune God is not complete until the end.[39] Therefore, he can speak of a trinitarian history of God. The difficulty with this view is that it ties God to his relationship to the world and makes the world a contributory factor to the ultimate nature of God. God is therefore not Father, Son, and Holy Spirit without this relationship and reciprocity between himself and the world. This is a position that cannot ultimately be maintained since it fails to give proper expression to the abiding perfections of the triune God.

Hans Urs von Balthasar

Balthasar begins with a much more traditional conception of the Trinity than does Moltmann.[40] The whole life of Jesus is for him a revelation of God and its supreme expression is the cross. Paradoxically, the death of Christ, which involves abandonment of the Son by the Father, is to be understood as the greatest revelation of God's love in a mutuality of giving and receiving. The opposition between Father and Son is involved in their common work to overcome our sin and rebellion. The negative relationship is embraced and overcome by the positive and this experience "remains within the scope of the ontologically, positive, divine love."[41] There is therefore no ontological separation in God. Balthasar sees this as analogous to the distinction and even distance within God between the Father and the Son by the Holy Spirit—a distance which is overcome by their unity in love. He sees it also as resulting in the reconciliation of the world with God through the Son's acceptance of God's judgment on our sin. This is brought out most clearly in Balthasar's original treatment of what he calls the theology of Holy Saturday.[42] In going down to death and its consequences Jesus Christ experienced the "second death," that abandonment which is hell and judgment. This is God's No in favor of his Yes confirmed by the resurrection and is "God's way, in his responsible love of creation, of taking the measure of all that is opposed to him."[43] God's love "being trinitarian may embrace difference and suffering, may allow and overcome evil, and in so doing it gives the greatest proof of its power without threat to its unity."[44]

This reflects a distinction and otherness in God who is love which is both a giving and a receiving. The drama of this event as a paradox of unity and otherness is possible only because it is based on the prior drama of the triune life, where, in the relationship between Father and Son, there is distance and distinction and yet unity by the Holy Spirit. O'Hanlon sums up by saying, "The scandalous paradox of the cross in which the Son who is God may be rightly said to die and to be separated from God, is illuminated, and a distant indication of its mystery given by this reference to the freedom and power of trinitarian love in which difference and otherness are positive."[45] This is close to Barth's view that what happens in its opposite on the cross is analogous to a distinction and otherness in the love and being of the triune God.[46] In this view Balthasar is setting out a clear and commendable trinitarian theology of the cross.

Karl Barth

Throughout the *Church Dogmatics* Karl Barth speaks as radically as any about the God-forsakenness of Jesus on the cross. "The cross means a conflict for God himself. The why of it is for Jesus an unheard of, inconceivable, unique question of doubt."[47] There is a large measure of agreement between Barth's and Moltmann's intention and language if not content. The cross as the culmination of the being and act of Jesus is the fulfillment of all God did with Israel and is the revelation of the life of God and of the deity of Christ. In the God-forsakenness of the cross we meet with God in the deepest act of humiliation as he bears our sin and his own righteous, just judgment on it, and so reconciles us to himself in his Son.

While the cross means the contradiction of God it also reveals his glory in its opposite. This cannot therefore be a self-contradiction in God or the ultimate separation of Father and Son. Barth affirms that, while the real hardness of the cross cannot be evaded, its fuller meaning is the unity of Father and Son in reconciliation. While the Son of God in union with the man Jesus on the cross did die, he did not give up his deity or his oneness with the Father. Barth writes, "He does not cease to be God. He does not come into conflict with himself. . . . [W]hen he dies in his unity with this man, death does not gain any power over him."[48]

Klappert, interpreting Barth, points out three possible views in relation to the God-forsakenness of Jesus on the cross and the opposition he encounters there:[49]

1. It could mean a real inner divine paradox of being (*Seinsparadox*) which would divide God's being in himself. This Barth rightly rejects, stating that God, while giving himself up, did not give himself away.[50]

2. It could mean an existential paradox associated with Heinrich Vogel in his Christology.[51] Here man is seen contradicting God by his sin and having a division in himself, but this does not mean a division in God. God makes this his own, however, on the cross but overcomes it by the sacrifice of Christ in reconciling us to himself.

3. It could mean a paradox of judgment. The Son of God undergoes the judgment of God on this contradiction, places "himself under the judgement under which man has fallen in this contradiction, under the curse of death which rests upon him."[52]

Klappert points out that for Barth the two paradoxes of existence and of judgment do not reach into the inner being of God and create a separation between Father and Son but are rather a moment in the act of reconciliation overcoming the contradiction against himself.[53] God's mercy and grace triumph over opposition and judgment in reconciliation. In this way and by the resurrection God the Father affirms the work of his Son and accompanies him in that work by the Holy Spirit. In fact for Barth the being of the one true God is to be seen here in all its fullness and truth. Here is a view of humiliation and God-forsakenness on the cross set in the economic perspective of our salvation and reconciliation which reflects the relationships of Father and Son to one another by the Holy Spirit in the eternal divine life of unity and love.

The Suffering of God

Modern theology—particularly in its christological and trinitarian perspectives—has been highly critical of the view expressed in much traditional thought that God is impassible. This view, known as *apatheia*,[54] was strongly influenced by Greek philosophical views which envisaged God as incapable of suffering and therefore of entering directly into the suffering of humanity. It would be wrong, however, to believe that this was the sole reason why the Patristics, the Reformers, and later writers continued to maintain something like the conception of a passionless God. The chief reason must lie in their view of the perfection of God as triune, having a life of perfect felicity in himself, which, when he came into our human sinful situation, did not alter him. The faithfulness and constancy of God as one of the attributes of the divine perfection also played a large part in this. Though God was a living, loving being in perfect communion with himself he could also, while maintaining his full deity, enter into relationship with our humanity and our world.

Central to our faith in the triune God are the incarnation and atonement where the Word or Son of God takes our humanity to himself. For much modern theology it is our sinful humanity that he assumed.[55] In it God overcame our rebellion and sin and all the evil that opposed him. This he did through the suffering and death of the Son on the cross. Since this is so, how does one envisage the relationship between a God of perfect beatitude and incomparable holiness and perfection and his entering into our sinful, hostile, suffering world, while still remaining the same? The answer generally given by Patristic writers was that it was only in his humanity that the Son of God suffered and died since God can neither suffer nor die.[56] This view, while plausible, had its dangers in incipient Nestorianism, which tended to divide the two natures in the one person of Jesus Christ. In other words, the unity of Christ was thereby threatened. One view that was put forward to ease the danger of dividing the person of Christ—the *communicatio idiomatum*—is still significant and valuable. This view taught that what one could attribute to either nature in the person of Christ could be applied to the person as a whole. For example, Jesus in his humanity was tempted, tried and suffered, but overcame; this is true of the one Lord Jesus Christ. Again the Son of God had power on earth to forgive sins—a divine prerogative. This is true also of the one Lord Jesus Christ. Thus Jesus Christ as divine and human suffered and died. Even with these qualifications and quite correct interpretations there was a hesitancy to attribute any idea of suffering to God. To do so, it was thought, would simply ascribe a human attribute to God, who was said to be "without body, parts or passions."[57]

This view has been challenged by theologians of many different outlooks in our time and the idea of a suffering God has been espoused by a large number of modern writers.[58] Process thought finds little difficulty with it since it sees God adapting himself in various ways to the chances, changes, and suffering of mortals. Modern awareness of the horrendous extent of human need, misery, and suffering requires a theodicy which can involve God in our sufferings and thus try to explain and eradicate them.[59] Pioneering voices in the last century and this[60] are few and far between but, for modern theology, some linkage of God and suffering is almost axiomatic. This is true both of those like Barth and Balthasar who take a more traditional view with very significant reinterpretations and of those more radical writers like Moltmann for whom God and suffering go hand in hand. Some argue with Moltmann and, to some extent, with Jüngel that because the nature of God is love, in creating our world and being concerned with it as it now is, he must inevitably suffer.

It would be impossible to cover the whole field of debate here, but we can look briefly at the writings of Barth, Balthasar, Jüngel, and Moltmann. The first two are close to one another, whereas Jüngel is some distance from them and Moltmann represents a more-or-less full-blown view of God as suffering in himself with us and for us. It is notable and important for us to see that all four relate suffering in some sense to God through a trinitarian theology of the cross.

Karl Barth

The trinitarian theology of Karl Barth can also be correctly described as one centered on the cross and resurrection. It is here that God is revealed as he eternally is in himself. He is made known to us as Father, Son, and Holy Spirit and has the fullness of life and blessedness in himself—is wholly light, glory, and perfection. At the same time in his Son Jesus Christ he identifies himself with our humanity and world in its sin and suffering and so himself can, in some way, be said to suffer. In line, therefore, with most modern theologians Barth rejects the idea of *apatheia*, of God as an unmoved, unfeeling being beyond the reach of suffering. But what can and does suffering mean for God? How does Barth attempt to answer this question? I suggest that there are two main areas that are involved in his attempted answers.

The Reality of God's Election in Christ. In his election God chose to be the God of our humanity while himself being separate from our sin. This is his eternal will and purpose for our good and is wholly good news. Barth writes,

> If we would know what it was that God elected for himself when he elected fellowship with man, then we can answer only that he elected our rejection. He made it his own. He bore it and suffered it with all its most bitter consequences. For the sake of this choice and for the sake of man he hazarded himself wholly and utterly. He elected our suffering (what we as sinners must suffer towards him and before him and from him). He elected it as his own suffering. This is the extent to which his election is an election of grace, an election to give himself, an election to abase himself for the sake of the elect.[61]

Reconciliation.[62] In Barth's doctrine the same idea is carried on. God is indeed high, holy, and exalted but he is known in the humiliation of the Son, in the real opposition to all that is divine. When God in his Son surrendered himself to our opposition to him he suffered even to death on the cross. This is seen in the depth of atonement where God in Christ took to himself the sin of humanity, bore the judgment it deserved, and took it away. The suffering of God is a clear implication of the incarnation and atonement and in this both the Father and the Holy Spirit are involved with the Son. The Spirit as the Spirit of truth leads us to both the Father and the Son. In the humiliation of God we see by the Spirit the mercy of the exalted Father but also at the same time with the Son in lowliness, allowing himself to be affected by our misery to such an extent that he gives and sends the Son to suffer and to reconcile.[63] It is therefore wrong to believe that the Father and the Holy Spirit are not associated with this act of suffering of the Son. Barth writes of the Father,

> It is not at all the case that God has no part in the suffering of Jesus Christ even in his mode of being as the Father. No, there is a *particula veri* in the teaching of the early patripassians. This is that primarily it is God the Father who suffers in the offering and sending of his Son, in his abasement. The suffering is not his own, but the alien suffering of the creature, of man, which he takes to himself in him. But he does suffer it in the humiliation of his Son with a depth with which it never was or will be suffered by any man—apart from the One who is his Son. . . . This fatherly fellow-suffering of God is the mystery, the basis, of the humiliation of his Son; the truth of that which takes place historically in his crucifixion.[64]

It is, however, significant that Barth states very carefully, and one must believe deliberately, that God's suffering is greater than man's and yet in another sense is not simply his own but that of the creature which in his Son he takes to himself. As W. J. Hill puts it, "While it is God who suffers and not just the manhood of Jesus, still he suffers in his 'other' and not in himself."[65] There is therefore no univocal sense in which the sufferings of God are spoken of. Rather, since God acts *ad extra* corresponding to his triune being *ad intra*, what Christ suffers on the cross has its basis in a self-giving in God, in a downward thrust from Father to Son which implies no inferiority but is, as we have seen, a form of obedience.

Barth, however, maintains throughout his writings that God lives in the perfection of life, in the fullness of his triune being as love. If then God is God without us yet only wills to be God with us and enters completely into and takes upon himself our suffering and alienated state, how, in the light of the foregoing theological perspectives, can we try to understand the suffering of a perfect God? The way in which an attempted answer may be given is similar to that of Balthasar, namely, that there is that in God which makes it possible for him to enter savingly into our situation so that his actions and suffering on the cross mirror his inner being. Jüngel correctly, though obliquely, interprets Barth here.[66] The inner being of God is that of the obedience of the Son to the Father, and this self-giving is seen in time and space in Christ's obedience unto death. There is therefore a direction downward in God, a humbling aspect which makes possible incarnation and atonement. Suffering is not, as with Moltmann, in God, but God has in his triune nature those aspects that enable him to remain himself while entering into our situation and being our reconciler in the passion and death of his Son by the Holy Spirit. In this self-relatedness yet unity of God as Father, Son, and Holy Spirit lies the possibility, not of a divine death, but, as Jüngel says, "God is able to suffer and die as man,"[67] while remaining essentially himself, at one with himself.

Hans Urs von Balthasar

Balthasar sees God as Holy Trinity, indeed as trinitarian event in the dynamic and liveliness of tripersonal self-giving. The trinitarian history of God's interpersonal relationships is seen in the distance and infinite distinction in unity which is the basis of the risks involved in the creation of free human beings who could and did sin. The consequence is the act of God for our salvation as the One who in himself is a relational being of giving and receiving. Since this is true of God, the self-emptying and self-giving in incarnation and cross are not foreign to his being, though the suffering of the Son on the cross and our human suffering cannot be ascribed univocally to God. On the cross the Son suffers the "second death" of the sinner on behalf of all of us. Yet the act of suffering and obedience to death is at one and the same time God's act of reconciliation between himself and us, the fruit of which is the presence of the Holy Spirit within us.

Several things are summarized by O'Hanlon in the relation of the triune God to the cross and Christ's suffering.[68] First, the suffering and death of Christ is a temporal form of the eternal give and take of the event of trinitarian love. The reality of our reconciliation takes this precise form because it images in flesh and blood the nature of the divine life of the triune God. Yet image and analogy are not used directly since there is no exact correspondence, only dissimilarity, between creator and creature.

Second, one must not say that suffering and death were attributed only to the human nature of Christ. It is the one Lord Jesus Christ in the totality of his being and action who suffered and died on the cross. Some form, therefore, of passibility must be attributed to the Son and so to God. Yet again it cannot simply be equated with ours.

Third, Balthasar parts company with Barth at one point. For him the cross in some measure affects God, who experiences "enrichment" thereby. This links on to the theme more prominent in Balthasar than suffering—the question of change in God, an "evermore" the same. Balthasar believes that the nature of God's love implies him becoming, in some way, greater.

Fourth, however we ascribe to God change, or something akin to suffering, it is clear that for Balthasar no creaturely suffering or change can be ascribed to God in his eternal being. He is God in beatitude and perfection. Balthasar thus holds firmly to traditional teaching yet moves from it perceptibly, but in a cautious manner, when he sees God as experiencing something corresponding to pain in Christ and in us. This he calls "suprasuffering." By this he means that there must be something in God which corresponds to human change and suffering. All three persons in God in some way "suffer" the event of the cross. Balthasar follows Maritain in stating that this has really no name but can be described as a kind of divine attribute which lays hold upon, accepts, and overcomes what opposes God and causes him "pain." This "pain" is transcended in the divine life and victorious love of the triune God.

Both Barth and Balthasar are right in the main thrust of their exposition, namely, that the cross (and resurrection) are the divine reconciliation and this reveals the true nature of God as self-giving, holy love. He is perfect in the divine life of giving and receiving as Father and Son by the Holy Spirit. Both are also correct in seeing that no univocal ascription of suffering, as we creatures know it, can be given to God. Nonetheless, since God has come and given himself in his Son in suffering on the cross, there is that in the divine life—obedience, humiliation, receptivity, giving, and receiving—which makes possible the passion of the cross yet in a joy transcending pain. This is close to traditional teaching yet counters a simple apathetic view and, in a nuanced way, relates the triune event of love to the cross and passion of the Lord.

These two theologians are also at one in seeing the suprasuffering of God related to the atonement and the judgment Christ accepts and undergoes for us and for our salvation. The soteriological interest central to modern trinitarian perspectives is clearly maintained by them.

There is, however, as we saw, a difference between Barth and Balthasar at one important point. Barth sees God's true nature revealed in the cross of Jesus Christ where suffering and death do not alter him but are potentialities of his triune being. Balthasar, on the other hand, sees a reciprocal relationship between God and the world which means a change in God. This latter, however, is not to be regarded as affecting his essential deity, but, analogous to human love, is an "evermore" of the same. Barth's view is to be preferred since Balthasar's could be seen as an expansion of or growth in God, though this is clearly not his intention.

It is unfortunate that as we interpret both theologians at this point we have to use abstract language to try to convey the nature of the immanent Trinity in relation to suffering since both seek to interpret God as triune in dynamic, concrete terms. This may, indeed, be unavoidable since in this realm all human language is inadequate and points beyond itself to the ultimate mystery of the living, triune God himself. While attempting positive statements both are also using a form of apophasis by describing God negatively since his suffering is not the same as man's but infinitely greater.

Eberhard Jüngel

Jüngel believes with Moltmann, Balthasar, and Barth that the cross is the key to the trinitarian nature of God.[69] With Luther God is known precisely in his opposite. Jüngel, however, speaks rather sparingly of suffering in relation to God. We derive his meaning, which is often indirect, from the main thrust of his arguments. These are threefold.

The Death of the Living God. Jüngel's thesis is that God identifies himself with the existence of the man Jesus put to death upon the cross.[70] The man Jesus is at the same time acknowledged as the Son of God; thus one can speak, after the fashion of Hegel, but with different meaning, of "the death of the living God." In this view God suffers in his encounter with death by submitting to it and overcoming it in Jesus his Son. In this way it becomes not the end of God but "a phenomenon which belongs to God,"[71] by which he defines his being.

The definition of God's being therefore relates very specifically to the death of Christ in suffering and God-forsakenness. Thus to identify the Son of God with the crucified requires "a confession that in and with the man Jesus God himself has suffered and died."[72] This points in two directions. On the one hand, it indicates a distinction between God and God, Father and Son—a self-differentiation in God. On the other hand, God is known as such only in the suffering, abandonment, and death of the Son. "Thus the crucified one belongs to the concept of God."[73] What Jüngel is indicating here is that in suffering death in the Son who is made alive by the Spirit, God is interpreting himself and is to be defined as triune. In this way Jüngel also seeks to maintain the aspect of ontological being in the Trinity.

"The Union of Life and Death in Favour of Life." This epigrammatic phrase echoes throughout Jüngel's exposition.[74] It means that God is life and love who meets death not simply as the friendly end of human life but as non-being, as that which is strange, opposed to God, similar to *das Nichtige* (the Nihil) of Barth. In the death of Jesus God meets, disarms, and so overcomes this enemy and shows his own true life. "In that God relates himself *creatively* to nothingness . . . he is the opponent of nothingness."[75] Since Jesus goes to this depth he enters into and suffers God's opposition to it in the abandonment of God-forsakenness but nevertheless as Son remains related to the Father. Thus by encountering death God does not contradict himself when Jesus dies. God is against God in one sense but at the same time the power of his life by the Spirit over death obviates any ultimate separation in the being of God. In fact quite the opposite is the case since it reveals a trinitarian view of God which shows his true nature and saves us from attributing contradiction to God.[76] "To say that the unity of life and death is in favour of *life* is to formulate in abstract terms how the Spirit is that bond of love which prevents intra-divine conflict"[77] between Father and Son. It is also to say that "in the midst of the most grievous separation, God does not cease to be the *one* and *living* God, but rather is precisely in this most completely himself."[78] As Webster states, "Trinitarian formulae thus prevent the explanation of God's being out of the concept of love from falling into problems with respect to the congruity of God with himself."[79]

The God Who Is Love. Jüngel not only takes over a framework from Hegel; he also uses that of the Augustinian psychological analogy of love requiring love, a lover, and a beloved. Love means selfless self-giving for another and this God shows in his love on the cross. The fact that he identifies himself with man in the suffering and death of Jesus counters the classical doctrine of God's *apatheia* and immutability.[80] This love involves not just ordinary suffering but that of the wrath and curse of God which every sinner deserves. Jesus suffers God's judgment on sin which no one else can or did and so takes our place as substitute. Jüngel thus sees the cross not simply as sacrificial love but as atonement. In this way, similar to Balthasar, it can be described as suprasuffering. "That the God who is love must be able to suffer and does suffer beyond all limits in the giving up of what is most authentically his for the sake of mortal man is an indispensable insight of the newer theology schooled by Luther's Christology and Hegel's philosophy. Only the God who is identical with the Crucified One makes us certain of his love and thus of himself."[81] As we saw, this implies a self-relatedness of Father and Son. This is because the love story of Father and Son on the cross, seen in the light of the resurrection and the Holy Spirit, is that of the triune God.

Jüngel's is an impressive attempt to link the union of God with the death of Christ and express this in trinitarian terms. He is not simply concerned with a theodicy but seeks "to work out the *ontological* dimensions of the issues, to try to state how language about God's suffering and death"[82] gives us insight into the divine being. Webster writes, "The doctrine of the trinity recasts the gospel narratives in conceptual form."[83] It is the mystery of God's being and action in Jesus Christ and the Holy Spirit.

The influence of Barth and Hegel is obvious throughout Jüngel's works. God exists from himself in nothingness. This means that by his life he overcomes the opposition of death and its enmity. Barth and Hegel "in their different ways . . . offer a means of stating how God is supremely himself in giving himself as the *human* God."[84] Moreover, Jüngel is to be supported in linking Christ's death not simply to abandonment and suffering, but to the judgment of God in terms of Luther's theology of law and Gospel. This gives implicit view of the atonement lacking in, for example, Moltmann.

However, Jüngel's position is open to criticism on at least three counts. In the first instance, like Pannenberg, he begins with a Christology from below which requires the retroactive power of the resurrection to confirm Jesus' unity with God as the Son.[85] This is not a very convincing way to seek to affirm the deity of Christ. A Christology from below, as distinguished from one from above, has the tendency to put the emphasis largely on the economic aspect of the Trinity. It is true, of course, as we have seen, that Jüngel seeks also to emphasize the ontological side, but he scarcely succeeds in doing so.

A further criticism of his position is that, while he demonstrates the victory of God's life over suffering, opposition, and death, his trinitarian framework still remains firmly within that of an identity of immanent and economic Trinity. God's selfless suffering in his Son on the cross and his self-relatedness as Father, Son, and Spirit are almost regarded as one. Here a distinction is necessary but in Jüngel's theology is scarcely possible or, at any rate, not really forthcoming.

Finally, in using the analogy of human love as a form of death in order to show the nature of God's love in the death of the Son, Jüngel is in danger of making this a preunderstanding of what love is and then applying it to God. The general conception of love can thus, probably contrary to Jüngel's intention, partially condition our understanding of God's love.[86]

Jürgen Moltmann

In line with most modern theology, Moltmann is critical of the metaphysical view of the *apatheia* of God. By contrast, he almost goes to the opposite extreme and makes suffering a central aspect of the nature of God who is love. Moreover, since God in his love identifies with suffering humanity, he is influenced by it so that he is both vulnerable and changeable.

Moltmann sees the suffering of God taking place not in a Jesus Christ who has two natures where only the human suffers, but by a trinitarian history of the cross. The Son is delivered up by the Father to death and "suffers dying in forsakenness but not death itself; for man can no longer suffer 'death' because suffering presupposes life."[87] The Son suffers Godforsakenness and the Father suffers the death of the Son in what Moltmann calls "patricompassianism" (an idea taken from Barth *C.D.*, IV/2, p. 357, but unacknowledged). This suffering is, however, not something that Father and Son merely identify with; it is "a suffering in God" himself in a dialectic where he takes the opposition of godlessness, alienation, sin, suffering, and evil into himself in order eventually to overcome it.[88]

Since Father and Son love and are open to the world, this history of God with man is inclusive of all human suffering. "The concrete 'history of God' in the death of Jesus on the cross on Golgotha therefore contains within itself all the depths and abysses of human history. . . . [A]ll human history is taken up into the 'history of God' i.e into the trinity."[89]

While there is opposition in God there is also a deep "communion of will of the Father and the Son on the cross."[90] Moltmann can sum all this up by saying "the Son suffers in his love being forsaken by the Father as he dies. The Father suffers in his love the grief of the death of the Son. In that case, whatever proceeds from the event between the Father and the Son must be understood as the Spirit of the surrender of the Father and the Son, of the Spirit which creates love for forsaken man, as the Spirit which brings the dead alive."[91] Here is a trinitarian theology that combines the cross and divine suffering.

At the same time Moltmann starts "from the assumption that this relationship between God and the world has a *reciprocal* character."[92] It is in the very nature of suffering love to be influenced by the one who suffers and whom one loves. In Moltmann's thought the suffering cross of the Son must, by its nature, act back on and change God. Moltmann adds the further idea that redemption is not only ours through the cross, but is also

God's own deliverance from the suffering of his love. In enmeshing himself with our suffering he must at the same time, in order to be God, involve himself in an act of self-deliverance.[93] Thus, one ends up with a God who, in his relationship to suffering humanity, is obliged to enter into a self-rescue operation.

A further aspect of Moltmann's thought involves not just redemption but creation. Creation is also known as a *passio Dei* for here God, by an act of kenosis, limits or contracts himself, making a space in himself for the world, and so, in the very act of creation, suffers within himself.[94] Moltmann relates this not only to the Father but also to the Holy Spirit.[95] As the One who commits himself to creation the Spirit shares in its groans and travails but is, at the same time, the source of hope for both believers and the cosmos. Moltmann writes, "The history of suffering creation, which is subject to transience, thus brings with it a history of suffering by the Spirit who dwells in creation. But the Spirit who dwells in creation turns creation's history of suffering into a history of hope."[96]

A final aspect of Moltmann's trinitarian theology of the cross deserves mention. Since Moltmann so firmly opposes the *apatheia* view that God cannot suffer, he puts in its place a strong emphasis on the divine *pathos*. Bauckham sums this up well:

> Moltmann's criticism of the concept of divine *apatheia* is not concerned narrowly with God's ability to suffer, but more widely with God's *pathos*. It rejects the unmoved, self-sufficient God of the philosophers in favour of the living God of the whole Bible whose "anthropopathisms" in the Old Testament and incarnate *pathos* in the New Testament are to be taken quite seriously as revealing God's *leidenschaft* and his *leiden*, his passionate interest in the world . . . and his readiness to suffer in his involvement with the world, which becomes most apparent in the cross. The dialectical love which embraces its own contradictions remains the cruciform centre of this divine *pathos*, but the latter provides a more comprehensive account of the love which God is in relation to the world.[97]

Since God's suffering love is so intertwined with ours and ours with his it is not surprising that Moltmann can say "there is no personal God."[98] God is rather a trinitarian event centered on the cross but involving all humankind and all history. This does not mean that Moltmann denies the reality of God but that he sees this as the event of the personal communion of Father, Son, and Holy Spirit. Prayer cannot, however, be made to an event but only through the person of the Son to the Father by the Holy Spirit.

This brief survey centers only on Moltmann's view of suffering in God. Later in his book on the Trinity he takes up the more common features of trinitarian theology in a positive way and almost leaves the whole question of suffering behind, though it is implied throughout.

Several points may be made by way of evaluation and critique of Moltmann's view. First, his anti-*apatheia* view is carried to extremes. Freedom and necessity are one in God.[99] God *must* suffer because he *is* love and this suffering is carried into the very nature of God himself. The retroactive view of the cross is unacceptable since it challenges the freedom of God, his redemptive actions, and his perfections. Can one really receive reconciliation from a God who is perfect only through his suffering relationship to humanity and who finds this perfection only at the end? Bauckham comments, "This conclusion results from the temptation, which Moltmann from *The Crucified God* onwards seems unable to resist, to see the cross as the key to the doctrine of God, not only in the sense that it reveals God as the kind of God who is willing to suffer, but in the sense that the actual sufferings of the cross are essential to who God is."[100] Moreover, can one legitimately apply the highly speculative view of a kenosis in God to his relation to creation—a view which requires another kind of suffering and sets a limit to God?

Perhaps the chief criticism which is to be made of Moltmann's theology is that his innovation lies in making the cross an inner, divine experience. Suffering is not simply something with which God identifies in becoming man in Jesus Christ, but rather suffering is in God himself. Miskotte gives a detailed critique of Moltmann at this point.[101] He shows how it is legitimate to state (with Karl Barth) that God suffers in Christ on the cross while remaining Lord over it. Moltmann, by contrast, reverses this and sees suffering as being *in* God in a manner bordering on pantheism. Miskotte sees the former as preserving God's freedom and sovereignty, whereas Moltmann's view endangers both since suffering is integral to God's being even though transcended at the last.

There is also in Moltmann an inadequate conceptuality. Remarkably, Moltmann never defines what he means by suffering. One of the chief defects of his whole theological approach is an almost total unawareness of the problem of applying human predicates to God. Or, to put it otherwise, he fails to see that in applying suffering to God he is in danger of using this term not in an analogical way but in an illegitimate, univocal manner.

Notes

1. Berthold Klappert, *Die Auferweckung des Gekreuzigten: Der Ansatz der Christologie Karl Barths im Zusammenhang der Christologie der Gegenwart* (Neukirchen: Neukirchener Verlag, 1971), pp. 85ff., 102ff.

2. Jürgen Moltmann, *The Crucified God*, tr. R. A. Wilson and John Bowden (London: S.C.M. Press, 1974). Eberhard Jüngel, *God as the Mystery of the World*, tr. Darrell L. Guder (Edinburgh: T. & T. Clark, 1977). Karl Barth *Church Dogmatics*, IV/1–IV/3 (hereafter cited as *C.D.*). Paul Fiddes, *The Creative Suffering of God* (Oxford: Clarendon Press, 1988).

3. Fiddes, p. 15.

4. *C.D.*, IV/1, pp. 176ff.

5. Ibid., pp. 305ff.

6. John Thompson, *Christ in Perspective: Christological Perspectives in the Theology of Karl Barth* (Edinburgh: Saint Andrew Press, 1978), p. 51.

7. Klappert, p. 154.

8. G. C. Berkouwer, *The Triumph of Grace in the Theology of Karl Barth*, tr. Henry R. Boer (London: Paternoster Press, 1956), p. 126.

9. *C.D.*, IV/1, pp. 303ff.

10. Klappert, pp. 291ff.

11. *C.D.*, IV/2, pp. 323ff.

12. See the Nicene Creed (381 A.D.), cf. Aloys Grillmeier, *Christ in Christian Tradition: From the Apostolic to Chalcedon* (*A.D. 451*), rev. ed. tr. John Bowden (London: Mowbrays, 1975), pp. 249–73.

13. Thomas Aquinas, *Summa Theologica*, I, q. 28, A.1, sees Father, Son, and Holy Spirit as subsistent relations, but also accepts the Spirit as divine.

14. Klappert, p. 195.

15. *C.D.*, IV/2, pp. 21–25.

16. Thompson, p. 53.

17. *C.D.*, IV/1, pp. 246–47.

18. Cf. Jürgen Moltmann, *The Trinity and the Kingdom of God*, tr. Margaret Kohl (London: S.C.M. Press, 1981), pp. 191ff.

19. P. T. Forsyth, "The Divine Self-Emptying," in *God the Holy Father* (1897; reprint, London: Independent Press, 1957), pp. 42–43.

20. Ibid., p. 42.

21. Ibid.

22. P. T. Forsyth, *Marriage, Its Ethic and Religion* (London: Hodder and Stoughton, 1912), pp. 70–71.

23. Ibid., p. 71.

24. *C.D.*, IV/1, p. 209.

25. Ibid., p. 203.

26. Ibid., p. 209.

27. John Thompson, "On the Trinity," in *Theology beyond Christendom*, John Thompson, ed. (Allison Park, Pa.: Pickwick Publications, 1986), p. 18. Cf. also Hans Urs von Balthasar, whose views are similar though not identical to Barth's and Forsyth's. He speaks of a creaturely obedience in Christ which mirrors an obedience that, in some mysterious way, is not foreign to God. This is not to be understood univocally but in terms of selflessness, self-giving, and receptivity between Father and Son by the Holy Spirit. See Balthasar, *Epilog* (Einsiedeln: Johannes Verlag, 1987), pp. 77–78; G. F. O'Hanlon, *The Immutability of God in the Theology of Hans Urs von Balthasar* (Cambridge: Cambridge University Press, 1990), pp. 44–46.

28. Moltmann, *The Crucified God*, pp. 235ff.

29. Ibid., p. 241.

30. Ibid., p. 152.

31. Ibid., p. 277.

32. Richard J. Bauckham, "Jürgen Moltmann," in *One God in Trinity*, Peter Toon and James D. Spiceland, eds. (London: Samuel Bagster 1980), p. 118.

33. Ibid.

34. *C.D.*, IV/1, pp. 157ff.

35. Hans Urs von Balthasar, *The von Balthasar Reader*, ed. Medard Kehl and Werner Löser, tr. Robert J. Daly, S.J., and Fred Lawrence (Edinburgh: T. & T. Clark, 1982), pp. 150–53.

36. Moltmann, *The Trinity and the Kingdom of God*, pp. 171ff.

37. Regina Radlbeck, *Der Personbegriff in der Trinitätstheologie der Gegenwart: Untersucht am Beispiel der Entwürfe Jürgen Moltmanns und Walter Kaspers*

(Regensberg: Verlag Friedrich Pustet, 1989), pp. 93–106, shows that the use of "subject" and "person" in modern terms has its dangers and is problematic in Moltmann. The "persons" in the Trinity do have as "subjects" centers of will, consciousness, and activity. Though for Moltmann the quality of a "person" is socially permeable, one cannot, in his view, speak of full unity in God until the eschaton. This will be discussed more fully in Chapter 6. J. J. O'Donnell, *Trinity and Temporality: The Christian Doctrine of God in the Light of Process Theology and the Theology of Hope* (Oxford: Oxford University Press, 1983), p. 90, also points to the weakness and problematic nature of Moltmann's attempts to define the unity of the three persons as three subjects uniting perichoretically.

38. Richard J. Bauckham, *Moltmann: Messianic Theology in the Making* (London: Marshall Pickering, 1987), pp. 107f.

39. Moltmann, *The Trinity and the Kingdom of God*, p. 161.

40. Von Balthasar, *Theodramatik II/2* (Einsiedeln: Johannes Verlag, 1976), pp. 480–2; G. F. O'Hanlon, *The Immutability of God in the Theology of Hans Urs Von Balthasar*, pp. 116ff.

41. O'Hanlon, p. 120.

42. *The von Balthasar Reader*, p. 153. O'Hanlon, pp. 26–29, 33–34. Hans Urs von Balthasar, *Mysterium Paschale: The Mystery of Easter*, tr. with an introduction by Aidan Nichols, O. P. (Edinburgh: T. & T. Clark, 1990) pp. 148ff.

43. G. F. O'Hanlon, "Does God Change? H. U. von Balthasar on the Immutability of God," *Irish Theological Quarterly*, vol, 53, No. 5, 1987, p. 164.

44. G. F. O'Hanlon, *Does God Change? The Immutability of God in the Theology of Hans Urs Von Balthasar*. Ph.D. diss., Queens University, Belfast, 1986, p. 274.

45. Ibid., p. 313.

46. Eberhard Jüngel, *The Doctrine of the Trinity*, tr. Horton Harris (Edinburgh: Scottish Academic Press, 1976), pp. 23–24, 88f.

47. Hermannus Heiko Miskotte, "Das Leiden Ist in Gott. Über Jürgen Moltmann's trinitärische Kreuzestheologie," in *Diskussion über "Der Gekreuzigte Gott,"* Michael Welker, ed. (Munich: Ch. Kaiser, 1979), p. 80.

48. *C.D.*, IV/1, p. 185.

49. Klappert, pp. 175ff.

50. *C.D.*, IV/1, p. 185.

51. Klappert, p. 176.

52. *C.D.*, IV/1, p. 185.

53. Klappert, p. 182.

54. J. K. Mozley, *The Impassibility of God: A Survey of Christian Thought* (London: Cambridge University Press, 1926), gives an early critique of this view.

55. *C.D.*, IV/2, pp. 27f. T. F. Torrance, *The Mediation of Christ* (Exeter: Paternoster Press, 1983), p. 50.

56. T. F. Torrance, *The Trinitarian Faith: The Evangelical Theology of the Ancient Catholic Faith* (Edinburgh: T. & T. Clark, 1988), pp. 188ff., to some extent defends this position.

57. See Westminster Confession of Faith, ch. II. Thirty-Nine Articles, "The Being of God," ch. 1.

58. Moltmann, *The Crucified God*; Fiddes, *The Creative Suffering of God*; Kazoh Kitamori, *Theology of the Pain of God*, tr, M. E. Bratcher (London: S.C.M. Press, 1966); *C.D.*, IV/1, pp. 157ff.; IV/2, pp. 357ff., in particular, but also II/2, pp. 164ff.

59. Moltmann, *The Crucified God*, passim; *The Trinity and the Kingdom of God*, pp. 21ff.

60. See Moltmann, *The Trinity and the Kingdom of God*, pp. 20ff., for a list of these writers.

61. *C.D.*, II/2, pp. 164–65.

62. *C.D.*, IV/1, pp. 157ff.

63. *C.D.*, IV/2, p. 357. See Thompson, "On the Trinity," where Barth is shown to approach the Trinity from the perspective of Jesus, the Holy Spirit, and the Christian community (pp. 22ff.).

64. *C.D.*, IV/2, p. 357.

65. W. J. Hill, *The Three-Personed God: The Trinity as a Mystery of Salvation* (Washington: Catholic University of America Press, 1982), p. 172.

66. Jüngel, pp. 85–87.

67. Ibid., p. 86.

68. O'Hanlon, "Does God Change?" pp. 165–66; *The Immutability of God*, pp. 37–40, 83–85.

69. Eberhard Jüngel, *God as the Mystery of the World*, tr. Darrell L. Guder (Edinburgh: T. & T. Clark, 1983); Jüngel, "Von Tod des Lebendigen Gottes," in *Unterwegs zur Sache* (Munich: Ch. Kaiser, 1972), pp. 105–25; Jüngel, "Das Verhältnis von 'ökonomischer' und 'immanenter' Trinität," in *Entsprechungen: Gott– Wahrheit–Mensch* (Munich: Ch. Kaiser, 1980), pp. 265–75.

70. Jüngel, *Unterwegs zur Sache*, pp. 105–25.

71. Ibid., pp. 120, 123; Fiddes, p. 198.

72. Eberhard Jüngel, "Das Sein Jesus Christi als Ereignis der Versöhnung Gottes mit einer gottlosen Welt. Die Hingabe des Gekreuzigten," *Evangelische Theologie*, vol. 38, 1978, p. 517.

73. Jüngel, "God as the Mystery," p. 372.

74. Ibid., p. 299.

75. Ibid., p. 223.

76. Ibid., p. 328.

77. J. B. Webster, *Eberhard Jüngel: An Introduction to His Theology* (London: Cambridge University Press, 1986), p. 73.

78. Jüngel, "God as the Mystery," p. 328 (Webster's translation).

79. Webster, p. 73.

80. Jüngel, "God as the Mystery," p. 373.

81. Ibid. In a private conversation in Tübingen in the winter semester of 1990 Professor Jüngel confirmed his belief that not only does God suffer, but God does so in a way far beyond anything we experience as creatures.

82. J. B. Webster, "Eberhard Jüngel," in *The Modern Theologians: An Introduction to Christian Theology in the Twentieth Century*, vol. 1, David Ford, ed. (Oxford: Basil Blackwell, 1989), p. 98.

83. Ibid., p. 99.

84. Ibid.

85. Klappert, pp. 160–63.

86. Paul D. Molnar, "The Function of the Immanent Trinity in the Theology of Karl Barth," *Scottish Journal of Theology*, vol. 42, no. 3, 1989, p. 391. Eberhard Jüngel, "What Does It Mean to Say, 'God is Love?'" in *Christ in Our Place: The Humanity of God in Christ for the Reconciliation of the World. Essays Presented to Professor James Torrance*, Trevor Hart and David Thimell, eds. (Exeter, Eng.: Paternoster Press, 1989), pp. 308–9, where Jüngel quotes Augustine, who saw human love for another as a form of death.

87. Moltmann, *The Crucified God*, p. 243.
88. Ibid., p. 244.
89. Ibid., p. 246.
90. Ibid., p. 244.
91. Ibid., p. 245.
92. Moltmann, *The Trinity and the Kingdom of God*, p. 98.
93. Ibid.
94. Ibid., p. 110.
95. Jürgen Moltmann, *God in Creation: An Ecological Doctrine of Creation*, tr. Margaret Kohl (London: S.C.M. Press, 1985), p. 102.
96. Ibid.
97. Bauckham, *Moltmann*, pp. 105–6.
98. Moltmann, *The Crucified God*, p. 247.
99. Bauckham, *Moltmann*, p. 109.
100. Ibid.
101. Miskotte, pp. 76ff.

4

The Triune God
and Mission

MISSION AND THE TRINITY

It can scarcely be said that the theology of mission has been a predominant feature of modern theological writing, much less a theology based on the Trinity. There has, however, been considerable reflection more recently on the nature of mission and its place in church life and theological thinking; this is so especially since the end of colonialism and the breakdown of the *Corpus Christianum*. The great Edinburgh Missionary Conference of 1910 was a landmark in this respect, but it has since been seen more as the beginning of the ecumenical movement than as a stimulus to missionary work and thought. Current thinking is very varied; here we concentrate on that which relates directly or indirectly to a trinitarian basis and the implication for our understanding of the nature and goal of mission.

Basis of Mission: *Missio Dei*

The term *missio Dei* was used, and became customary in many circles, as a result of the missionary conference in Willingen in 1952.[1] It indicates that mission is not primarily a human work but the work of the triune God. It is based on and reflects his nature, will, and action. What he does in and for the world corresponds to who he is in himself. In this way it reaches back to the unity and distinction of immanent and economic Trinity, and at the same time reaffirms that the Trinity is the mystery of our salvation.[2] This is in contrast to the view that the Trinity is a barrier to outreach to others in mission and dialogue. This attitude often assumes that God is one but not triune; it is basically unitarian in outlook.[3] Colin Gunton rightly argues the opposite, namely, that the theology of the Trinity is the heart of our appeal to the unbeliever as the good news of God's creation and redemption.

The nature of God as Father, Son, and Holy Spirit is not to be conceived as a static being beyond us, unconcerned with us, and unrelated to us. Rather he is movement and fellowship within himself and moves down and out into our world to manifest his glory, to bring us salvation, and to lift us up to participate by his grace in the communion of his eternal life. That participation, however, owes its origin and power not to our doing but to his own action as the triune God. God is a God of mission, which means a God who sends. "The sending of the Son and of the Holy Spirit into the world was the highest expression of the divine missionary activity."[4] The real divine mystery of mission, by which it lives, is the coming of the Son, who is both sent by the Father and is the content of that mission, and, in turn, is moved by and sends the Holy Spirit. While it is possible and necessary to distinguish the persons and to ascribe to each a particular activity (*appropriationes*) as creator, redeemer, and sanctifier, it is wrong to separate these since each is involved in the work of the other. Treated under the perspective of the Trinity it means that the one undivided God is present in his mission in all three persons, though each has a particular and special work to perform in conjunction with the others. As Father, Son, and Holy Spirit it is God's will to bring salvation to humanity.

This view of mission, based on God's activity toward us and his sending of his Son and Spirit into the world, implies a critique of other bases, however valid in themselves, where the emphasis is more on the church and its work than the mission of God. Rather we should see these others taken up and integrated into the activity of the triune God and indeed only made possible by his mission. In the past mission theology suffered from attempts at apologetic proofs based on the Bible, or as necessary for people, or as a task of the church, or to spread Christian culture and civilization. Again, it is not based on a conscious or unconscious need of non-Christians or on a subjectively or objectively illuminating need of Christians to communicate, but on the will of the triune God.[5] Nor is it a view based on sinful man— one F. D. Maurice criticized in the last century—though it involves an action and coming of God in the totality of his being as salvation from sin.[6]

This latter approach is also criticized by Hardy and Ford, who see it as problem-based, "sniffing out sin and misery, making people feel guilty and inadequate, and then offering the Gospel as the answer. Instead, the essence of mission and evangelism is in the intrinsic worth, beauty and love of God, and the joy of knowing and trusting him."[7] They continue, "This approach is in line with a transformation of mission by many christian churches in the twentieth century. There has been a change in the dominant perspective. Beginning as the mission of the Western church to the rest of the world, it shifted to the mission of the worldwide church, and finally to the 'mission of God' in both church and world."[8] This is in line with Karl Barth's general approach giving priority to Gospel over law and beginning with the victory of Christ in principle over the opposing forces.

Now, by his prophetic word, he makes known to all who are in bondage, guilty of sin and in need of salvation, the reconciliation he has accomplished for them.[9]

Given then that the triune God is the sender and the sent, the one who comes; given also that distinction of persons and activities is relatively necessary, how can we conceive the distinctive mission of each person in this unitary perspective? We cannot see it as God sending anyone other than himself as his emissary as in Arianism, or as involving any infringement of his Lordship. He acts and comes as Lord in the fullness of his Godhead and in the form of great humility, lowliness, suffering, and service yet also in majestic power and love.[10]

This exposition basically follows the document drawn up by the Lutheran World Federation at a conference in Addis Ababa in Ethiopia in 1988. The Lutherans make several important points.[11] First, the mission of God is based on his revelation in Jesus Christ. Second, it has a twin thrust, the proclamation of the Good News to the nations and the establishment of the Kingdom of God. The purpose of the triune God is thus to bring salvation to humanity and to establish righteousness. In this respect the interrelationship of creation and redemption is indicated but not fully spelled out. Third, while accepting the unity of action of the divine persons it tends to treat them too much in isolation from one another. In the following discussion we make use of the main outline of the Lutherans but also seek to show how each person's work is intimately bound up with that of the other two and cannot be properly understood otherwise.

The Mission of God as Creator

As Luther said, creation is grace. As Calvin said, the universe is God's work created *ex nihilo* to be the *theatrum gloriae Dei*. God maintains the creation in being as a sphere for peace, freedom, and righteousness. Imprisoned by human sin and evil, creation is promised freedom by God. "The mission of God the creator is the determination, basis and promise for the whole creation"[12]—the promise of freedom from the slavery of decay to share in the glorious liberty of God's children. God's promises embrace not just a "new creation" for persons in their conversion to him from sin, but also a new created cosmos which includes a changed natural order. The two are intimately interrelated, as Romans 8 points out. In order to maintain the creation he made by grace and to save it from chaos he sent his Son. P. T. Forsyth writes of this, "The first missionary was God the Father, who sent forth his Son in the likeness of sinful flesh. That is the seal and final ground of missions—the grace, the ultimate unbought, overwhelming grace of God, the eternal heart and purpose of the Father, who gave us not only a prophet but a propitiation."[13] One can and should see the redemptive work of God as the basis and meaning of creation, as Newbigin and Barth point out. Newbigin sees it focused in Jesus' proclamation of the reign of God which "is the true secret of universal and cosmic history";[14]

Barth sees it centered in election and covenant as the will of the Father by the Son for the creation and reconciliation of the cosmos.[15] God's mission is thus universal and cosmic in extent. While the Father is primarily Creator, the Son is the agent of creation and has a cosmic role holding all things together, preserving creation from chaos and bringing righteousness.[16] At the same time the Spirit with the Word is the Creator Spirit (Gen. 1:2).

The Mission of the Son

God acts in a unique way in sending his Son as the Word incarnate who not only proclaimed but embodied the kingdom in his own person. This good news is of his mission to the world, assuming our sinful human nature, accepting and undergoing God's wrath and curse, his judgment on our sin, and effecting victory over sin and death and all the powers of darkness by his death and resurrection. The mission of the Son as our reconciliation is an exclusive work yet has an inclusive missionary perspective and is at the heart and core of the *missio Dei*. "The second missionary was that Son, the apostle of our profession as the New Testament calls him, the true primate of the apostles, of those that he sent forth who himself came forth from the bosom of the Father to declare him; who exiled and emptied himself in this foreign land of earth, and humbled himself to death, even the death of the cross."[17] The Lutherans put it succinctly: "The sending of Christ to redeem the world is at the heart of the mission of God in human history, between creation and its renewal in glory."[18]

The Father is involved with the Son, suffers with him, reveals his own name and nature through him, glorifies him, raises him from the dead, gives him the kingdom, the power, and the glory, receives back from him the power and reign of his mediatorial work. He is with the Son the source of life of the Spirit.[19]

The Mission of the Holy Spirit

The mission of the Holy Spirit is closely related to that of the Son. He comes upon Jesus and endows him with the ability to go out preaching, teaching, healing, and performing miracles, so fulfilling his messianic vocation. He enables the Son to rejoice in God, acknowledges the glory of the Son and the Father and with the Son glorifies the Father. At the same time he is often almost identified with the Son (1 Cor. 3:17). He is nonetheless distinct; he is, to use Barth's phrase, the subjective reality of revelation, of which Jesus is the objective reality.[20]

The Holy Spirit thus comes from Christ, makes people new creations in him, creates a community of faith, and conforms us to the image of the Son. He gives many gifts and tasks and enables mission and service. The Spirit is the firstfruits and foretaste of our inheritance.[21] As the one who unites us with Christ this reflects his role in the Trinity as the union and communion of Father and Son.

God's continuing mission is his action in the world by the Holy Spirit. "The Spirit of God empowered the prophets, came down upon Jesus at the beginning of his work, sent and equipped the young church as his witness."[22] In the same way the Holy Spirit sends and enables the people of God in every age to participate in his mission. "The third missionary is the Holy Ghost whom the Saviour sends forth into all the earth, who comes mightily and sweetly ordering all things, and subduing all lands to the obedience of the Kingdom of Christ."[23]

The Spirit shares in the mission of Son and Father in creation and redemption, in the coming and life of the Son, and himself is sent and comes to be with us. He is like and with Christ intercessor and advocate with the Father pleading our cause at God's right hand (Rom. 8).

Father, Son, and Holy Spirit are so interrelated that the work of each, while distinctive, is so joined with and related to the others that it becomes and is one work. It is a sending and a coming in the unity of purpose and will as well as of divine being. Only in this way are the *opera trinitatis ad extra indivisa*; they are not uniform or simply that of God, whose oneness outweighs the distinctions of the persons and their own appropriate activities. Rather, each is in and with the others the one triune God active in the world to glorify himself and to bring us and the world redemption.

One can sum up what we have said to date as follows. The *ultimate basis* of mission is the triune God—the Father who created the world and sent his Son by the Holy Spirit to be our salvation. The *proximate basis* of mission is the redemption of the Son by his life, death, and resurrection, and the *immediate power* of mission is the Holy Spirit. It is, in trinitarian terms, a *missio Dei*. Thus mission is based on the will, movement, and action of the grace and love of God—Father, Son, and Holy Spirit. Forsyth sums it up as follows: "We owe ourselves, our faith, hope, and eternal destiny to the eternal God redeeming us to his eternal self in Father, Son, and Holy Ghost. These go forth into each other, into all the world, into the depth of the soul."[24] This interpenetration of Father, Son, and Holy Spirit reaches into the depth of our sinful situation and brings salvation, justice, and peace to the whole of creation and humanity and gives it the hope, with us, of new life with God.

The Mission of the Church

Participation in the Missio Dei

The *missio Dei*, which sees mission as primarily God's activity, is not intended to exclude humanity from participation in this work. The earlier critique was not aimed at setting aside the church or the human communication of the gospel, but was intended to see them in a role subordinate to the mission, which is primarily that of God himself. Under God, however, each has its place. It is not as if God is and does everything and we can do nothing. In the light of the triune God as the basis and agent of mission we are called and enabled by him to be his human instruments in his exclusive divine work, to be participants in it.

"The mission of the church takes its lead from God's own mission."[25] One way in which this can be expressed is to see it as analogous to the place of Jesus' humanity in the divine scheme. Just as the man Jesus participates in the life of God by union with the Son, so we, by grace, are exalted into communion with Christ by the Holy Spirit and do share—not in his original work—but in the meaning, power, and direction of it as human salvation, righteousness, and peace. George Vicedom quotes Karl Hartenstein as follows: "Mission is not only obedience to the word of the Lord, it is not only an obligation to gather a church [community]; it is participation in the sending of the Son, the *missio dei*, with the comprehensive goal of setting up the Lordship of Christ over the whole redeemed creation."[26] The Lutheran World Federation document speaks similarly. "The main object of the church is to participate in the mission of God. The mission of the church comes from God's own mission and is anchored in God's self-revelation."[27] It participates not by repeating God's work, but "in word and action proclaiming the presence and the coming of the kingdom of God and bringing the world the message of salvation in Jesus Christ."[28] Here there is a twin thrust—the kingdom of God and its righteousness and the message of salvation in Christ. The one possibly points to right relations in society and the other to a right relationship with God and with one another in the Christian community. It would be wrong to play off the one against the other, as sometimes happens. They belong integrally together as part of the mission of God and his people to the world.

As the church belongs to God, is the body of Christ, the temple of the Holy Spirit, so mission belongs to the very being of the church. The New Testament metaphors for the church—the body of Christ, people of God, bride of Christ—are not meant to describe a static group but a living community in and for the world but not of it. All church offices, all church activities, even those regarded as building up fellowship internally, have this character of outreach to the world.[29] The church as a whole and each member of it is called upon to participate in mission in these ways. To this mission also belongs the unity of the church, which is both God's gift and, under him, our task to seek to realize visibly on earth.[30]

Two further things must be said about the church and its mission. It is carried out on the completion of Christ's work of reconciliation, which is inclusive in character, embracing all humanity and the whole cosmos. It is thus exclusively the work of Christ in union with the Father and the Holy Spirit, but it includes everything in its scope and redemptive purpose. The other significant factor is that this participation of the church in mission is to be carried out by the power of the Holy Spirit (Acts 1:8). It is the Spirit who enables the church to witness not only to all nations and peoples, but throughout all time to the end of the ages. It has thus a pneumatological and also an eschatological perspective based on the very nature and action of the triune God.

As P. T. Forsyth sums it up, "The fourth missionary is the church and these four missionaries are all involved in the one divine redemption to which we owe ourselves utterly."[31]

Mission as Witness

We have already used the terms mission and witness. Both are central to the New Testament message about the mission of the triune God and the church's participation in it. This has been taken up in our century by Karl Barth in particular.[32] Barth's missiology is, as indicated, indirectly trinitarian. It is related to the third or prophetic office of Christ who bears witness to his own reconciliation, revealing it as a transforming light for the nations. Jesus, by his cross and resurrection, is victor and speaks his own direct word of reconciliation to the world. Because of the inclusive nature of this reconciliation the world is his de jure but not de facto. The word of revelation bears witness to that truth, calls all people to hear and believe in Christ and themselves to be a witnessing fellowship. All this is possible only because the crucified One has been raised from the dead to the glory of the Father and lives forevermore. The task of the church is to bring people not simply to salvation, which could be self-centered and have a certain aspect of egoism in it. Rather, it is to enable them to be witnesses. For Barth, Christ is "The True Witness"[33] yet the One who also uses us as witnesses. To be a true witness to Christ is the real meaning of being a Christian.

In contrast to the general *missio Dei* theology Barth does not speak of a participation in God's work—that would seem an ambiguous phrase to him, as in many respects it is. In his later writings Barth even set aside the whole idea of Word and sacrament being means of grace. They bear witness to Jesus Christ the Son of God but are not instrumental means. They are significatory rather than instrumental and sacramental. Barth's christological concentration centers all on a *missio Christi*, who proclaims God's act of reconciliation. However, this is not without the Spirit, nor ever can it be. In the time between the ages of the first and second coming it is the Spirit who is the Victor's instrument going into all the world, calling and enabling people to believe, to be a Christian community, and themselves to be witnesses. Barth would undoubtedly concur with Newbigin's view that "in sober truth the Spirit is himself the witness who goes before the church in its missionary journey. The church's witness is secondary and derivative insofar as it follows obediently where the Spirit leads."[34] In this understanding Barth's view is close to that of the *missio Dei* with the church caught up in Christ's action by the Holy Spirit and thus being a witness to him. It is, therefore, indirectly a trinitarian perspective on mission.

Two main criticisms have been made of Barth's view. The first is that it is too objective, that reconciliation has already been accomplished on the cross. "This . . . is too objective, too inclusive a view,"[35] leading inexorably to universalism. Human beings must respond moved by God's Spirit and so believe. Few would object to this position; Barth would not, for it is only by the Spirit we can respond and believe. Barth's inclusive view, based on an exclusive reconciliation, means on the one hand that, in principle, we live in a reconciled world, de jure belonging to God; in practice there are many who do not believe.[36] The fact of unbelief may contradict God's sovereign universal purpose but can never overcome it. The thrust may be toward universalism but this is in fact never implied or taught in any of Barth's writings.

Barth's missiology and general theological position are more vulnerable in his view of witness as a sign or pointer to Christ rather than as a means of grace. Manecke points out that one would have expected between Christology and pneumatology a section on preaching the word of reconciliation as a means of justification.[37] When Barth does mention proclamation in this context it is seen as a sign indicating the word Christ himself proclaims as he engages in conflict with evil and sin in the world.[38] There is truth in the criticism that was put to Barth himself by his friends[39] who felt he had made both Word and sacrament no longer means Christ uses but simply signs, echoes, pointers. Christ himself is the one true witness, his word eliciting a faint echo from us, just as the server at the Mass rings a bell and indicates the action of Christ himself in the eucharist. Like John the Baptist, a witness is one who points to Christ and says "Behold the Lamb of God who takes away the sin of the world." This is an area of considerable debate; it indicates Barth's concern to eliminate any intermediary who could, in any sense, claim some control over the Word and the sacraments. The object of witness and the agent of witness is Christ, Son of the Father, by the Holy Spirit who reveals his own reconciling work effectively to human beings and so enables them to believe and to be witnesses to others. But whether one should regard the word of human agents and the sacraments God has given as no longer means of grace is quite a different matter and goes further than the main traditions have so far gone. Does God in fact speak directly without human agency and means? Is a pointer or sign not a means God uses?

The Goal and Method of Mission

The Goal of Mission

"The primary goal of the participation of the church in the mission of God is, as expressed by Christ in his missionary mandate, to make disciples (Matthew 28:19)."[40] Put otherwise, it is to bring men and women into living fellowship with the triune God and with one another through him. The church is thus not a static product of the Spirit's work, but a dynamic instrument in the service of others. "You are God's own people that you may declare the wonderful deeds of him who called you out of darkness into his marvellous light" (1 Pet. 2:9). The church is, on the one hand, the provisional result of mission but, on the other hand, it is God's agent of it.[41] The goal of the church is thus not itself but the world. "The church participates in God's mission to bring to humankind righteousness and salvation and to reconcile a broken creation."[42]

Here, as we have seen, a double thrust—the salvation of humankind and righteousness in society and in the world as a whole—becomes obvious. Theo Sundermeier points out how, roughly speaking, two opposing models of mission are presented today.[43] One starts with witness leading to spirituality and then socially liberating action. The second goes in the opposite direction, though it could be said that both have the same aim—to see the work of the triune God *ad extra* as one work with one goal summed up by the preceding quotation from the Lutheran Conference as "righteousness" and "salvation," the redemption in total of a broken creation and creatures. The starting point is less important than the goal, though it may indicate what one aims at and intends. If one has to choose, the former is the more traditional and, one may say, biblical model—evangelical and catholic in one. The latter is the way of liberationists and of some political theologians and is also advocated by some ecumenical missiologists.[44] These twin thrusts are often though not always contrary to one another. Seen in proper perspective they may be complementary. What one aims at is a holistic vision and approach.

Such a comprehensive view of the mission of the church and its goal in the world is set out by Karl Barth in his *Church Dogmatics*.[45] He points out that there are six conditions of true missionary activity.

First, missionary activity presupposes that everything has already been done for the world and humanity in the reconciliation accomplished in Jesus Christ. Second, mission is not an optional extra or the preserve of a few, or simply the task of missionary societies, but is that of the church as a whole. It is true that only individuals can act as missionaries to go abroad, but the church as a whole should be missionary in outlook. Third, the sole purpose of mission is to proclaim the Gospel and to convert men and women to Christ; it is not the strengthening or confirmation or the extension of Western or any other culture, civilization, or politics. One can say, in line with Barth, that in the past the faith followed the flag and there were established little colonies, not only of Christians, but denominations of Methodists, Anglicans, Presbyterians, and others in India, to take but one example. It was then discovered that the Indians might believe in Christ but our denominational habits were and are largely alien to them, hence the church unions of North and South India. Fourth, on the human level, mission should be carried out with the greatest respect for the values of others who have a different religion from us but with a sincere lack of respect for them from the point of view of the Gospel. The Gospel must be opposed to theism and these religions in all its uniqueness and novelty with no attempt to compromise or vitiate its truth but offered in the spirit and reality of love. Fifth, mission involves the whole person and so a care for humanity in its totality. Education, healing, and help in need, though never the main goal, have always rightly been associated with mission. Sixth, the goal of missionary work is to make a missionary church, to testify to the nations the God who wills to make them too his witnesses and missionaries. Barth's holistic vision centered on God's activity in Christ by the Spirit claims all humankind and creation for the triune God.

Method in Mission

There are clearly many ways in which this task can be carried out. The chief ways are by speech and by service in order that the church may grow both spiritually and numerically. A new movement within the church concerned with method, and active particularly in the United States, is the Church Growth Movement, where numerical growth at home and abroad is important and seems for some to be almost central.[46] Waldron Scott writes of this movement, "When evangelicals speak of church growth today more often than not they refer to quantitative growth only."[47] He continues, "One wonders whether the current focus on numerical expansion is not simply a reflection of the modern American preoccupation with success."[48] The danger here is both a counting of heads and an emphasis on human agency and methods. But if the previous emphasis on mission as God's work is correct, and if, as we have seen, this is a work of the Holy Spirit in particular, then we cannot measure results in purely quantitative terms. As Scott says, "It is perfectly true, of course, that quantitative expansion may mirror qualitative growth. But not always."[49] The New Testament speaks of people being added to the church but in the power of Pentecost. It equally, if not more frequently speaks of growth into Christ.[50]

William Abraham, writing of the modern Church Growth Movement,[51] sees one of its main weaknesses as being its largely pragmatic character. It is based on looking in a very practical way at certain situations, evaluating them, and seeing how they should be approached. In many ways this is not incorrect since one must act with knowledge. Abraham, however, speaks of the serious lack of theological balance and the many penetrating objections that have been raised to standard church growth exegesis of the great commission.[52] It can be grafted onto various theologies or little theology so that, as he states, we "are tempted to domesticate the Holy Spirit in structures and requirements of a prosaic profession."[53] In other words, the message of the triune God is reduced too often to research programs. Research can be necessary, but the work of mission must be carried out in accordance with the will of God and his action and in fact by and through him.

It is precisely the concept of mission as the work of God, Father, Son, and Holy Spirit, that saves any church growth movement from shallowness and too strong an emphasis on human methods. And it is the same God as Holy Spirit who enables us to grow into Christ and to live in his image and likeness as a community and as individuals. Much of the New Testament is occupied with this aspect of qualitative growth and holiness as well as human zeal and enthusiasm.

Trinity and Dialogue

It is generally recognized that, roughly speaking, there are

> three different types of Christian attitudes to other religions: the exclusivist, the inclusivist and the pluralist. The first sees genuine knowledge and experience of God confined to Christian faith. The second grants that genuine knowledge and experience of God may exist in other traditions but holds that the fullness of that knowledge and experience of God can be found only in Christianity. The pluralist view represents the different traditions as differing expressions of a knowledge and experience of God that is common to many traditions.[54]

Pluralism so interpreted assumes that the unity of mankind and cooperation between the various religions should be our main object in dialogue and that the old claims to the uniqueness of the Christian faith should be abandoned. While some religions have more truth value than others, no one can make exclusive claims or provide for human unity. A form of relativism becomes the prevailing "orthodoxy."[55] The exclusivist view may lead to separation of the Christian faith from other faiths in an attitude of opposition or hostility, though it can also lead to mission and evangelism in love. This exclusivist view will not be very receptive to dialogue with its supposed dangers of watering down the faith. The inclusivist view has been held in the churches by many people throughout the centuries. It accepts the uniqueness of the Christian revelation but does not exclude knowledge of the true God outside this sphere. In this view dialogue is possible since there are points of contact and common beliefs with many other faiths.

From a trinitarian perspective the preceding pluralist view leads to a basic denial of what is distinctively Christian. The doctrine of the Trinity makes truth claims that are unique and to that extent affirms a form of exclusivism since only in Jesus Christ is there salvation. To meet with others will not lessen our conviction of the truth of the triune God but it may correct false interpretations others have had or have of our Christian faith and also lead us more deeply into the knowledge of our own faith and its implications for relations with others. Positively, since God as Father, Son, and Holy Spirit is a being in a community of personal relationships, the fact of personal encounter with others can prove invaluable, especially if it acts, as God has done, in the greatest humility and love. The very nature of the Trinity can also be shown to others as a paradigm and basis for true relationships in community with others. Moreover, since in Christ God has united our humanity with himself by the Holy Spirit, "we seek to find in trinitarian doctrine, in our beliefs about the very being of God, the foundation for the unity of humankind."[56]

At the same time, from the Christian perspective, the trinitarian view of God offers a critique of all other views of God and forms of "religion," including the Christian, as Karl Barth points out.[57] The temptation to create idols, making gods in our own image, is as old as humanity and a continuing danger today. One cannot therefore simply accept that the other faith claims have equal validity with the Christian. "While it is right that we should take seriously and, where appropriate, with due penitence, the charge made by members of other faiths against the way our theology has sometimes been used oppressively, we should not be afraid to face sincerely the differences between trinitarian and other forms of monotheism."[58] This would apply even more to polytheism.

The trinitarian view of God claims that in Jesus Christ the true God has revealed himself uniquely to humankind. Yet this exclusivity has by its nature, through reconciliation in Christ, a universal perspective, inclusive of humanity and creation as a whole. This being so, the best paradigm for interfaith dialogue in the Christian perspective is the exclusivist–inclusivist one, which is basically that of Karl Barth.[59] In this respect Newbigin comes close to Barth by stating that "it is the doctrine of the trinity that provides us with the true grammar of dialogue."[60] This means three things which Newbigin believes parallel the three persons in the Trinity.[61] First there is a given unity in humanity since all are the objects of God's creation and reconciliation. This will imply a readiness to cooperate with people of other faiths for the common good without compromise of principle. It will also mean, as Barth points out, that there is an ontological relationship between the man Jesus, who includes all in himself, and all other human beings.[62] Since this is so and Jesus Christ is Lord by virtue of his reconciling the world to himself, we may expect "parables of the Kingdom" *extra muros ecclesiae*. These cannot, however, contradict or supersede the Christian revelation but only confirm the one truth of God in Jesus Christ. This view of these signs of the truth and love of God in others may also be applicable to other religions, though it does not mean that they are in the same sense as the Christian means of salvation.[63] Second, dialogue is carried out on the basis of the uniqueness of Christ. The universality of his person and work gives a common basis for all—all share in it though not all know it. "The meeting place is at the cross, at the place where he [the Christian] bears witness to Jesus as the judge and saviour both of him and of his partner."[64] This may call in question some of our received ways of thinking, which need to be reformulated, but in no way lessens the truth of the person and claims of Christ. Third, "we participate in the dialogue, believing and expecting that the Holy Spirit can and will use this dialogue to do his own sovereign work, to glorify Jesus by converting to him both the partners in the dialogue."[65]

In these senses, while one is open to learn and receive, basically dialogue is an aspect of the mission of the triune God to the whole of humankind and the world.

THE TRINITY AND THE CHURCH

One of the aspects which has been a feature of Orthodox and some Anglican doctrines of the Trinity is its social nature.[66] God is not lonely or sin-
gular but is a fellowship of life and love in his being in himself as Father,
Son, and Holy Spirit. This results quite clearly from beginning with the
persons of the Trinity more than the unity. From a quite different perspective, but nonetheless clearly, Karl Barth[67] has underlined the community
aspect of the life of God. God has the fullness of life and fellowship within
himself. Yet in the freedom of his will and grace he has created us and our
world and in our sin reconciled us to himself. For the exponents of both
views what God does *ad extra* corresponds to who he is in himself. Hence
the church as a community of God's people reflects, in some measure, the
community nature and life of God. As God is a unity in communion those
called by him through Christ by the Holy Spirit will show this, however
imperfectly, and be drawn to participate in the fellowship of God within
himself as Father, Son, and Holy Spirit.

Historical Review

That this is no new conception is shown by Heinz Schutte[68] in an article
on the trinitarian nature of the church and the need to develop it. Many of
the patristic writers took the metaphors applied to the church in the New
Testament and saw them as implicitly pointing to a trinitarian basis. The
church is the people of God (*Father*), the body of *Christ* (*the Son*), and the
Temple of the *Holy Spirit*. In this perception "the Church is a trinitarian
reality"[69] called and enabled to be God's people through union with Christ
as his bride by the Spirit who also makes this fellowship his temple.[70] Schutte
points out that this strain is seen in Clement of Rome, Hippolytus, Clement of Alexandria, and Tertullian. Tertullian wrote, "Where the three, Father,
Son and Holy Spirit are there the church is to be found, the body of the
three."[71] Cyprian of Carthage, though championing a view of the church
not all would follow, stated that the church is "the people made one in the
unity of the Father, the Son and the Holy Spirit."[72] Schutte writes, "The
unity of the church is related to the mystery of the trinity."[73]

Thus in the patristic era there were clear signs showing an awareness of
the church as a trinitarian reality emphasizing the mystery of God's being
and action, creating the unity and fellowship of the church reflecting his
own divine life of love.

In the Middle Ages, while the church did not wholly lose this perspective, in the West it became known as "Christendom" and was virtually identical with the whole community viewed as Christian. It also took on a form
of papal monarchy. The break between East and West is seen not only in
relation to the *Filioque* controversy; it is also related to the fact that the
earlier view of the church as a trinitarian reality was largely left behind.

Schutte writes, "The churches in the West and East retained the view in common that the church is the people of God, body and bride of Christ and mystery of the faith. In the West this took a secondary place to a juridically structured ecclesiology which was increasingly developed."[74]

The Reformers reacted strongly against the errors and abuses of their day, reaffirmed the Trinity, and to some extent related it to the church. Luther could speak of the church, the body of Christ, as "one body, as Father and Son are one God."[75] Calvin's ecclesiology is more oriented toward the Holy Spirit, who makes us one with Christ and without whom we cannot call God Father.[76] Yet it is also a fact that neither these nor other Reformers, nor later Protestant orthodoxy, while affirming the Trinity, drew out the significance of the relationship of the church to the triune God. It has been left to modern times both to reaffirm and think through the Trinity in a new way and to demonstrate its centrality, normative place, and significance for the doctrine and life of the church in its unity and community.

If it is true that God is one yet three in one and that in both East and West we can (however differently) view God as one in a community of persons, this, when appropriated and applied, has important consequences for the doctrine of the church and for interchurch relations and dialogue. This has, of course, been said many times from the perspective of Christology and as such is valid and true, since the church is where Christ is and is one in him. But we do less than justice to the conception of the church if we omit its trinitarian basis, especially since it is the Holy Spirit who unites us with Christ, enabling us to be sons and daughters of God and know and call him our Father. It is the Spirit who through the Son draws us up to participate in the life and love of the triune God in and with the fellowship of his people.

There are two immediate consequences that follow from such a conception of God. On the one hand, the life of the church, reflecting the Trinity, will be a life of unity in community; on the other, this unity in community belongs to the very being of the church. We look briefly at four examples of how this is being understood and interpreted today.

Unity and Community

Jürgen Moltmann

Moltmann's view of the trinity emphasizes strongly the personal fellowship of God as Father, Son, and Holy Spirit. He believes, with some justification, that "theological ecclesiologies in the West have traditionally concentrated on establishing the ground for the authority of a ministry in the church. Finding a basis for the community of the people of God lagged far behind."[77] Given this understanding he is critical both of his own Reformation traditions and of Roman Catholicism in particular. The Reformation view—both Lutheran and Reformed—defined the church as the place where the Word of God was truly preached and the sacraments rightly administered. This implied that by these means of grace Christ speaks, calls people to himself by the Holy Spirit, and creates a community of faith. While one assumes Moltmann does not disagree with this, he clearly thinks it is not enough. In his view it underestimates the charismata of the Holy Spirit, who leads to the charismatic congregation, and this congregation is, in the older perspective, reduced to the charisma of the one ministry. Moltmann sees the New Testament church not only as a charismatic community, but as having a charismatic structure without defining too clearly what he means by this.

The view that the ministry constitutes the church and that the community is almost entirely dependent on just such a ministry has clearly need of broadening in the direction Moltmann indicates. But to put ministry contra community is an exaggerated critique which is scarcely biblical. Moltmann's view is critical of a monarchical episcopal Anglican or Roman view. This can take several forms—*Ubi Episcopus ibi ecclesia* or a papal universal episcopate—*Ubi Petrus ibi ecclesia*.[78] While these may guarantee some form of unity of the community, they too bind the Spirit to the ministry in an even stronger way, "so that it is hardly possible for the community which is charismatic in itself to develop because the community remains passive, a recipient of the actions of the church ministry."[79]

Moltmann sees the foregoing views as a form of dominion based on a particular conception of God's sovereignty. In place of this he sees the church as a trinitarian fellowship, "the very fellowship of the Son with the Father into which the Holy Spirit takes it, as John 17:20 implies. The unity of the congregation is in truth the trinitarian fellowship of God himself, which it mirrors and in which it participates."[80] Although this is to some extent acceptable, it leaves out how, humanly speaking, this fellowship is called into being and maintained and what form of ministry and structure it implies. Moreover, Moltmann sees the Holy Spirit, who brings us into this fellowship, as the feminine person of the Trinity so that we have God as our Father, are brothers of the Son, and are children by the maternal Holy Spirit. This leads to a brotherly and sisterly community in which all are equal and there is no superiority or subordination but a community of men and women set free by love. Moltmann's view points clearly to a unity and community reflecting the triune God and reminds us that all our forms of ministry are for such an end and service as well as to the glory of God.

His ecclesiology further emphasizes the Christian community as the mature and responsible congregation. His polity is basically congregational, against a state church which often operates like a government bureaucracy.[81] It is a "relational ecclesiology," related to others inside as freedom and equality and to those outside in openness, solidarity, and readiness for dialogue. In both cases it reflects the Trinity as community and as one that is open to the world and the future of the Kingdom.

Moltmann's ecclesiology is also one "from below," where fellowship should prevail. This should also characterize synodical and church government actions and attitudes since these are not "above" the congregation.

"The fellowship of the fellowships should be lived as fellowship [and] the affairs that have to be ordered must be settled in the fellowship of the Spirit."[82] This unity expresses itself not only in Word and sacrament, but in identification with the poor and all oppressed. Here doctrine may unite but politics divide. But both must go together in real unity. Internal unity is not enough; these other issues are "questions of faith as well" and must be tackled in the field of interchurch relations.[83] Moltmann has, however, remarkably little to say on the nature of this unity.

With Barth this is basically a charismatic and congregational polity which varies considerably from the structures of most present-day churches. Yet these are properly challenged by Moltmann to see if, in the light of the reality of fellowship, they are genuinely biblical and trinitarian.

Agreement with Moltmann that trinitarian ecclesiology involves a community of brothers and sisters does not preclude acceptance of official ministerial forms. Nor can obedience be excluded from the life of the community any more than it can from the Trinity. Nor can one say that the church has little need of structure, order, and authority.[84] These ideas do not deny, nor need they conflict with, equality and community, but they are to be exercised as a body in a love which liberates. One cannot simply set aside the *kephale* theology, as Moltmann does, as "still undeveloped from the trinitarian point of view."[85] A general critique has been stated persuasively by Bauckham:

> Perhaps the most cogent criticism of Moltmann's concept of the church as free fellowship is that in simply opposing power and authority, on the one hand, and love and freedom, on the other, Moltmann too easily equates the former with domination. He neglects the inevitability of some kind of power and authority in human society and therefore misses the opportunity to explore the way in which power and authority can be based on consent, exercised in love, and directed to fostering, rather than suppressing, freedom and responsibility. However his brief discussion of *leadership* in the congregation and the more general discussion of the relationship between community and the particular assignments of its members have potential in this direction and show that he is not wholly unaware of the issues.[86]

Eastern Orthodox Perspectives

The Orthodox, like Moltmann, begin with the community of the three persons in the Trinity, Father, Son, and Holy Spirit, rather than with the unity. Fellowship or community is central to the being of God since it presupposes not an abstract being of God, as is supposedly the case in the Western view, but persons who are capable of fellowship. With dogmatic definiteness Larentzakis declares, "A God who does not exist in concrete persons, i.e. hypostases can neither be known nor indeed exist."[87] He does not accept an abstract ontology of being but opts rather for a metaphysic of love—a relational metaphysic where at the center person, not substance, stands. He claims that the Greek fathers had overcome the metaphysics of the time and had developed and replaced them by a Christian ontology. That is, they put a biblical presentation of God in place of a Greek philosophical one. In this view the Father is the source or *arche* of the Godhead; the Son and the Holy Spirit receive their being from him.

Reflecting the Trinity of three persons in mutual love and fellowship and called into being by it is the church. Taking up the patristic view mentioned earlier, Larentzakis writes, "The church is the people of God the Father, the body of Christ and the Temple of the Holy Spirit"[88] and thus a community of persons. "The knowledge of God wrought by the triune God has soteriological and community character."[89] Church membership and eternal life are not possible without this basis of the mystery of the triune God. It begins with baptism, which brings new life and fellowship, and continues its community character in the eucharist. It is basically a eucharistic ecclesiology.

Here the emphasis is on full personal fellowship analogous to the Trinity yet which claims that we can have this only if we accept the Orthodox view of the triune God. Here there is no equating of the church with the fellowship without hierarchy, which is viewed in Orthodoxy as a development of tradition in the undivided church. A question, however, arises: What is the relationship between a hierarchically structured church and the Trinity? Here too is a view of baptism and eucharist which is based on tradition, with little consideration given to their relation to Scripture and the God revealed there.

In a more nuanced theological approach John Zizioulas states that there are four elements in an Orthodox ecclesiology: a trinitarian, christological, pneumatological, and iconological.[90] It is the economy of the Trinity that is the prime basis of the church. "The church is built by the historical work of the divine economy but leads finally to the vision of God 'as he is', to the vision of the triune God in his eternal existence."[91] In other words, in his works of salvation God founded the church to reflect his being so that persons in community are the ikon or image of God and this points to the triune God as he is and will be known at the end. While Christ does the work of God and the church is the body of Christ, it is primarily the Spirit who is active both in Christ and in the church. A form of Spirit Christology informs this whole conception. Zizioulas writes, "The Holy Spirit, in making real the Christ-event in history, makes real *at the same time* Christ's personal existence as a body or community."[92] Again he sums up, "Thus the mystery of the church has its birth in the entire economy of the trinity and in a pneumatologically constituted christology."[93] Christ is thus a corporate personality, a being in communion, in whom we are included by the Holy Spirit. To this should be added a valid hierarchically structured ministry as essential to the givenness of Christ and the church. This is, however, to be seen not as an apostolic succession of bishops as individuals, but in the bishop as the head of his community. Ordination is not the direct transmission of authority simply through a clerical succession but is to be viewed in the context of the church as a whole.

While the emphasis in this exposition is on community in variety based on the Trinity, certain specific Orthodox traits manifest themselves and call for considerable qualification. The economic Trinity is sharply distinguished from the immanent since God in his being is known only by "vision." There is truth in the fact of the church by the Spirit being incorporated into Christ so that to be in Christ is to be in his fellowship.[94] The Spirit as creating the Christ event is only a partial truth that needs to be balanced by a Logos Christology or one ends up, as is the tendency here, with a mainly Spirit Christology which is quite inadequate. Finally, in this view the nature of ministry has its strength in its relationship to the church, but it identifies too closely the church's ministry with that of Christ.

Karl Barth

A similar view of the church as community is expressed by Karl Barth, whose whole theological enterprise, including his ecclesiology, is based upon and structured on the Trinity.[95] His view of the Trinity is more Western than Eastern, stemming primarily from Augustine but, rather than basing it on the one divine substance as so much Western thought does, he follows the Cappadocians and understands God's revelation as that of the one divine Lord who exists as subject in three distinct personal modes of being. God repeats himself three times as the one God in three personal distinctions of his being.[96] He is not in need of the world or another with whom to have fellowship, but as a being in dynamic, loving movement he has the "other" within himself as Son and Spirit with the Father.[97] This view of the inner trinitarian relationships is reflected in the church where its being is a community. Barth prefers to omit the word church and follows Luther in using the word community to bring out more clearly the basic nature of those called out by God and constituted a fellowship of believing people.[98] From a quite different perspective than the Easterners, Barth comes close to them and to Moltmann in his ecclesiology. He sees the community as called out by God the Holy Spirit to faith, built up in love, and sent out into the world in mission, in hope.[99] Barth's views are thus closer to Moltmann's than to those of Larentzakis and Zizioulas since he does not accord baptism and the Lord's Supper sacramental character, nor does he, in his later work, say much about the ordained ministry.[100] The church is primarily the community God calls and uses as a precursor of a hope for all and as God's instrument for his service in the world. It is the whole people of God in its membership who minister and serve. Barth's basic views of the Trinity and ecclesiology have both elements of East and West in them, a possible pointer to future ecumenical consensus.[101] Moltmann is more in line with the East.

A traditional element which is agreed on by all three is perichoresis, the mutual indwelling of Father, Son, and Holy Spirit. It is centered first in this relationship of divine persons and then in the relationship of the believer to Christ by the Holy Spirit as indicated in Saint John's Gospel. There is not only a mutual being for one another in love, a being together as community, but there is a being in Christ and with him by the Spirit in the Father. This is a relationship not only of mutual interpenetration of triune love in the community with God, but of sanctification in the truth. God as triune is both *holy* and *true*. In these conceptions we express and experience the mystery of the triune life of God but can only from afar state it in terms of concepts and language. Here all runs out into mystery.

Roman Catholic Perspectives

T. F. Torrance states that in the Dogmatic Constitution on the Church in Vatican II, entitled *Lumen Gentium,* we find "the first fully authoritative formal declaration of the doctrine of the church ever made by Rome in its long history."[102] This view sees the church as a mystery of revelation— mystery meaning a sacramental reality united with Christ, who is the *Lumen Gentium,* the light of the nations. The church has its basis in the nature, action, will, and election of the triune God, Father, Son, and Holy Spirit. The Father elects the church from all eternity and in Christ, his Son, he founds and effectuates this in time in a life sustained by the sacraments, especially the eucharistic sacrifice. The church is at the same time sanctified, guided, and renewed by the Holy Spirit. Therefore its existence it owes in its entirety to the triune God, that is, in its beginning, continuation, and destination or direction to its goal.[103] The important thing to notice here is the very definite trinitarian, predestinarian view of the church as the people of God, the vineyard of God, the temple of the Holy Spirit, the bride and body of Christ. It is through this body that Roman Catholics receive the divine life and this comes via the sacraments. In the church there is unity and diversity with the apostolic position of Peter and the Apostles holding the chief place but Christ nonetheless the head. The church is also a visible unity with a given structure and conforms to Christ's likeness. This visible unity and structure points also to the fact that it has the other side as well, the invisible side, and corresponds to the divine-human in the one Lord Jesus Christ. The mystical body and hierarchical agencies of the church thus reflect and convey the mystery of the incarnation, which both reveals and conceals the divine reality.[104]

To the question of where this church is to be found today, the answer is given that this church "subsists in the Catholic church, which is governed by the successor of Peter and by the Bishops in union with that successor, although many elements of sanctification and truth can be found outside her visible structure."[105] In this statement there is a considerable amount of very good biblical material, a new and marked feature of Vatican II with its trend toward the Bible. This is in contrast to previous statements which are more juridical, scholastic, and hierarchical, though the latter features are by no means omitted in Vatican II. Here the church is given a trinitarian basis and an attempt is made to put greater emphasis on the dynamic community aspect than on the institutional. Again, the statement which defines where the church is to be found includes in intention all who name the name of Christ but are at present (sadly in Roman Catholic eyes) out of full communion with the Roman Catholic church.[106] This definition of the church has been interpreted in two ways. On the one hand, the church in its fullness exists within the Roman Catholic church, yet aspects of this are to be found in other "ecclesial communities"; on the other hand, more often it is expounded to mean that the Roman Catholic church imperfectly but closely approximates to this ideal fullness and the others in doctrine (not so much in practice) approximate very much less so. Yet, because of their Catholic character, the others have and possess "an inner dynamism towards Catholic unity."[107]

This is to be welcomed as far as it goes, but there are serious objections to the view which defines the Roman Catholic church as the God-given church, yet, while involving itself in ecumenical dialogue and meetings, refuses, because of its ecclesial definition and nature, to join in the fellowship of the World Council of Churches. The claims made by the Roman Catholic church exclude closer fellowship in this sense since Vatican II still emphasizes the divinely given right of its hierarchical structures and the virtual identification of the community aspect with these.[108] In practice, the growth of a more conservative Catholicism under the present pope and the appointment of bishops who follow this line are all indicative of the fact that even the limited vision of Vatican II is not being fully realized in practice. At best *Lumen Gentium* represented a step forward toward a more dynamic, biblical, and trinitarian ecclesiology. But by the nature of Roman Catholicism with irreformable dogma, Vatican II is a basic compromise between its own biblical insights and earlier, more fixed tradition.

Unity and Diversity

Local and Universal

The triune God in his life is both one and three in his being and relationships. This insight is applied in relation to the church in two areas, the local and the universal. The New Testament speaks not only of the church but also of the churches. By this is not meant denominations in our modern sense of the term, but the various *ecclesiae*, the various local communities wherever found. In this sense the churches represent the universal church. Each particular congregation shares in this fullness and totality in both locality and universality. In the diversity of churches or communities the one church appears in each place. One can put it in picture form by saying that the whole universal church looks out in the local church.[109] The Conference of European Churches (C.E.C.) made the point clearly: "The whole church of Christ is constituted not by adding together part church to part church, but is expressed by the communion of local churches in mutual interpenetration (perichoresis). Conciliar community of churches is thus an integral part of the concept of the trinity."[110] By this it means not that each church can and should seek to live by and for itself but, by its very basis and existence, is one with the church universal and must express that relationship analogous to the Trinity, in concrete structured form, however one may interpret this.

The British Council of Churches (B.C.C.) report believes that, because the church has not been considered sufficiently in the light of the Trinity, institutional and legal forms have predominated. It also states that a "related matter of great ecumenical importance is the relation between the local and the universal church. It might be argued that a strong stress on the unity of God may lead to an excessively centralizing view of the church, and it was asked whether the Second Vatican Council, for all the progress it made in developing a more dynamic ecclesiology, gave adequate place to the local as distinct from the universal church."[111]

Ecumenical

Larentzakis writes, "The trinitarian principle of diversity in unity can be used in ecclesiology but can also be helpful for the *oikumene*."[112] The C.E.C. document expresses the same idea when it states that "it is intrinsically important too, however, that the trinity should be accepted as the model for Christian unity. . . . [I]t is not, then, a case of a model dictated from outside with the command to reproduce it but of the mode of being in which our triune God exists and acts concretely in the history of humankind."[113] In other words, he acts to bring us into the fellowship of his own being and life and so into the real relationships of love and unity with one another which the Trinity implies.

Concretely this means a recognition that there is a basic unity within and between the "churches," yet the actual division into denominations contradicts our calling and the very nature of the triune God. Hence there is the need to seek to express in concrete form and action the unity and diversity (communion) of the church analogous to the triune God. The C.E.C. document expresses the well-known New Testament truth, which some seem still to misunderstand, that unity is not uniformity but diversity or "pluriformity." It also realizes that achievement of this unity is still beset with many difficulties:

> Many ecumenical problems such as inter-communion and mutual recognition of ministries have been studied seriously and carefully by the churches for years on end. It grieves us all the more that no official agreement on inter-communion and recognition of ministries has yet come about between all churches. We do, however, regard the insight that all congregations participate in the universal church on the model of the trinity and that the universal church exists and is expressed in the various particular churches and congregations, as a spur to further advance.[114]

Larentzakis sees this as meaning "unity in diversity, or communio and independence . . . without this serving to explain or even justify *all* confessional, substantial, dogmatic differences. The theological, ecumenical dialogue must still be regarded, even today, as significant and necessary."[115]

This implies that despite our confessional differences each congregation and "church" belongs in some measure to the universal church. It also involves no simple acceptance of the status quo but a critique of confessional stances and traditions. This may happen and growth in unity and love may be fostered by using the Trinity with its reconciling power as basis and paradigm.[116] Popescu writes,

> We need to see the organic unity of the church as the body of Christ as inherent in the diversity of local churches just as the persons of the trinity are inherent in the divine nature and the divine nature in the persons of the trinity. . . . Organic unity of the body of Christ is thus no longer a structure representing an outward threat to the churches' local identity, but the power which affirms that local identity from within, an identity open to other churches in the perspective of the reconciling power of the trinity.[117]

This is clearly envisaged as a two-stage process, recognizing a given unity in the Trinity as fellowship but with an openness toward organic unity as the will of God for all his people. In this way local identity would not be ignored or annulled but ultimately included and enriched in one church by the reconciling power of the Trinity. This has actually happened in the united churches of North and South India, to take but two modern examples.

Notes

1. Dieter Manecke, *Mission als Zeugendienst: Karl Barths theologische Begründung der Mission im Gegenüber zu den Entwürfen von Walter Holsten, Walter Freytag und Joh. Christiaan Hoekendijk* (Wuppertal: Theologischer Verlag Rolf Brockhaus, 1972), pp. 183–84. Manecke points out that this was in part influenced by Barth's doctrine of the Trinity.

2. See Chapter 2 for a discussion of this affirmation.

3. Colin Gunton, *The Promise of Trinitarian Theology* (Edinburgh: T. & T. Clark, 1991), p. 7.

4. Lutherischerweltbund—Dokumentation, *Gottes Mission als Gemeinsame Aufgabe: Ein Beitrag des L.W.B. zum Verständnis von Mission* (Stuttgart: Kreuz Verlag, 1989), p. 5 (hereafter cited as *L.W.B.*)

5. Georg F. Vicedom, *Missio Dei: Einführung in eine Theologie der Mission* (Munich: Ch. Kaiser, 1958), p. 12.

6. F. D. Maurice, writing of the Evangelical Movement of the last century, states, "I cannot but perceive that it made the sin of man and not the God of all grace the foundation of Christian Theology" (*Theological Essays, p. XVI*), quoted in A. R. Vidler, *The Theology of F. D. Maurice* (London: S.C.M. Press, 1948), p. 37.

7. Daniel W. Hardy and David F. Ford, *Jubilate: Theology in Praise* (London: Darton Longman and Todd, 1984), p. 149.

8. Ibid., p. 150.

9. Karl Barth, *Church Dogmatics*, IV/3, 1, pp. 165 ff. (hereafter cited as *C.D.*). For Barth, Christ's reconciliation has also the character of revelation demanding expression. As such it is the christological basis of the church's missionary task. (See *C.D.*, IV/3, 1, pp. 18, 38, 154.)

10. *C.D.*, IV/1, pp. 163–66.

11. *L.W.B.*, pp. 5ff.

12. Ibid., p. 7.

13. P. T. Forsyth, *Missions in State and Church: Sermons and Addresses* (London: Hodder and Stoughton, 1908), p. 270.

14. Lesslie Newbigin, *The Open Secret: Sketches for a Missionary Theology* (1978; reprint, Grand Rapids, Mich.: William B. Eerdmans, 1981) p. 110.

15. *C.D.*, IV/1, pp. 22ff.

16. John 1:3, Col. 1:16, 17; Heb. 1:2.

17. Forsyth, pp. 270–71.

18. *L.W.B.*, p. 8.

19. John. 17:11, 21; Gal. 1:1; Rom. 6:4; 1 Cor. 15:20–28.

20. *C.D.*, I/2, pp. 203ff. See also *C.D.*, IV/2, pp. 322ff. for the Spirit in relation to reconciliation.

21. Luke 4:18f., 10:21; John 16:13–15; Rom. 8:23; Eph. 1:4; 1 Cor. 12–14.

22. *L.W.B.*, p. 8

23. Forsyth, p. 271.

24. Ibid.

25. *L.W.B.* p. 8.

26. Vicedom, p. 12.

27. *L.W.B.*, p. 5.

28. Ibid.

29. Ibid., p. 9. *C.D.*, IV/3, 2, p. 766, where Barth is critical of the Reformation definition of the church, which seems to limit it to internal activity to the detriment of its task of mission to the whole world.

30. *L.W.B.*, p. 10.

31. Forsyth, p. 271.

32. *C.D.*, IV/3, 2, pp. 681ff.

33. Ibid., pp. 368ff.

34. Newbigin, p. 68.

35. Waldron Scott, *Karl Barth's Theology of Mission* (Exeter: Paternoster Press, 1978) p. 40.

36. *C.D.*, IV/2, pp. 511ff.

37. Manecke, p. 262.

38. *C.D.*, IV/3, 1, pp. 221ff.

39. Berthold Klappert, *Promissio und Bund: Gesetz und Evangelium bei Luther und Barth* (Göttingen: Vandenhoeck und Ruprecht, 1976), pp. 266ff.

40. *L.W.B.*, p. 10.

41. Hendrikus Berkhof, *The Doctrine of the Holy Spirit* (Atlanta: John Knox Press, 1977), pp. 38–39.

42. *L.W.B.*, p. 9.

43. Theo Sundermeier, "Begegnung mit dem Fremden. Plädoyer für eine Verstehende Missionwissenschaft," *Evangelische Theologie*, vol. 50, no. 5, 1990, pp. 390–400. Sundermeier rejects both paradigms as outdated today and opts for one oriented on the stranger—an understanding of those religiously and socially strange to us. Only such a view, he believes, overcomes the defect of the other models where "the other" becomes an object of the self. In the model Sundermeier proposes God chose the rejected, the unexpected. For mission this will mean being drawn to all such, with the possibility of new thinking and action toward them.

This understanding leads to proclamation, spirituality, and socially liberating action. But are these elements not already involved in other views of mission?

44. See Newbigin, pp. 102ff., 146ff.

45. *C.D.*, IV/3, 2, pp. 874–76. Barth sees theism as assenting to the possibility that human beings can by reason, reach and have knowledge of a Supreme Being. Such an approach he believes to be impossible, since only by God is God known.

46. Donald A. McGavern, *How Churches Grow* (New York: Friendship Press, 1959), and many other writings, has pioneered this approach.

47. Scott, p. 33.

48. Ibid. See also Newbigin, pp. 135ff., for a good summary and critique. A balanced statement and defense of this movement is given by Eddie Gibbs, *I Believe in Church Growth* (London: Hodder and Stoughton, 1990).

49. Scott.

50. Cf. *C.D.*, IV/2, pp. 644ff., for a fine exposition of the New Testament concept of growth. It is intensive but also extensive and both depend on the Holy Spirit's work.

51. William J. Abraham, *The Logic of Evangelism* (London: Hodder and Stoughton, 1989), pp. 20ff.

52. Ibid., pp. 70–80.

53. Ibid., p. 81.

54. David Lochhead, *The Dialogical Imperative: A Christian Reflection on Interfaith Encounter* (London: S.C.M. Press, 1988), p. 89. Pluralists are represented by, among others, John Hick, *God Has Many Names: Britain's New Religious Pluralism* (London: Macmillan, 1990); Alan Race, *Christians and Religious Pluralism: Patterns in the Christian Theology of Religions* (London: S.C.M. Press, 1983); Paul Knitter, *No Other Name? A Critical Survey of Christian Attitudes toward the World Religions* (Maryknoll, N.Y.: Orbis, 1984). For a penetrating critique of these views see Lesslie Newbigin, *The Gospel in a Pluralist Society* (London: S.P.C.K., 1989), pp. 155–70. Reinhold Bernhardt, "Ein neuer Lessing? Paul Knitter's Theologie der Religionen," *Evangelische Theologie*, vol. 49, no 6, 1989, pp. 516–28, also gives a critical analysis. The exclusive view is represented in many Reformation confessional statements and the inclusivist by Karl Rahner and others.

55. Newbigin, *The Gospel in a Pluralist Society*, pp. 155ff.

56. *The Forgotten Trinity. Report of the B.C.C. Study Commission on Trinitarian Doctrine Today* (London: British Council of Churches, Inter-Church House, 1989), vol. 1, p. 40 (hereafter cited as *B.C.C. Report*).

57. *C.D.*, I/2, pp. 280ff.

58. *B.C.C. Report*, vol. 1, p. 40.

59. This is based on Karl Barth's combination of the exclusive revelation of God in Christ with an inclusivist reconciliation.

60. Newbigin, *The Open Secret*, pp. 206–7.

61. Ibid.

62. *C.D.*, III/2, pp. 134ff.

63. *C.D.*, IV/3, 1, pp. 110ff.

64. Newbigin, *The Open Secret*, p. 209.

65. Ibid., p. 210.

66. For a brief summary of some of these see Donald Baillie, *God Was in Christ: An Essay on Incarnation and Atonement* (London: Faber & Faber, 1956), pp. 133–47.

67. *C.D.*, IV/1, p. 561. For a discussion of Barth's view see Claude Welch, *The Trinity in Contemporary Theology* (London: S.C.M. Press, 1953), pp. 200–202.

68. Heinz Schutte, *Im Gespräch mit dem Dreieinen Gott. Elemente einer Trinitärischer Theologie. Festschrift für Wilhelm Breuning*, Michael Bohnke und Hanspeter Heinz, eds., (Düsseldorf: Patmos Verlag, 1985), pp. 361–75.

69. Ibid., p. 361.

70. Ibid., pp. 361–62.

71. Ibid., p. 363.

72. Ibid.

73. Ibid.

74. Ibid., p. 366.

75. Ibid., p. 369.

76. John Calvin, *The Institutes of the Christian Religion* (1559), John T. McNeill, ed. (Philadelphia: Westminster Press, 1961), III/1.

77. Jürgen Moltmann, "The Reconciling Power of the Trinity in the Life of the Church and the World," in *The Reconciling Power of the Trinity. Conference of European Churches*, C.E.C Occasional Paper No.15 (Geneva: C.E.C., 1983), pp. 53–54.

78. Ibid., p. 54.

79. Ibid.

80. Ibid. In John 17:21 Jesus prays that all christians "may be one, Father, just as you are in me and I am in you."

81. Richard J. Bauckham, *Moltmann: Messianic Theology in the Making* (London: Marshall Pickering, 1987), pp. 129–30. Moltmann, *The Church in the Power of the Spirit*, tr. Margaret Kohl (London: S.C.M. Press, 1977), pp. 224, 318–19, 326–28, 334.

82. Moltmann, p. 345.

83. Ibid., pp. 346–47.

84. Joseph Trutsch, "Second Comment on Moltmann's Speech," in *The Reconciling Power of the Trinity*, p. 71. Heindrikus Berkhof points out that it is wrong to set community and institution against one another. The Spirit not only creates fellowship but uses means of grace—Word, Sacraments, and Ministry, all of which have institutional aspects—to call together and enable the community to be, to grow, and to serve. *The Doctrine of the Holy Spirit* (Atlanta: John Knox Press, 1964), pp. 51ff.

85. Ibid., p. 69.

86. Bauckham, p. 135.

87. Grigorios Larentzakis, "Trinitärischer Kirchenverständnis," *Trinität: Aktuelle Perspektiven der Theologie*, Wilhelm Breuning, ed. (Freiburg: Herder, 1984), p. 77.

88. Ibid., p. 84.

89. Ibid., p. 85.

90. John D. Zizioulas, *Being as Communion: Studies in Personhood and the Church* (Crestwood, N.Y.: St Vladimir's Seminary Press, 1985), p. 19.

91. Ibid.

92. Ibid., p. 111.

93. Ibid., p. 112.

94. Ibid., p. 210.

95. *C.D.*, IV/1, pp. 643ff. Colm O'Grady writes, "In Karl Barth's dogmatics the doctrine of the church is the description of the subjective realization in cer-

tain men, by the Holy Spirit, of the reconciliation of the Father, objectively realized in the Son. The trinitarian scheme of his ecclesiology is immediately apparent." *The Church in the Theology of Karl Barth* (London: Geoffrey Chapman, 1968), p. 99.

96. *C.D.*, I/1, p. 350.

97. *C.D.*, II/1, pp. 257ff.; IV/2, pp. 756ff., 777ff.

98. *C.D.*, IV/1, p. 651.

99. *C.D.*, IV/1, pp. 643ff; IV/2, pp. 614ff; IV/3, pp. 681ff.

100. *C.D.*, IV/4 passim; IV/3, 2, pp. 830ff.

101. Thomas F. Torrance, "Towards an Ecumenical Consensus on the Trinity," *Theologische Zeitschrift*, vol. 31, no. 6, 1975, pp. 337ff.

102. T. F. Torrance, "Ecumenism: A Reappraisal of Its Significance, Past, Present and Future," in *Theology in Reconciliation: Essays towards Evangelical and Catholic Unity in East and West* (London: Geoffrey Chapman, 1975), p. 59.

103. Walter M. Abbott, ed., *The Documents of Vatican II* (London: Geoffrey Chapman, 1967), pp. 14ff.

104. Ibid., pp. 20ff.

105. Ibid., p. 23.

106. Ibid., p. 33f.

107. Ibid., p. 23.

108. Torrance, "Ecumenism," p. 65, regards the hierarchical agencies (wrongly to my mind) as simply scaffolding in contrast to the real church as community, as the people of God. The definition of the church given in Abbott, p. 33, clearly contradicts this. See Chapter 3 for the place and necessity for hierarchical structures.

109. P. T. Forsyth, *The Church and the Sacraments*, 1st ed. (1917; reprint, London: Independent Press, 1947), p. 65.

110. Peter Wilhelm Bøckman, "Trinity, Model of Unity—Relationship between Unity and Communion the Universal and the Local," in *The Reconciling Power of the Trinity*, p. 89. Cf. Moltmann, who speaks of unity and community of the church and churches in similar terms (p. 342f.).

111. *B.C.C. Report*, vol. 1, p. 28. It also states that, since all churches tend to justify their own history and life, "there is a crying need for ecumenical conversation" (ibid).

112. Larentzakis, p. 90.

113. Bøckman, "Trinity, Model of Unity," *The Reconciling Power of the Trinity*, p. 89.

114. Ibid., p. 90.

115. G. Larentzakis, "First Comment on Prof. Moltmann's Speech," in *The Reconciling Power of the Trinity*, p. 65.

116. Dumitru Popescu, "Introduction to the Consultation," in *The Reconciling Power of the Trinity*, pp. 11, 12.

117. Ibid., p. 12

5

The Trinity and Worship

Faith and Worship

"It is in our *worship* that most of us become aware of the *doctrine* of the trinity. We all sing hymns that address each of the three persons in the one Godhead and in the more liturgical traditions, we end our recital of the Psalms and Canticles with a threefold ascription of glory to the Father, Son and Holy Spirit."[1] In this there is implied a coordinated relationship between a trinitarian doctrine of God and what we do when we worship him. The B.C.C. report states that the distinctive name for God is Father. Yet this has to be qualified in various ways, by stating, as the report does, that to say Father we must also speak of the Son and of the Holy Spirit.[2] The Fatherhood of God has true meaning only in relation to Son and Spirit. For the New Testament God is conceived not simply as the Father in general to whom one adds Son and Spirit later. He is from eternity the Father of the Son by the Spirit. While we must make this affirmation of faith in relation to the Trinity, in practice a great variety of approaches is possible.

Thus worship can be offered to God the Father by the Spirit through the Son or directly to the Father, the Son, or the Spirit. The B.C.C. report sums this up as follows: "There are various ways in which the trinitarian character of worship is understood: as being offered to the Father through the Son and in the Spirit; or to the Father, to the Son and to the Spirit; or to the one triune God. But all alike witness to the reality of relationship, of communion."[3] The report tends to favor the first, as we have already noted. Genuine confession of the triune God—whatever form it takes—is not to be divorced from what is seen as at the same time an act of worship, a worship which is most properly celebrated in the community of faith. In other words, profession of faith and worship of the triune God go together. While it is in a sense true, as the B.C.C. report indicates, that we call God Father "not so much when we are speaking *about* him as when we are speaking *to him*,"[4] any separation between the two would, properly understood, be a spurious distinction. Our faith in and our knowledge of God and our worship of him belong together in the community of his people.

In our worship we need continually to be corrected by the riches and variety of the New Testament witness. Modern trinitarian statements rightly point out that although each person of the Trinity can be addressed in worship, to do so in any exclusive sense courts danger.[5] Overemphasis of one person to the exclusion of the others is in fact a virtual denial of the true God. The Father without the Son and Spirit may be treated as a first cause but not as creator; the Son without the Father and Spirit leads to a Jesuology of one who does not lead us in salvation to the Father or give the Spirit. And the Spirit without the Father and the Son may emphasize our subjective experience or the variety of gifts but is loosed from his true context in the divine life. Such separation of faith and worship in the church can lead to idolatry. "The idol could be a transcendent God who is not really free to take a personal part in history; or a divine-human being who himself receives all worship; or a God who is within human beings or in some other way immanent in the world. Those three basic ways of absolutising one dimension of the Christian God roughly correspond to the Father, Son and Holy Spirit."[6] The writers continue, however, and say that "taken as a unity, the trinity continually dispels illusions and fantasies about God."[7]

Distinctive Aspects of Worship

Prayer

Most modern perspectives on the Trinity and worship see prayer as a central aspect of this relationship. "The passages in the New Testament that distinguish most clearly between the Father, the Son and the Holy Spirit are those that deal with prayer."[8] Christ as our reconciler and peacegiver is the one through whom "we have access by one Spirit to the Father" (Eph. 2:18). "It was when he was thinking about prayer that Paul also thought about how in their different ways the Son and the Spirit enable us to approach the Father."[9] While all three persons in the Trinity are necessary properly to speak of God as one it is primarily to the Father that the Son and the Spirit lead us in prayer. This is summed up by Paul when he says, "God sent the Spirit of his Son into our hearts crying 'Abba, Father.'" (Gal. 4:6). Central to this is the Son who reveals the Father, and whom, when we see, we see the Father. This leads us back to our Lord's Prayer and his relation to God where the distinctive name he gives him is "Father." Prayer is "through Jesus Christ our Lord," that is, through all he was and said and did in his life, death, and resurrection. He is the way, as well as the truth and the life.

If prayer is to the Father and through the Son, it is enabled by the Spirit. "Only the Spirit enables us to know God as Father (Gal. 4:6) or to confess Jesus as Lord (1 Cor. 12:3) or to pray to the Father in a way that is acceptable to him (Rom. 8:26–27)."[10]

The role of Son and Spirit in this is profoundly expressed in Romans 8. Christ who died for us is now our great High Priest and Intercessor by his presence with the Father in the power of his finished work on the cross (v. 34). Yet we can know this and be able to enter into its meaning only by the Holy Spirit. He is the One who lays hold upon our weaknesses by his strength and intercedes for us with sighs too deep for words (v. 26). Through Christ we become children of God and this relationship is made possible, continued, and brought to its completion by "his Spirit which dwells in you" (v. 11). He is the gift and power of the present and the hope of immortality. It is the Spirit (who is divine) who intercedes for us. God the Father who knows us and our weaknesses knows his own Holy Spirit and God, speaking to us through God, as it were, prays for us and with us as the Spirit, as God wants and as prayer ought to be. At the same time, paradoxically, it is not simply the Spirit's prayer but ours as well. So close is the work of Son and Spirit in bringing us to the Father that each is spoken of as Advocate and Intercessor. The trinitarian aspect of prayer has profound significance for worship. It is not seen primarily as our work but God's own gift through Christ and the Holy Spirit. Thus "prayer and worship are not primarily hard tasks that God sets us; they are gifts that through his Son and in his Spirit he shares with us."[11]

The Word

Much modern trinitarian theology of worship focuses on the Trinity in relation to prayer and the sacraments but less, if at all, on the Word and preaching. However, the earliest Christian community had a way of faith, life, and worship founded on the apostolic preaching and focused on Jesus and the resurrection. Their preaching was explicitly trinitarian. The apostolic testimony is that the Jesus who was crucified "God raised up . . . being therefore exalted at the right hand of God, and having received from the Father the promise of the Holy Spirit, he has poured out this which you see and hear" (Acts 2:33). It was this implicit trinitarian revelation which produced the church, united the Christian community as one, inspired its worship, and gave it a message to proclaim. The content of the apostolic preaching, well summed up by C. H. Dodd,[12] is basically a kerygmatic statement of the faith of the New Testament community as a whole. It was later expanded in the form of letters and gospels and has this essentially trinitarian revelation at its heart.

The original Word was the Word Incarnate, who was with the Father and who was manifested to us in Jesus Christ himself and written testimony to him by the Holy Spirit is given us in Holy Scripture. It is true that Christ is primarily the Word of God, yet the Scriptures, as analogous to him as divine-human, have throughout Christian history been rightly called the Word of God. This testimony is not of human origin but comes from God the Father through the work of the Son and the inspiration of the Holy Spirit. The unity of Word and Spirit—the latter as the *testimonium internum Spiritus sancti*—is central to our knowledge of the triune God. To worship God is to listen to and embrace his Word and this can be properly received and experienced only by the Holy Spirit. This is what John means when he writes "they that worship him, must worship him in Spirit and in Truth" (John 4:24). Worship must be by the Holy Spirit, who through the written and preached Word leads us to the living Word. Through the ministry of the Word the Spirit speaks to the church and leads us to the Father. "Apart from the operation of the Holy Spirit Christian worship would be merely a human act. . . . [I]t would be human effort to please God and merit his favour. Because of the Holy Spirit, Christian worship is actually a work of God in and through the believing community gathered unto him."[13] An essential aspect of this is the ministry of the Word by the same Holy Spirit.

The character of Christian worship is thus based on Jesus Christ, who is the Truth of God. As such it must correspond to Christ and, while it is essentially trinitarian, it is centered in him:

> The trinity constitutes a basic morphology which cannot be violated if liturgical theology is to be Christian. As we explore the triune character of Christian revelation as basic for thought, however, we still must understand that here, as elsewhere, the integrating reality is Jesus Christ . . . so the decisive center of liturgical theology lies not in the trinity in general but in Jesus Christ in particular.[14]

In this way Christ as word and truth of God by the Holy Spirit is the one through whom and by whom we worship God the Father.

J. J. O'Donnell points out how, from a Roman Catholic perspective, both Balthasar and Rahner have a similar view, as does Vatican II. Like many others he sees a close relationship not only between the Word and Spirit but between the Word and Prayer. He writes, "Christian prayer is both made possible by and is bound to the Word."[15] However, he regards prayer as less our enabling by the Spirit than our receptivity as exemplified supremely in Mary's fiat. Here the Reformation and Roman Catholic ways part. O'Donnell also states that it is by the Holy Spirit that "we see how the life of prayer exists within a trinitarian framework. Its origin is the Father's love and election of us. This love comes to visible expression in God's ikon, his word of life in Jesus Christ."[16] O'Donnell also recognizes that "our response to the Word would not be possible without the action of the Spirit within us."[17] It is, as we have seen, both God's act in us and our response. The Spirit opens up the Word to us and us to the Word and in this way leads us to the Father. "The Word becomes alive within us by the Spirit."[18]

The Sacraments

New Testament trinitarian formulas are based upon the fact of God's revelation, namely, that in Jesus Christ God is made known to us as Father and through him as our Father. After the resurrection believers were brought into this relationship and communion of Father and Son by the Holy Spirit. These affirmations are grounded in the revelatory event itself and are already implicit in the synoptic tradition of the baptism of Jesus foreshadowing his death.[19] Indeed his death is also referred to as a baptism, and in the New Testament the church began to baptize in the name of Jesus for the forgiveness of sins on the basis of his work on the cross.

However, the most explicit trinitarian formula in the New Testament is that of the baptismal command "go and make disciples of all nations baptising them in the name of the Father, and of the Son, and of the Holy Spirit" (Matt. 29:19). Since the early baptismal formula was "in the name of Jesus" this one is unlikely to represent the *ipsissima verba* of Jesus. The words are, however, "a summary of the early Church's development and practice which had been guided by the Spirit of Jesus Christ and to that extent were authorised by Jesus himself."[20] In this way baptism "is not a novelty but simply gives concise expression to the basic trinitarian structure of the Synoptic tradition and even of the entire New Testament."[21] Thus it is no theoretic or speculative formula with which we are dealing but one based on the central affirmation of the faith related to salvation in Christ by the Holy Spirit. It is, therefore, rightly and centrally a form of worship. Nor can baptism in the triune name be seen as different from the early practice in Acts of that in the name of Jesus. The name signifies the reality of the one God who is known to us as Father, Son, and Holy Spirit. The trinitarian formula is thus a legitimate expansion of the earlier one in the name of Jesus since he is divine, one with the Father and the Holy Spirit.

The question may be asked at this point: In the baptismal formula, has one not the possibility of starting with the unity of God as in the West? Here at any rate unity and threefoldness are not separated or given any priority the one over the other. Baptism is thus associated with preaching, forgiveness, repentance, and faith. It is from the very earliest days linked with people becoming Christian and entering into membership of the Christian community. "Baptism is universally administered in the Church in the threefold name of Father, Son and Holy Spirit, and by it we are initiated into the community of God's people. The theme of baptism is of great importance in this context, because it opens out other aspects also of the theology of the trinity."[22] By this is probably meant that, on the one hand, it sets the seal on the nature and life of Jesus, on the person and work of the Spirit and their relationship to the Father, and on the other hand it points forward to the way we should seek to understand the relationship of unity and threefoldness in God.

In the same way the Lord's Supper has a trinitarian structure built into it as an act of worship. In it "there is prayer to God the Father to send the

Holy Spirit that Christ may be present with his people in worship, and that we might share with him his communion with the Father. The Holy Spirit lifts God's people into the presence of the Father as he brings the risen Christ into their midst, and through him enables them to offer to God both themselves and the life of the whole creation in thanksgiving and praise."[23] This comprehensive definition does not mention a primary aspect which recalls and remembers the work of Christ on the cross for our salvation. It does, however, center on prayer that Christ may be known not simply as past event but as present. He comes from the Father and enables us to share fellowship with him and so participate in his own communion with the Father. This takes place by the power of the Holy Spirit. Another way of putting it is to say that the Holy Spirit exalts the community in Christ to God the Father. This reflects the twin thrust of much theological reflection in relation to our faith—from God to humanity and from humanity to God, but set within a trinitarian movement from above to below and vice versa.

Since Christ is present as the One who by the Spirit offered himself once for all upon the cross, the sacrament is also our sacrifice of praise, a self-offering to God in gratitude for his salvation. But it is not a self-enclosed action; it is open, as the triune God is, to the world. What is meant by the phrase "to offer to God . . . the life of the whole creation in thanksgiving" is not made clear. One may interpret it to signify that the eucharist reminds us of God's goodness and mercy in creation as well as redemption. Moreover, like the church, it is a provisional representation of what God wills for the whole of creation: life, liberty, and wholeness.

The definition also fails to include the eschatological aspect by which the Spirit points us forward to the consummation at the last in the coming again of the present Lord and the doxological character of our future hope by which we continually join in giving glory to God, Father, Son, and Holy Spirit as we share in his own glorification. These aspects of worship will be taken up in the next section though applied more generally.

Theology and Worship

The B.C.C. report rightly begins its work in and with worship which encloses all "else we say within a statement of what we believe to be the most fundamental reality; 'where we stand' is before the triune God in worship and praise."[24] What has been said here leads naturally to one important conclusion. If one understands the New Testament and the view it gives of how we meet with and know God and worship him as triune, then worship is not primarily our act but, like our salvation, is God's gift before or as it is our task. While it is trinitarian, the focal point is christological and has a doctrine of incarnation and atonement at its heart.[25] Christ is both the priest who offers himself on the cross and the high priest who, at God's right hand, continually intercedes for us. He is the One who as the God-man comes as God to us, reveals himself, but is also representative man, being and doing in our place what we cannot be and do for ourselves. He makes the perfect, sinless offering of holiness to the Father in an act of suffering service that can be called worship. Jesus Christ is thus the one true worshiper, the one for the many who, through his representative humanity, includes all humanity in himself. By the Holy Spirit we are drawn into the worship and response Christ offers to the Father. Ours is a response to a response. The Spirit enables this and so gives what he demands, the worship of our hearts and lives.[26]

In our prayers and worship the two things are held together: first, we worship Christ as God, but second, we meet him as man "praying for us and with us to the Father." Thus "by sharing Jesus' life of communion with the Father in the Spirit we are given to participate in the eternal Son's communion with the Father."[27] The essence of this is of grace and gracious. God does not accept us because of anything we do or are—because of our worthy worship—but because of what Jesus Christ in his vicarious humanity has done for us and all humanity. By his Spirit we are united with Christ, adopted as children in the Son and so brought to the Father. The nature and structure of all true worship is thus trinitarian, incarnational, and pneumatological. It also involves an objective view of the atonement.

In this interpretation we are drawn up to God, Father, Son, and Holy Spirit to share in the fellowship of the divine life of holy love. Torrance points out that worship is thus not primarily what we *do*—sing, pray, listen to the Word, offer and give ourselves. This he regards as basically Pelagian, possibly even unitarian, against both New Testament teaching and that of the Reformers. Medieval Christendom obscured the true nature of worship and tended "to substitute the priesthood, the sacrifice, the merits, the intercession of the Church—the vicarious humanity of the *ecclesia* (Mary and the saints)—for the vicarious humanity of Christ, in a way which obscured the Gospel of grace, the good news of what God has done for us in Christ."[28] Much modern Catholic writing seeks a more biblical basis for faith and worship and is basically trinitarian.

There is in this understanding of theology and worship in relation to the Trinity two movements, as we have noted, that of God to humanity—from the Father through the Son by the Spirit to our humanity—and that of humanity to God—by the Spirit through the Son to the Father in a reverse direction. The *ordo cognoscendi*, of experience, is not that of the *ordo essendi*, of the Trinity itself, but moves back, as it were, to God from the point where through Christ and by the Spirit he touches and changes life and accepts us as his sons and daughters. The movement of the Son is from the Father by the Spirit and back again, drawing our humanity up into relationship with the Father.

The general thesis of Torrance is to be warmly welcomed. Where he could have given more guidance is in the nature of our response. It can be understood like the paradox of faith at its center as both God's gift by the Spirit and our act inspired and enabled by it. In this way the danger of objectivism is avoided and the subjective element of revelation—the Holy Spirit—is specifically drawn into this whole movement. In consequence, our willing and free response to Christ's response on our behalf is given adequate attention.

T. F. Torrance states the two sides well when he writes that "our worship and prayer, in as much as we freely and fully participate in the Sonship of Christ and in the whole course of his filial obedience to the Father . . . are derived from and rooted in a source beyond themselves, in the economic condescension and ascension of the Son of God."[29] Our worship is thus truly ours but only as it participates in the Spirit's uniting movement through the Son to the Father. Torrance also makes the important comment that, given this basis, content and action of worship, which is permanent, actual forms of worship, are "open to change in variant human situations and societies, cultures, languages and ages even with respect of differing aesthetic tastes and popular appeal."[30] The fact that this is based on the invariant form in Christ by the Spirit to the Father will free us from imprisonment in forms of the past or slavery to current and possibly passing trends.

The worship we offer, therefore, is not only something that is within the area of the church but is a form of testimony before the world. It is part of our witness to the world and has this trinitarian dynamic both drawing us into the fellowship of the life of God and at the same time equipping us to be witnesses to Christ. That it is a gift which includes the task is well stated by the B.C.C. report:

> The Liturgy of the Church as well as the inmost prayer of the heart are the gifts of the Spirit to us. The triune God lives in an eternal self-giving of love between the three divine persons. By that self-giving love the world is made and is redeemed. Through the work of the Spirit in our worship we are caught up into that creative and recreative self-giving. In the Spirit and through the Son, the Father gives himself to us: by the same Spirit and through the same Son we give ourselves on behalf of the world to the Father, so that what the trinity made in love may be made new, and that we may have part in that renewal.[31]

In other words, the triune God who is in action for our salvation is concerned not simply with human beings but with the renewal of the whole created order and with us as his instruments in that service.

The Trinity and Doxology

Doxology means to praise God for his excellent glory.[32] Christians are those who live to the glory of God and give him glory. This is expressed in various formulas as a climactic expression of all acts of public worship.[33] But before it is our doing, and as such, it is God's own act as triune—one could say an act of self-glorification—an inner trinitarian event. Or, to put it in other words, as Father, Son, and Holy Spirit in the unity of being and interrelationship of the persons the triune God lives as an act of worship. Kasper has pointed out how both aspects—our giving glory and the origin of it in the glorification of God—are both based on the great high-priestly prayer of Jesus in John 17:1: "Father, the hour has come, glorify the Son that the Son may glorify Thee."[34] In one sense this is completed on the cross in the economy of salvation. But what the Son does there reflects his eternal relation to the Father. "When the Father glorifies the Son by exalting him, the Father himself is in turn glorified by the Son; in the glorification of the Son the Father's own glorification is made manifest. The Son's glory is that which he has from eternity with the Father."[35] Father and Son—and one must assume also the Holy Spirit—give each other the glory and live as such in fellowship. The revelation of the eternal being of God is "a revelation of the Godness of God. It is said that from eternity God possesses the glory of his Godness because the Father glorifies the Son and the Son in turn glorifies the Father."[36] Those who are disciples "are incorporated into this eternal doxology"[37] and the Son is glorified in them. But this cannot take place except through the action of the Holy Spirit, who guides us into the truth of Son and Father. "He too acknowledges the glory of the Son and the Father" (John 16:13–15). "The Spirit is, and effects the concrete presence of the eternal doxology of Father and Son in the church and in the world."[38]

Kasper distinguishes correctly between *trinitarian confession* and *trinitarian doctrine*. The former has doctrinal content but is essentially doxology; the latter is simply the grammar of the doxology.[39] Doxology is, therefore, closely linked to salvation since it praises God for the majesty of his being and acts and is an expression of our communion with him. In full agreement with Kasper, it has been pointed out that the basis of our knowledge of the Trinity is salvation and doxology. "Praise is properly the new song because in the trinity doxology and salvation are joined."[40] The liturgy is seen as the context and point of departure for theological reflection. It gives us primary theology since we must worship in the presence of God (*coram Deo*) and are always in a relationship to him and to one another. In other words, further reflection on the nature of God as triune should never lose its basis in worship and doxology nor, as Scholasticism did, give it too rationalistic an emphasis, leading to "rational discourse in 'a far country,' at a troubling remove from its experimental basis"[41] in worship and praise of God's saving act.

Similarly, Moltmann argues for a distinction between economic and immanent Trinity based on doxology and related to salvation.[42] We praise God for his mighty acts in the economy. In this way, "the triune God is not made man's object"[43] in the form of his possession; rather we know in order to participate in the divine life, and this Moltmann calls doxological knowledge. In doxology we thank the giver not merely for his good gifts but for his goodness. We glorify and glory in God not merely for his salvation but for himself as the One who saves and is to be worshiped in and for himself. Salvation points from the economic doxology to the immanent Trinity.

This is a distinction that is valid as stated. Moltmann, however, qualifies and thus changes this in two ways. First, he sees the economic as retroactive in a mutuality between God and man which alters both sides. Moreover, the immanent trinity is both open from behind and to the future and is not fulfilled until the end.[44] These views seriously qualify and impair Moltmann's more acceptable statements on the relationship between salvation and doxology.

A very fine treatment of doxology from a biblical and trinitarian standpoint is A. M. Ramsey's chapter on "The Praise of His Glory."[45] God's glory has its human counterpart in our praise and worship.

Creation and redemption intertwine and redeemed humanity gives creation its voice so that both praise the Lord together. However, "the perfect act of worship is seen only in the Son of Man. By him alone there is made the perfect acknowledgement upon earth of the glory of God and the perfect response to it. . . . In him too man's contrition for his own sin and the sin of the race finds its perfect expression; for Christ made before God that perfect acknowledgement of men's sin which man cannot make for himself."[46] The whole life, death, and resurrection of the Son of God confesses the Father "and in this glorifying (which was from all eternity) the human nature, assumed in the incarnation, now shares."[47] The glorying of the Son in John and the high priesthood of Christ in Hebrews have essentially the same meaning—an offering of praise and worship by the Spirit to the Father in which the church joins as it is in union with Christ. "In the ascended Christ there exists our human nature rendering to the Father the glory which man was created in order to render."[48] This makes possible our godward offering and giving glory worthy of the Redeemer and Creator.

In turn, this results in the twin thrusts of unity and mission. The work of the triune God is through the church, in and to the world. "The common life of the Christian fellowship is not only a witness to the glory, but is itself the glory of the Father and the Son shown forth to the world."[49] This can again be expressed as manifesting Christ's own glory to the world. This mission is no mere corollary of the church's worship but is "a very part of that life."[50] In this combination of worship, unity, and mission we see the church giving God the glory which is due to him through the Son and by the Holy Spirit.

In his much acclaimed book Geoffrey Wainwright sets before us a comprehensive vision of the interrelationship between worship, doctrine, and life.[51] Worship as the central, coordinating act of the Christian community in its varied forms has both an implicit and explicit trinitarian content and context since it is giving glory and praise to God the Creator and Father, to Jesus Christ the Son, and to the Holy Spirit. Likewise, doctrine as expressed in creeds, confessions, and more formal extensive theological statements has a trinitarian structure—or should have—despite much writing to the contrary. These, in turn, influence the nature of the church, its preaching, life, and mission to the world as well as how the various churches interrelate positively though sometimes critically and negatively to one another.

Wainwright's title indicates that the various aspects of Christian doctrine are a giving glory to God, a form of doxology. He traces this to its basis in God's action for us as Creator (Father), Son, and Holy Spirit. Through the Spirit and in the Son, we worship the Father. Each aspect of worship, preaching, praying, sacraments all involve the glorification of God on the basis of what he has already done for us. It is also the heart of the missionary task of the church. [52] It is the final joy of the saints, who rest from their labors, and the goal and purpose of all creation.[53] "Our being changed from glory into glory is itself for the greater glory of God."[54] In contrast to Ramsey, Wainwright indicates that this praise is an enrichment of God, who is perfect love. This is an issue that is debatable. I favor the view that although giving glory to God is the essence of the Christian faith in its totality, God is eternally rich and does not through our glorifying him gain a new dimension or richness that was not there before.

Notes

1. *The Forgotten Trinity. The Report of the B.C.C. Study Commission on Trinitarian Doctrine Today* (London: British Council of Churches, Inter-Church House, 1989), vol. 2, p. 5 (hereafter cited as *B.C.C. Report*).

2. Ibid., pp. 5–6.

3. Ibid., vol. 1, p. 3.

4. Ibid., vol. 2, p. 5.

5. Ibid., pp. 21–23.

6. Daniel W. Hardy and David F. Ford, *Jubilate: Theology in Praise* (London: Darton Longman and Todd, 1984), p. 55. Thos. A. Smail, *The Forgotten Father* (London: Hodder and Stoughton, 1980), p. 185, writes in similar vein.

7. Hardy and Ford, p. 55.

8. *B.C.C. Report*, vol. 2, p. 5.

9. Ibid.

10. Ibid., p. 6. Smail, p. 185.

11. *B.C.C. Report*, vol. 2, p. 7.

12. C. H. Dodd, *The Apostolic Preaching and Its Developments* (London: Hodder and Stoughton, 1936), p. 28.

13. Robert G. Rayburn, *O Come, Let us Worship: Corporate Worship in the Evangelical Church* (Grand Rapids, Mich.: Baker Book House, 1980), p. 109.

14. Paul W. Hoon, *The Integrity of Worship* (Nashville: Abingdon Press, 1971), p. 115, quoted in Rayburn, p. 112.

15. John J. O'Donnell, *The Mystery of the Triune God*, Heythrop Monographs 6 (London: Sheed and Ward, 1988), p. 148.

16. Ibid., pp. 149–50.

17. Ibid., p. 149.

18. Ibid., p. 150.

19. Walter Kasper, *The God of Jesus Christ*, tr. Matthew J. O'Connell (New York: Crossroad, 1989), pp. 244–45.

20. Ibid., p. 245.

21. Ibid.

22. *B.C.C. Report*, vol. 1, p. 3.

23. Ibid.

24. Ibid., p. 4.

25. James B. Torrance, "The Vicarious Humanity of Christ," in *The Incarnation: Ecumenical Studies in the Nicene–Constantinopolitan Creed, A.D. 381*, Thomas F. Torrance, ed (Edinburgh: Handsel Press, 1981), p. 128.

26. Ibid., p. 144.

27. Ibid., p. 130.

28. Ibid., p. 129.

29. T. F. Torrance, "The Mind of Christ in Worship: The Problem of Apollinarianism in the Liturgy," in *Theology in Reconciliation* (London: Geoffrey Chapman, 1975), p. 212.

30. Ibid., p. 214.

31. *B.C.C. Report*, vol. 2, p. 7.

32. The Westminster Assembly of Divines, which met in London in 1643–47, states as first answer in *The Shorter Catechism* that "Man's chief end is to glorify God and enjoy him for ever."

33. Kasper, p. 261.

34. Ibid., p. 303.

35. Ibid.

36. Ibid.

37. Ibid.

38. Ibid.

39. Ibid.

40. C. M. LaCugna and K. McDonnell, "Returning from 'The Far Country': Theses for a Contemporary Trinitarian Theology," *Scottish Journal of Theology*, vol. 41, no. 2, 1988, p. 196.

41. Ibid., p. 201.

42. Moltmann, *The Trinity and the Kingdom of God*, tr. Margaret Kohl (London: S.C.M. Press, 1986), pp. 152–53.

43. Ibid., p. 152.

44. Moltmann, *The Church in the Power of the Spirit*, tr. Margaret Kohl (London: S.C.M. Press, 1977), pp. 50ff.

45. A. M. Ramsey, *The Glory of God and the Transfiguration of Christ* (London: Longmans, Green, 1949), pp. 91ff. The phrase is taken from Eph. 1:12.

46. Ibid., p. 93. This is very much in line with the thought of John McLeod Campbell in *The Nature of the Atonement*, 6th ed. (London: Macmillan, 1895), and is closely followed by J. B. and T. F. Torrance (see note 25).

47. Ramsey, p. 94.

48. Ibid.

49. Ibid., p. 99.

50. Ibid.

51. Geoffrey Wainwright, *Doxology: The Praise of God in Worship, Doctrine and Life: A Systematic Theology* (New York: Oxford University Press, 1980).

52. Ibid., p. 355.

53. Ibid., p. 461.

54. Ibid., p. 462.

6

The Trinity, Society, and Politics

THE TRINITY AND SOCIETY

Model for Society

Jürgen Moltmann

"The trinity is our social programme." "This statement is found in the 19th Century in the Orthodox theologian Nicolai Fedorov and also in the Anglican theologian F. D. Maurice and the Danish Lutheran Nicolai Gruntvig." So writes Jürgen Moltmann in an address given at the Conference of European Churches in Goslar, Germany, in 1982.[1] Moltmann's concern to relate the Trinity to society stems from his particular view of God as a union of three divine persons or distinct, but related subjects. The Trinity forms the social paradigm since it is a mutually loving, interacting, sustaining society. It is, as he puts it, "the exemplar of true human community, first in the church and also in society."[2] Moltmann believes that the concept of person, stemming largely from the Christian doctrine of God, has had a permanent effect upon Western political thought. It has had much less of an impact on the social aspects of life. This stems from the fact that God was conceived too much in a monotheistic way rather than as a God of trinitarian unity and community. Moltmann therefore sees the social view of the Trinity as being both a proper paradigm for society and a critique of a false idea of God.

He writes,

> The triune God is reflected only in a united and uniting community of Christians without domination and subjection and a united and uniting humanity

without class rule and without dictatorial oppression. That is the world in which people are defined by their social relationships and not by their power or their property. That is the world in which human beings have all things in common and share everything with one another except their personal qualities.[3]

On the one hand, this points away from individualism and egoism where self-interest rules. At the same time, it does not consist in a collectivism, where human personhood and freedom are submerged. Moltmann opts for that kind of society and social order which seeks to hold both together, the one and the many, the personal and the social. Clearly, he is thinking both of the capitalism of the West and the collectivism of the East, although things have changed rapidly in the former Soviet Union in particular and in Eastern Europe since he wrote these words. He does not choose any particular social order but sets before us a vision of what we are called to be as we seek to reflect in life and society the very nature of the triune God. This will, however, involve the twin aspects of true society and the value of each person within it.

Moltmann writes, "Social personalism and personalist socialism could, with the help of the social trinitarian doctrine, be brought theologically to converge."[4] The triune God breaks through our divisions and isolation. "In Jesus he comes beside us as a brother, we approach him as Father, we live from our Mother, the Spirit. The whole human being in complete community with other human beings is to live before, with and from God in his wholeness. That is the goal of human reconciliation with God."[5]

Leonardo Boff, whose views closely mirror Moltmann's, states that "when set against the ideal of trinitarian communion, modern society in its two principal current embodiments—socialism and capitalism—shows considerable aberrations."[6] Liberal capitalist society leads to individualism, to great divisions between rich and poor, to misery in the Third World. "Societies with a socialist regime are founded on a right principle, that of communion with all and the involvement of all in the means of production."[7] These valid insights are, however, debased by being enforced collectivistically, through the party and its dictatorship.

As a general evaluation and critique, there are large elements of truth in both Moltmann's and Boff's views since capitalism tends to lack community and has flourished on exploitation and often greed even though it depends also on freedom and individual initiative. On the other hand, the collapse of socialism in Eastern Europe and the Soviet Union shows that in practice, however meaningful and correct aspects of its social theory may have been, it is at least as damaging as capitalism if not more so and endangers true freedom and community. In fact, there is no ideal form of society since all forms are corrupted by sin. Moltmann is wise, therefore, not to choose a particular view as the only correct one. Nonetheless, the nearest to the trinitarian model must always be the society that furthers social solidarity, freedom, and community.

While these presentations of the social implications of the trinitarian doctrine have much to commend them, there are certain weaknesses which stem from their view of the Trinity as a simple fellowship of persons. There is the danger of tritheism, and also the fact that a social view has community but requires also, as we saw in the previous chapter, order and some kind of authority. These do not seem to be very clearly envisaged by either Moltmann or Boff, in what is in itself an attractive vision. Nonetheless, the thrust of their position is in general to be followed but should also include the positive aspects of the views they reject.

Orthodox Perspectives

From the Orthodox perspective a similar though slightly different view is set out by Gregorios Larentzakis in the section of an article entitled "The Social Dimension of the Trinitarian Mystery." This, he says, can be properly understood only if we know the meaning of "person" and "community" as seen in the trinitarian fellowship of persons. He writes, "The person, distinguished from the *individual*, will be properly understood only in *fellowship* with others."[8] Person in other words is a relational, social concept and points in the direction of community or fellowship. The life of the Trinity is therefore a society of persons and is seen as the original or archetype for the social teaching of the church. Again, the form for society is to be understood as corresponding to the fellowship of persons within the Trinity. Larentzakis quotes G. Manzaridis:

> The social idea of Orthodoxy is largely summarised in the Orthodox doctrine of the Trinity. The triune God represents a fellowship of love. The characteristic nature of this love is a lack of need. Each person of the trinity is perfect God. Therefore, the fellowship of love of the persons is not to be understood as pressure to receive what one needs but is the expression of perfection and of lack of need.[9]

Here Eastern and Western views of the Trinity show a considerable appearance of identity, for does not the West speak strongly of the deity of each person, of the oneness of God, of the unity consisting in each person sharing a common deity? The hidden difference is that the East gives greater priority to the Father, sees the reality of the Godhead centered in him, personal distinction deriving from him and mediated to the Son and the Holy Spirit. There is a danger here of subordinationism of Son and Spirit to the Father, or, as John Zizioulas admits, of a hierarchy of persons. This does not fit in well with the other claims of Orthodoxy.

The Orthodox view also claims that God seen as a community of persons contradicts the idea of God as abstract being. Larentzakis believes that the Orthodox conception contains its own ontology of love, since the three persons exist in love and this love is the very being of God. It is clearly implied that the West has not a personal but a substantial metaphysic and so must, in some measure, repeat the errors of the philosophical abstract view of God. Moreover, it is hard to see how a proper social view of humanity can be set out if there is such a fault at its source.

Karl Barth

That the social aspect of God can be emphasized following a largely Western tradition, which Moltmann so strongly criticizes, is clear. Karl Barth, for example, uses the term "modes of being" for persons but thereby means that each is distinctly personal together with the others, these being the ways in which the triune God expresses and reveals himself. From a quite different perspective—that of analogy—Barth states that since God has life, love, and fellowship within himself, what he does *ad extra* in creation, reconciliation, and redemption will correspond to who he is in himself. In Jesus Christ, he creates a community of faith corresponding to his nature; in turn, the civil community should reflect this in its life. Being in personal relationship or, if you will, community is true of God in himself and thus of his works in the world.

In the trinitarian conception of God, therefore, the personal God has this unmistakably social nature or being in fellowship. The God witnessed to in the Scriptures is the God who chooses people for fellowship with himself and with one another and, in doing so, enters into covenant with them. Following Barth, Jan Lochman writes, "This God does not rest in his eternal perfection. He is not the prisoner of his sovereign interests. It is not so much his 'aseity' as his 'Pro-seity' and pro-existence that is his distinguishing mark."[10] In other words, while he is perfect in himself he reaches out to others, is one who both lives in fellowship and communicates it to and with his people. Lochman further points out that we can speak of this fellowship, especially from the perspective of the Holy Spirit, since the "being" of God is Father and Son in the fellowship of the Holy Spirit. "The trinitarian dogma seeks to stress the sociality or social nature of God. God means fellowship because he is fellowship in his own being. His covenant with man is not arbitrary, his history of salvation not capricious, his coming in the flesh does not contradict his own being. All this corresponds to the 'inner logic of his heart.'"[11]

The history of Israel and of Jesus Christ were in the heart of God from all eternity. All of this is clearly in line with Barth's views on election and covenant and uses language borrowed therefrom. Yet, although God has willed from all eternity so to act, these events are not simply a repetition of eternity but occur in history in contingent happenings so that "in the history of Israel and of Jesus Christ God went the way of his being."[12] In other words, God acts in a way that corresponds to his very nature as triune. This conception of God means that, since he has reconciled the world to himself in Jesus Christ, society and life in the political realm will have this social dimension, this will to be a fellowship of people for and with one another. The task for a social ethic, and particularly an ecumenical one, is not only the Christian duty to set before others this vision, but the obligation to seek to fulfill it and thereby to be socially involved in carrying out the task and thus in some measure realizing the vision. This can be credible only if we have more than a general concern for people or a mere general conception of God. It needs to be based in the center of our faith, where the Trinity belongs.

The Conference of European Churches

We look finally at the report of the Conference of European Churches on the Trinity and Society. In this connection the report begins with human analogies rather than with God's nature and revelation. It speaks of anthropology pointing us to the unity of mankind in diversity, of sociology and the attempt at social integration of the individual, of ecology and the community of creation and the relation of its life to ours, and of the political divisions which demand communion. In the light of the Bible and tradition and the experience of the church, "we can recognise that the movement towards community is a reflection of the communion which exists in God himself. The deepest aspiration of human life corresponds to the dynamics of the life of the Trinity."[13] This is a way of putting things that seems at first sight to be based primarily on experience and human observation which point us beyond themselves to the community of God. That there are such signs of the social dimension in all these aspirations is not to be denied. Nonetheless, from the Christian perspective, the primary basis of our knowledge of the possibility and power of such sociality is in the divine revelation, in the reality, love, and action of the triune God.

The C.E.C. report, however, does speak in practical terms of those social areas of life which the Trinity helps and indeed inspires. It states, "The Holy Trinity offers us not only the model of unity, but also the power of love to overcome egoism and effectively to imitate that model in the life of the Church and the world. The trinity thus supports us in our activity for reconciliation, unity and peace in the world today."[14]

A further section of the report asks how, in an increasingly secular society, the witness of the church to the triune God in sociopolitical affairs can be made. Once more we see that it is the triune God who is the fundamental motive of all our actions. To live out the mystery of the Trinity (as Augustine and Congar in their writings and lives sought to do) leads to a profound spirituality. This is no ingrown individual affair but, like God himself, outgoing in love, social responsibility, and action. The deepening of spiritual life and the formation of real community and willingness to serve will alone lend credibility to our professions of faith in the triune God.

The third section of the report makes three specific suggestions for practical social action:

> To devote ourselves to peace by opposing the build-up of deadly weapons. This is now in the process of taking place, although not every area of the world is necessarily free from fear of them or their use.

To strive for the creation of an international economic order in which less injustice prevails, to seek justice between peoples.

To aim at a life-style more in keeping with the maintenance of ecological balance so that the world may remain habitable for ourselves and future generations.[15]

The conclusion reads: "We are of the opinion that genuine spirituality necessarily leads to responsibility for the world. . . . We have learnt and experienced that that road holds many further promises for us of even deeper ecumenical co-operation."[16] And this spirituality, as we have seen, is based on a profound perception of the love and communion of the triune God.

Anthropology and the Image of God

We have seen that modern theology is rightly critical of defining human beings in purely individualistic terms. Individualism contradicts the true being of humanity since we are not meant to be alone. Various other anthropological theories also come in for censure in the modern debate—humanity viewed simply as rational beings (monism) and the dichotomy between body and soul (dualism).[17] The B.C.C. report states, "By concentrating on reason or freedom or our moral sense as the basis of our distinctive humanity, the tradition has been frequently tempted into an individualistic, or, indeed, merely secular anthropology: the image of God is that which human beings *individually* possess."[18] The biblical perception is based rather on the nature of our real humanity as seen in the person of Jesus Christ.

One of the most profound, indeed revolutionary modern treatments has been given by Karl Barth. There are, roughly speaking, three areas of Barth's thought that are of relevance here. In the first place, God does not exist in splendid isolation or loneliness but as Father, Son, and Holy Spirit in a relationship of "co-existence, co-inherence and reciprocity."[19] Second, in incarnation and reconciliation in Jesus Christ, God and man live together in union and communion. Third, the humanity assumed by the Word in the incarnation is ours and Jesus lives in it and in our history a life which can be called radical co-humanity. He is thus *from, for,* and *with* others "the man for others." This implies a total solidarity with humanity in its sin and need (*from*), a work of identification and reconciliation which means he acts pro nobis *for* us, and a being *with* us. Further, Jesus' being for others reflects the very relationship which God has in himself as Father, Son, and Holy Spirit. God's works *ad extra* in the man Jesus create another relationship not alien to but appropriate to him. Barth writes, "It is this relationship in the inner divine being which is repeated and reflected in God's eternal covenant with man as revealed and operative in time in the humanity of Jesus."[20] Again, he writes, "The humanity of Jesus is not merely the repetition and reflection of his divinity or of God's controlling will; it is the repetition and reflection of God himself, no more and no less. It is the image of God, the *imago Dei*."[21]

It is in this way through the person of Jesus, and in this instance his humanity, that we have revealed to us and know the true nature of our humanity and its likeness to God. It is in the man Jesus that we discern what Barth calls "the basic form of humanity." To live in isolation, for ourselves alone, is to be inhuman and is the essence of sin. We are human only when we exist as persons in a relationship lived as those who are made to be with and for one another. It is in Jesus that we see this true being in relationship and know that his being for others is the true image of God. This is perceived by faith. Nonetheless, it is given in and with the very structure of our being and belongs inherently to all people, whether they know it or not. It continues despite the Fall and in and through our reconciliation in Christ. With others, Barth finds the biblical basis not only in the humanity of Jesus but also in our creaturely nature as male and female. This points beyond marriage and the family to the wider human community and more profoundly to the covenant relationship between God and man.

Barth's view finds support in the Greek Orthodox theologian Gregorios Larentzakis, who states: "In the anthropomorphic Genesis narrative of the creation of woman, we observe precisely this community-related action of God."[22] Man and woman are given to one another by the God who is and creates fellowship in order to be one with him and in union and communion with one another. The Orthodox even speak of a "homoousian" between man and woman, indicating also persons of equal worth. This unity, love, and community is the highest purpose of marriage—all others are subordinate to it, including procreation, which is, or should be, an expression of love. In creating humankind in this way God corresponds to himself. He "shows himself to be the God of love and community who creates the human community on the foundation of love. One can quite certainly also accept that this social and community form also constitutes an expression of the human beings as image and likeness of God, which is also Moltmann's view."[23]

Colin Gunton sees two weaknesses in these approaches, particularly in Barth's. "The first is the tendency to be binitarian: the anthropology reflects a Father–Son duality reflected in that of male and female rather than expressing a theology of communion."[24] But does not Genesis speak of the image of God, male and female, reflecting God's being as such and is it not simply meant to convey the nature of communion, the personal relationships between humans, the basic form of humanity? Further, Gunton believes that "the second weakness is a tendency to anthropocentrism in Barth. Andrew Linzey's analysis of Barth's treatment of the creation sagas has shown that Barth underplays the way in which Genesis brings the non-human creation into the covenant."[25] Barth does, however, show that creation and covenant are interrelated, the creation being the outer basis of the covenant and the covenant the inner basis of creation, so that it is indirectly at least related to the image of God, the *imago Dei*.[26]

Gunton makes the point that since humankind is related to the cosmos as well as to other persons, the image, the essence of which is relatedness, should be seen in both. This is true as far as relation is concerned, but there is little biblical evidence that the image of God is seen in other than personal relationships. Gunton virtually grants this by stating, "To be made in the image of God is to be endowed with a particular kind of personal reality. To be a person is to be made in the image of God: that is the heart of the matter. If God is a communion of persons inseparably related, then surely Barth is thus far correct in saying that it is in our relatedness to others that our being human consists."[27] There are also, it must be said, two further weaknesses in Gunton's approach. First, he scarcely mentions the christological perspective of Barth's whole trinitarian and community aspects; second, he does not indicate Barth's varied understanding of the image of God as an analogy to both Trinity and the incarnation. Barth's complex conception of analogy is largely ignored.

One may sum up the position of Barth in this way: our humanity in Christ and so in us as co-humanity is the image of God. Our humanity, therefore, has the nature and possibility of partnership; *imago Dei* is the very nature of our creatureliness and so cannot be lost by the fall. Thus in its very being humanity reflects God. It cannot be an analogy of being (*analogia entis*), as in Roman Catholicism where God and humanity have something in common. It is rather an analogy perceived by faith (*analogia fidei*) and furthermore one of several relationships (*analogia relationis*). It is thus not a correspondence of likes but an analogy of dissimilars, since humanity is not similar to God in being but only in certain relationships. These are revealed in Christ and not perceived per se or naturally. Furthermore, although the image of God is seen in humanity and in our nature as such, it is possible for us to exercise it fully only when by the Holy Spirit we are elevated to a new birth, reborn as members of Christ's body, and in this relationship are able to be for others—in the image of God.

We are indebted to Stuart D. McLean, who gives a perceptive view of Barth's writings and points out the nuanced, sophisticated, and special kind of relationship that Barth has in mind and how he developed it in what McLean calls a dialectical-dialogical way. By this he means that God enters into the negative side of our nature in a dialectic. In this way he overcomes the negative and has dialogue and fellowship with our humanity in Jesus Christ. McLean makes three main deductions from Barth's view which are highly significant. He writes, "Relationship is the key to understanding God and persons. . . . [P]ersons are entities that not only *have* relationships with other entities, but *are* in fact constituted by such relationship."[28] In the second place, to be for and with others does not exclude but in fact characterizes us as distinct and properly individual. McLean states, "Relationship involves *being with* (unity) and, because of this *being with*, interaction and differentiation (separation). . . . The greater the unity (and community) of this particular kind, the greater the possibility of personal identity (individuality)."[29] Third, McLean writes, "*Being for* another or God's *being for us* . . . points to the actional, interactional and event character" of these relationships and dialectic and is "complemented by the equally important receptivity and openness to what is done *for* one." There is thus a complex, rich, dynamic of relationships "of giving and receiving, of agency and receptivity."[30] All this is involved in the basic form and content of our humanity as the image of God. McLean succinctly summarizes the essence of Barth's view: "The form of our humanity is the dialogical structure of the I–Thou relationship, of being in relationship-to-the-other, of mutually seeing, speaking, and listening, assisting, and doing all this 'gladly.'"[31]

The Trinity and Feminism

One of the strongest challenges to traditional forms of thought including modern reinterpretations of the Trinity comes from the feminist critique. There are, roughly speaking, three aspects of the modern debate: the feminist approach; the reaffirmation of the Trinity, however varied the content and form of it may be, as Father, Son, and Holy Spirit; and a mediating position between the feminist and traditional views.

The Feminist Critique

The main criticism by feminist writers is that trinitarian language, through use of the masculine gender, reinforces the paternalism of the church. The Father in particular implies this. Trinitarian language is in fact sexist. There is a gender stereotyping where "masculine terms such as Father or Son are heard as referring to males. The constant use of such terms and the absence of comparable female terms increases exclusivity according to gender in church and society."[32] No doctrine can be divorced from its context in what are still overall predominantly male-dominated, paternalistic, or, worse still, patriarchal societies. There is a natural conditioning by which male language and theology excludes the female and implies and encourages male dominance. On the other hand, society is already so structured that the male prevails and this in its turn influences the church, its worship, theological thinking, and language. The result is domination by the male sex.

It is further argued that the trinitarian theology and language which emerged during and after the long debates in the early church were influenced by Greek metaphysical ideas where the male rational principle was more divine than the female material principle. This philosophical idea gained influence, it is argued, within the church. Moreover, "The whole framework for thinking about God in these early centuries was set as hierarchical and anthropomorphic, drawing on the biases of the patriarchal cultures of the period."[33]

As an alternative, language has to be retrieved and emancipated from its bondage, the Trinity seen in economic nonsexist terms as, for example, Creator, Redeemer, and Sustainer. This emphasizes not God's apartness or maleness but God's closeness and relationship to the world and humanity. In other words, the feminist critique in this understanding often seeks a radical alternative to both the male language and the actual content of the doctrine of the Trinity.

The Traditional Response

It is generally granted "that exclusively male imagery has actively oppressive effects,"[34] but this is due more to our human sin than to any desire to attribute male characteristics to the triune God. In fact, such attribution would be a form of idolatry, a fashioning of God after our own image. This would be equally true if we regarded God as female. There is, it is argued correctly, no gender in the deity and male domination is sanctioned neither in the Bible nor in the Christian tradition. That tradition goes back, however, to biblical precedent where "Father" is used in two senses, as a term for God's care and love but also specifically as the Father of Jesus where he is called Abba. This is no mere metaphor but the distinctive term for a special, unique relationship which, while manifest in time, has an eternal dimension.[35] Jesus is thus called *the* Son. Moreover, that he became man in no sense means that the deity is male, but rather that the eternal Son took to himself our "humanum," humanity in its wholeness. Nor does it do anything but confuse the issue to speak of the Holy Spirit as female.

A further point in reply is also made. Theological language is apophatic; that is, it does not speak of God as it does of humans. Rather by means of a determined "thinking away" of the inappropriate connotations of the term—in this context that means masculine—we come to a better understanding of the nature of God.[36] Or, to put it differently, it is linguistically and theologically improper to make univocal attribution of human terms to the divine. Trinitarian terminology is meant to speak of God relationally and "reminds us that when we are called to enter into the communion of the divine love, we enter a community of three persons in which gender has no place."[37] The triune God transcends our human perceptions and "reveals personal being that is inclusive of all human and created existence."[38] This means that the male language we use is appropriate but not necessarily exclusive, provided any other usage implies the Trinity of persons in unity of being.

Geoffrey Wainwright is highly critical of the most favored alternatives to the traditional trinitarian language current in North America at the present time. One very much favored is that of Creator, Redeemer, Sustainer. He believes, rightly, that it has a flavor of Sabellianism and tends to separate God into three offices or functions. But "the Christian doctrine of the trinity recognises a divine communion of persons who cooperate undividedly in all their creative, redemptive and sanctifying work towards the world for the sake of bringing redeemed creatures into the glorious life that they themselves share from, in and to all eternity."[39] These are not merely economic acts but express relations internal to the very being of the one God.

An ontology of personal, communal being is replaced by an imperfect functionalism. The interrelationship and involvement of each person in the work of the others is set aside in the alternative feminist view. Wainwright writes, "Consideration of creation, redemption and sanctification shows that an account of these that is true to the biblical narrative will also imply and depend on the trinitarian communion and cooperation of Father, Son and Holy Spirit."[40]

A Mediating Position

A more mediating position is the tendency seen in some of the writings of Moltmann. This is particularly connected with the person and work of the Holy Spirit, the neglect of which has been so strongly criticized in modern trinitarian theology. Moltmann draws on Count Nikolaus von Zinzendorf, who in 1741 in Pennsylvania recognized the maternal office of the Holy Spirit. The Father of Jesus is our true Father, the Son our true Brother, and the Spirit our true Mother. Zinzendorf took this over from the Homilies of Macarius/Symeon, who based his thesis on exegesis of John 14:26 with Isaiah 66:13. The Holy Spirit, comforts us as a mother her child. Moreover, since we are born anew of the Spirit, we are "children of the Spirit." "The Spirit is their 'mother.'"[41]

"This idea helps to overcome masculinism in the idea of God and in the church. It serves to justify a liberated brotherly and sisterly community of men and women such as Paul had in mind in Galatians 3:28–29."[42] Moltmann retains the traditional terminology of Father, Son, and Holy Spirit throughout his work on the Trinity, and yet at the same time he seeks to make some accommodation to the feminist critique by way of attributing a maternal aspect to the Spirit. He believes that this gives more credibility to the Christian church, where male and female should be equal. But does it not, at the same time, confuse the issue by giving masculine qualities to two persons of the Trinity and a feminine to the third person? The B.C.C. report is right to reject both the attribution of human gender to the Trinity and the particular feminine one to the Holy Spirit.

Yves Congar shows how, historically, the preceding views have their source in certain aspects of the Christian tradition. He writes, "Tradition recognises in the Spirit a certain maternal function. In Genesis 1:2, the Spirit is shown in a sense as God's *ruach*, hatching the egg of the world. It is likewise the principle of the second creation."[43] It recreates us as new creatures so that we become God's children, his sons and daughters. Congar continues, "The part played in our upbringing by the Holy Spirit is that of mother—a mother who enables us to know our Father, God, and our brother, Jesus."[44] Roman Catholic writers are also tempted, as Matthias Josef Sheeben is, to compare "the procession of the Word, the Son with the production of Adam and the procession of the Holy Spirit with the production of Eve."[45] Later, Christian tradition saw the church as the new Eve and almost identified the Spirit and the Church. The Word calls for a response of love, which in the Trinity is the Spirit and in the church is the

Virgin Mary. "The new Eve, the Church . . . is the Spirit in a human existence. Woman then is the great symbol of the response of love given to
God. In God that response is the Holy Spirit."[46] Here Spirit and feminin-
ity are closely linked, although not necessarily absolutely identified. There
is an affinity between who the Spirit is and what a mother is and does. These
parallels are forced and unconvincing as biblical exegesis.

Moltmann adds another dimension to the feminist debate when he suggests that the fatherhood of God should be complemented by the divine
motherhood. The source of Godhead is not just the Father principle. The
first person of the Trinity not only begets the Son but also bears the Son in
his womb, hence he has both a fatherly and a motherly aspect. The nature
of the Godhead is both masculine and feminine. God is not only our heav-
enly father but is also our divine mother. Here, clearly, attempts are made
to take a middle way between traditional views (even if in modern guise)
and the feminist rejection of this tradition.[47]

What conclusions then should we draw from this discussion? There are
certainly lessons to be learned from the feminist critique, though one cannot follow feminist arguments more than partially. The first is to recognize
the dangers, past and present, of a form of domination based on exclusively
male language. The retrieval of language and its inclusive nature is one feminist achievement. The second lesson is that no particular language is absolutely sacrosanct. Yet, as far as the Trinity is concerned, it must enshrine
the essence of the doctrine. Sometimes it does seem that the feminist re-
statements do not. Colin Gunton rightly points out that while the Trinity
is an expression of the being of God in personal relations, it is never a static
datum but seeks to articulate the dynamic of the living being of God in
these relationships.[48] This can be done in various ways while reaffirming
the essence of the doctrine. The third point is that "we cannot lightly toss
aside the linguistic context which encapsulates the content of the Gospel.
We have been reminded of the words of St. Athanasius, that the only reason we have for calling God Father is that he is so named in Scripture."[49]
This, while true, is not a wholly convincing argument. Fourth, as has been
stated, this does not imply a male deity since such gender attribution to
God is quite inappropriate to the personal relations of the Trinity. Rather,
we use the traditional language as the most appropriate and also because
many alternative proposals which are put forward today virtually deny the
reality of the triune God, of the one divine being in personal relationships.

THE TRINITY AND POLITICS

Both Jürgen Moltmann and Jan Lochman see the view of God as strictly
monotheistic mirrored on earth in the form of an imperial ruler. "The one
monarch on earth . . . corresponds to the one monarch in heaven."[50] The
idea of God was influenced by this and became monarchical, imperial, and

authoritarian. Lochman points out that a trinitarian view, if properly understood, would have a liberating effect. Any identification of an earthly monarch with the triune God is excluded. The social nature of the Trinity is proof against a personality "cult" in the political realm. Thus, while ancient monotheism tended toward monarchical politics, the trinitarian conception is properly directed toward community, sociality, participation both in theory and practice.[51] Moltmann is in substantial agreement.

Moltmann goes further and seeks to show how the early church controversies leading to the christological and trinitarian definitions have had as background a false conception of God as monotheistic and a form of what he calls "monarchical theism." He writes, "The Arians were not concerned to disparage the Son, but with the sublime monarchy of the one God, and that is why they subordinated the Son."[52] It is possibly the main reason why the same happened with the Spirit, as seen in the case of the Pneumatomachians, who had the same concern. This can all be granted. Moltmann, however, goes on to state that because the Western tradition in theology began with the unity of God, it gave only a secondary or subordinate position to the three persons. When Hegel, for example, substituted Subject for Substance, the same imbalance prevailed. Moltmann quite uncritically brings together Hegel, Dorner, Barth, and Rahner in modern times, though they differ very greatly in many respects. He does not go so far as to say that their view is simply monotheism. Nonetheless, he believes they all speak in a one-sided way by giving priority to the oneness of God over the personal aspects and relationships in the Trinity. He sees the fellowship of the three persons preceding their unity or, in fact, creating it. Moltmann continues on this basis to give a critique of political views based on this supposed monotheism. But are not unity and threeness equally ultimate in God?

Wolfhart Pannenberg in his *Systematic Theology*, while supporting Moltmann's critique of the Western trinitarian view, also agrees with Barth that one cannot speak of monotheism as if it meant oneness only. The unity of God must be, is, and always has been a unity in trinity. He writes that to be against Barth's view of revelation as expressed in the one divine Subject "in no way means that the idea of monotheism should be dropped and made an object of theological polemics as Moltmann does."[53]

J. J. O'Donnell and others largely follow Moltmann's line in believing that historically there is a strong link between monotheism and monarchy. One God–one Führer went together in Nazi Germany, for example.[54] In a similar way, some views of lordship and omnipotence lead to sociopolitical domination. Trinitarianism may not necessarily be a sure defense against tyranny, but it does point in the right direction, toward a view of the worth of persons and the need for community, cooperation, and consent in social and political life.

The view that monotheism is to be interpreted in the way in which Moltmann and others do must be challenged, since in this debate there is often lack of clarity and different perceptions about the meaning of the terms used. Monotheism can be and often is interpreted as a belief in God as one, or in the primacy of unity over threeness. But monotheism can also be interpreted as specifically Christian since it is in the threeness of God that the unity consists, a point made from earliest times by Christian theologians. Trinity and monotheism are or should be one. It is only a false monotheism that can in any sense be said to legitimize tyranny. David Brown strongly and correctly criticizes Moltmann in this regard:

> Moltmann has an extraordinary chapter (Chapter 6) in which he argues that the unity model has reinforced patriarchy and dominance within society rather than encouraged mutual cooperation and respect. Whether this is true historically is questionable, but, even if true, the plurality model would not necessarily lead to the latter objectives. After all, three-man juntas are almost as common in the world as one-man dictatorships. One hopes that such thoughts played no significant part in leading Moltmann to advocate the latter model.[55]

The British Council of Churches report, while granting that "monistic theologies tend to legitimise totalitarian regimes," also states that "recent historical studies, however, have suggested that it is not easy to draw direct lines between theological positions and political theories."[56] This is a timely warning which also urges advocacy of the priority of persons in community, social, and political affairs over concepts, as the Trinity itself implies. In a similar vein, Walter Kasper writes,

> The trinitarian understanding of unity as communion has implications for the political sphere in the broadest sense of this term and therefore for the formulation of the goals of unity in the Church, in society and in the human race; in other words, for the peace of the world. E. Peterson has proposed the thesis that the doctrine of the Trinity puts an end to political theology. It would be more accurate to say that it puts an end to a particular political theology that serves as an ideology to justify relations of domination in which an individual or a group tries to impose its ideas of unity and order and its interests to the exclusion of others. The doctrine of the trinity inspires an order in which unity arises because all pool what they have and make it a common store.[57]

Kasper agrees with others that this communion cannot simply be identified with left- or right-wing political stances. He writes,

> Such a vision is as far removed from a collectivist communism as it is from an individualistic liberalism. For communion does not dominate the individual being and rights of the person but rather brings these to fulfilment through the giving away of what is the person's own and the reception of what belongs to others. Communion is thus a union of persons and at the same time maintains the primacy of the always unique person. This primacy, however, finds its fulfilment not in an individualistic having but in giving and thus granting participation in what is one's own.[58]

What form in political terms would parallel this may vary greatly from time to time and from place to place, but it would always involve freedom, community, and personal rights as well as integrity, wisdom, and responsibility among both leaders and people.

THE TRINITY AND THE THEOLOGY
OF LIBERATION

The theology of liberation, which largely accepts the Marxist critique of society and identifies its vision for social and political life with the oppressed against the oppressors, with the poor and the needy in society, seeks from this basis and in the light of its understanding of the faith to write and support a theology of liberation. Many of these theologians are often critical of the West, whose theology they regard as produced in a context of oppression and therefore suspect.[59] Yet when it comes to giving doctrinal content and expression to their own insights, they largely take over material or terms rooted in the West. This is true both of Jon Sobrino's Christology and of Leonardo Boff's doctrine of the Trinity.[60] Boff spends the greater part of his book writing on the doctrine of the Trinity following the main lines of Moltmann's argument and only periodically and briefly engages the basic terms of liberation theology which he espouses. One must state that in fact much of what he says, if not all of it, is already stated by Moltmann and others.

Boff notes three things that can be said in favor of a trinitarian understanding of God in relation to liberation:

1. It is archetypal and inspirational. The Trinity as saving mystery touches the lives of each of us, especially those struggling to be free from oppression. The Trinity is an open and egalitarian community of persons, the archetype of what we are called and may be enabled to be and to do. "If the trinity is good news it is so particularly for the oppressed and those condemned to solitude."[61] It is also an inspiration to persevere and to struggle for a more equal human society. "If oppressed believers come to appreciate the fact that their struggles for life and liberty are also those of Father, Son and Holy Spirit, working for the kingdom of glory and eternal life, then they will have further motives for struggling and resisting; the meaning of their efforts will break out of their restricting framework of history and be inscribed in eternity, in the heart of the absolute mystery itself."[62] By this, Boff seems to be saying that God the Father in his Son by the Holy Spirit enters into the struggles and needs of our humanity by taking them to himself in Jesus Christ and that this is a foretaste of the ultimate kingdom of God and of eternal life. This is so since God in his action overcomes what is oppressive and wrong and inspires people to be united with him in this struggle. In other words, Boff's understanding of this is that we are caught up through our struggles and our faith into unity with the triune God himself and so commune with the final mystery of life itself. The triune God wills and acts for human liberation and communion and so inspires human struggles and effects freedom and fellowship.

2. It is a profession of faith based on the concept of perichoresis (in Moltmann's sense of the mutual interpenetration of the three persons), and this principle of unity in the Trinity leads to a unity which is "not to be

found in the solitude of One but in the coexistence and communion of Three."[63] Boff writes further, "From the perichoresis-communion of the three divine persons derive impulses to liberation: of each and every person, of society, of the Church and of the poor."[64]

For him this has a double significance in that it offers a critique of all mechanisms of egoism. He writes, "Society offends the trinity by organising itself on a basis of inequality."[65] By contrast, it honors it the more it favors sharing and communion, for only thereby can one bring about justice and equality for all. The oppressed and the poor reject their lot as sin against trinitarian communion. The interrelatedness and unity of the Trinity of persons is, on the contrary, a model for a humane society. This is true also, not only of society within nations, but for the relationship between nations and peoples in the world.

3. It is significant not only for social and political life but for the life of the world as a whole. This view of the Trinity reaches out to the whole universe; Boff states, "The universe exists in order to manifest the abundance of divine communion."[66] Creation is, to use Calvin's phrase, the *theatrum gloriae Dei*, or, in Boff's terms, it is "created to allow the divine persons to communicate themselves."[67] To this extent it points to a future fulfillment "culminating in man and woman in the likeness of Jesus of Nazareth and Mary . . . inserted into the very communion of Father, Son and Holy Spirit. Then the trinity will be all in all."[68] Here a Roman Catholic strain is evident, as is also Moltmann's view of the trinitarian history of God, which takes our human history into it and is complete only at the end. Neither view is valid. In the first case, it is based on relating the male to Jesus and the female to Mary in a way contrary to much of Boff's other writing. In the second place, one cannot agree that God as triune comes to himself at the last through his participation in history and is only properly triune through that particular experience.

When one examines Boff's views on society and political life in relation to the Trinity, one finds little that is new. The mainly Eastern view of Moltmann is its chief inspiration, a view of a Trinity which is one-sided and makes it incomplete until the end. The value of both writers is the strong emphasis on community, but this needs to be supported by a better view of the nature of the Trinity and its relation to society and to politics.

Notes

1. Jürgen Moltmann, "The Reconciling Powers of the Trinity in the Life of the Church and the World," in *The Reconciling Power of the Trinity. Geneva Conference of European Churches*, C.E.C. Occasional Paper No. 15 (Geneva: C.E.C., 1983), p. 56.
2. Ibid.
3. Ibid., p. 57.
4. Ibid., p. 56.
5. Ibid., p. 57.

6. Leonardo Boff, *Trinity and Society*, tr. Paul Burns, Liberation and Theology Series 2 (London: Burns and Oates, 1988), p. 149.

7. Ibid., p. 150.

8. Gregorios Larentzakis, "Trinitärisches Kirchenverständnis," in *Trinität: Aktuelle Perspektiven der Theologie*, Wilhelm Breuning, ed. (Freiburg: Herder, (1984), p. 91, quoting J. Zizioulas in *Die Spontangruppe in der Kirche*, 1971, p. 178.

9. Ibid.

10. Jan Milič Lochman, "Zur Praktischen Lebenszug der Trinitätslehre, *Evangelische Theologie*, vol. 35, no. 3, 1975, p. 244.

11. Ibid.

12. Ibid.

13. *The Reconciling Power of the Trinity*, Report of Section 1, p. 84.

14. Ibid., p. 87.

15. Ibid., Report of Section 3, p. 93.

16. Ibid., p. 94.

17. Colin Gunton, *The Promise of Trinitarian Theology* (Edinburgh: T. & T. Clark, 1991), p. 104f.

18. *The Forgotten Trinity: Report of the B.C.C. Study Commission on Trinitarian Doctrine Today* (London: British Council of Churches, Inter-Church House, 1989), vol. 1, p. 23 (hereafter cited as *B.C.C. Report*).

19. Karl Barth, *Church Dogmatics*, III/2, p. 218 (hereafter cited as *C.D.*).

20. Ibid., pp. 218–19.

21. Ibid., p. 219.

22. *The Reconciling Power of the Trinity*, p. 64.

23. Ibid., p. 65.

24. Gunton, p. 115.

25. Ibid., pp. 115–16.

26. *C.D.*, III/1, pp. 94ff.

27. Gunton, p. 116.

28. Stuart D. McLean, "Creation and Anthropology," in *Theology Beyond Christendom: Essays on the Centenary of the Birth of Karl Barth May 10, 1886*, John Thompson, ed., (Allison Park, Pa.: Pickwick Publications, 1986), p. 112.

29. Ibid.

30. Ibid.

31. Stuart D. McLean, *Humanity in the Thought of Karl Barth* (Edinburgh: T.& T. Clark, 1981), p. 43.

32. Susan Brooks Thistlethwaite, "On the Trinity," *Interpretation*, vol. 45, no. 2, 1991, p. 159. See also Elisabeth Moltmann-Wendel and Jürgen Moltmann, "Menschwerden in einer Gemeinschaft von Frauen und Männern, *Evangelische Theologie*, vol. 42, no.1, 1982, p. 87.

33. Thistlethwaite, p. 164.

34. *B.C.C. Report*, vol. 1, p. 39.

35. Ibid., vol. 2, pp. 32–33. Geoffrey Wainwright, "The Doctrine of the Trinity, Where the Church Stands or Falls," *Interpretation*, vol. 45, no. 2, 1991, p. 119.

36. *B.C.C. Report*, vol. 1, p. 39.

37. Ibid., vol. 2, p. 32.

38. Ibid.

39. Wainwright, p. 121.

40. Ibid., p. 123.

41. *The Reconciling Power of the Trinity*, pp. 54–55.

42. Ibid.

43. Yves Congar, *I Believe in the Holy Spirit*, vol. 3, *The River of Life Flows in the East and in the West*, tr. David Smith (London: Geoffrey Chapman, 1983), p. 161.

44. Ibid., p. 161.

45. Ibid., p. 159.

46. Ibid., p. 160.

47. Jürgen Moltmann, "The Motherly Father. Is Trinitarian Patripassianism Replacing Theological Patriarchialism?" *Concilium*, vol. 143, 1981, p. 51f.

48. Gunton, pp. 163–64.

49. *B.C.C. Report*, vol. 1, p. 39.

50. E. Peterson, *Monotheismus als Politisches Problem*, p. 81, quoted in Jan M. Lochman, "Zur Praktischen Lebenszug der Trinitätslehre," *Evangelische Theologie*, vol. 35, no. 3, 1975, p. 245.

51. Ibid.

52. Moltmann, "The Reconciling Powers of the Trinity," p. 48.

53. Wolfhart Pannenberg, *Systematische Theologie*, (Göttingen: Vanderhoeck and Ruprecht, 1988), vol. 1, p. 363, n. 220.

54. John J. O'Donnell, *The Mystery of the Triune God*, Heythrop Monograph 6 (London: Sheed and Ward, 1988), pp. 128–34.

55. David Brown, *The Divine Trinity* (La Salle, Ill.: Open Court, 1985), p. 308.

56. *B.C.C. Report*, vol. 1, p. 36.

57. Walter Kasper, *The God of Jesus Christ*, tr. Matthew J. O'Connell (New York: Crossroad, 1989), p. 307.

58. Ibid.

59. Pablo Richard, "Latin American Theology of Liberation: A Critical Contribution to European Theology," in *European Theology Challenged by the World-Wide Church*, C.E.C. Occasional Paper No. 8 (Geneva: C.E.C. 1978), pp. 30ff.

60. Jon Sobrino, *Christology at the Crossroads* (Maryknoll, N.Y.: Orbis, 1976). Boff, *Trinity and Society*.

61. Boff, p. 158.

62. Ibid., pp. 157–58.

63. Ibid., p. 139.

64. Ibid., p. 236.

65. Ibid.

66. Ibid.

67. Ibid., p. 237.

68. Ibid.

7

The Trinity, Language, and Modern Thought

Trinitarian Language

The Trinity is a divine mystery, yet we must seek as far as possible to interpret it in human language. It may be about God in heaven but theology, as Karl Barth reminded us, is done in Basel, or wherever—that is, on earth. What, therefore, the theology of the church seeks continually to do is to articulate conceptually faith in the triune God in a manner that corresponds as closely as possible to its truth claims and eliminates erroneous conceptions. We do so in the modern age, post-Enlightenment. Speaking of one important aspect of this enterprise—the basic concept of person in the Trinity—Walter Kasper writes, "At issue in this question is . . . the correct conception of the centre and basic structure of the Christian message in the context of modern thought. The issue is the Christian answer to the situation of atheism that has been brought about by Christian theism."[1] This gives us the twin themes of our chapter: first, the most acceptable concepts and language to employ when speaking of the Trinity, and second, the Trinity in relation to the present age, especially the practical issues of atheism and theism.

Trinitarian language is not a direct transcript (except occasionally) of biblical language but it does attempt to interpret biblical teaching. It was forged in the early centuries and modified often since in the process of debate about the true meaning of the Christian revelation and the best terminology to use. To that extent R. P. C. Hanson is correct in his portrayal of the development of the Christian conception of God as a process of trial and error.[2] Nor can it be said that one common terminology emerged to express the truth of the Trinity. Nor, when to some extent it did, was that terminology always used with exactly the same meaning. The difference between the East and the West in the interpretation of a formula like "one being in three persons" to state the essence of the doctrine was and is a case in point. The church and its theologians used the best available terminology in dialogue with each other and with the world and often in disagreement with each other. Terms were used, developed, and took on new shades of meaning in the course of controversy in the attempt to maintain and state the apostolic faith against one-sided, dangerous views of it. Hence the doctrine of the Trinity was the product of reflection on revelation, the result of a process of thought, conflict, and disagreement about its validity, content, and viability.

The basis for thought was Holy Scripture, though the terms employed were often nonbiblical. On this basis Yves Congar sums up what was attempted then and since. "To a very great extent the treatises on the Trinity consist of a search for a way of speaking. Is it possible to say this or that, is it wrong to utter a certain sentence? . . . What is sought is an understanding of what is believed."[3] This latter point is crucial: faith grasped the revelation and reconciliation of God in Jesus Christ by the Holy Spirit according to the Scriptures. But this faith, as Anselm put it, continually sought and required understanding: *Credo ut intelligam.*

Language and Meaning

Up to the fourth and fifth centuries not only did controversy rage over the content of the faith—particularly in its christological and trinitarian aspects—but there was confusion as to the right terms to use and their meaning. By this time both in East and West there was general, although not complete agreement that the Son was of one being or nature with the Father—the famous *homoousion.* The Holy Spirit was also regarded as of one being with both Father and Son. There was not simply a single being God, or three Gods, but the one true and living God was manifest in three ways of existence or persons. In the Eastern development the original term for the being of God, *hypostasis,* was gradually transferred to signify the three distinctive or special personal characteristics in which this *hypostasis* existed. Thus the term *hypostasis* was changed to mean "person," and *ousia,* or being, was used exclusively for the unity of the three persons. John Zizioulas points out that the identification of *hypostasis* with person was a revolutionary development and meant that person is "no longer an adjunct to a being," as was the tendency earlier; it is itself the hypostasis or distinctive way in which the being of God exists.[4] J. N. D. Kelly summarizes: "The badge of orthodoxy in the East was one *ousia,* three *hypostases.*"[5] In the Latin West this became one essence or substance, *substantia,* in three persons, *personae.* Thus in form at any rate the theologies of East and West were one. But while the East had at its disposal a more subtle Greek language that was also more dynamic and nuanced, the West used a more static, less flexible language. When to this was added both a different starting point—in the East with the persons and in the West with the unity—and a varied use of the terminology adopted, it indicated a somewhat different emphasis and understanding of the way the doctrine was to be interpreted and applied.

The two main approaches are seen best in the Cappadocians in the East and in Augustine in the West—both largely influential still. One prominent aspect in modern trinitarian theology is a strong critique from a number of Western theologians of their own Augustinian heritage and the growing acceptance of the importance of the Cappadocian approach. It is seen as helpful in understanding the Trinity; in applying its insights to the present-day church, society, and politics; and in its dialogue with philosophy and science. While this is so, theologians and historians of dogma like G. L. Prestige[6] and Yves Congar[7] believe in a large measure of agreement between the two. Congar, for example, writes, "Faith in the mystery of the trinity, then, goes beyond any theological terms and constructions that can be formulated by man. It is therefore clear that it is possible for several different trinitarian theologies to exist and even several dogmatic formulae and constructions dependent on these theologies."[8] What is sought is an understanding of what is believed, however varied the form. But this understanding should also attempt to reach, if possible, a greater measure of consensus.

The Cappadocian Conception of the Trinity

The Eastern theologians and those from the West who are dismissive of Western Augustinianism claim to find support for their views from the Cappadocians, particularly in seeing "person" in the Trinity in terms of "being in relation" or communion. The B.C.C. report states, "There was remarkable unanimity in the Study Commission in looking for resources to the three Cappadocian Fathers St. Gregory Nazianzen, St. Gregory of Nyssa and St. Basil of Caesarea as well as to some Latin thinkers such as Tertullian, St. Hilary of Poitiers and Richard of St. Victor."[9]

The Cappadocians, while differing from each other in some respects, shared a basically common view of God as triune. Their conception of God had five main strands based on the unity of God in three persons.[10] First, they affirmed the fullness of the deity in each of the persons with the correlative idea of their equality. God is one and undivided. Second, he is manifested in three distinct modes of being, three personal subsistences or persons. Third, the person of the Father is the source of the being of the Son and the Holy Spirit—the Son coming from the Father as source (*aitia*) and the Holy Spirit proceeding from the Father through the Son. Each has a distinct *schesis*, or relationship of origin, which characterizes its personal being.[11] The Father is unbegotten, the Son begotten, and the Spirit proceeding. It is in these relationships of persons, or distinctive ways of being, that God is and expresses himself and that he comes to be known by us. Fourth, the Eastern theologians qualified the unity of God in two ways. God is inexpressible in his nature, a divine, unknowable mystery. Further, he is at the same time manifest in his energies, known as the *energeia*. Fifth, the concept of three *hypostases* in one *ousia* and the ontological significance of the persons is further emphasized by the idea of perichoresis. This means that each person or hypostasis inheres in the other two in the fullness of deity and personhood.

Modern commentators on the Cappadocians see the prime contribution of their trinitarian theology as relational—the relationship of the persons in communion which at the same time constitutes them ontologically as the very being of God. The B.C.C. report sums up the views of many in this regard: "The basis of the theological contribution to the concept of person is to be found in the fact that, under pressure of the Christian gospel and in the light of their particular concerns, the Cappadocian Fathers developed a new conception of what it is *to be*. . . . The being of God is a relational unity."[12] This has two main effects: it gives concrete particularity to the persons who interrelate and so constitute the deity, and at the same time it conceives God's being in these distinctions as creative of or in fact existing as communion. As a paradigm for humanity it sees personhood as basically relational, concrete, and communitarian. In this way it has reciprocity and relationship as its very essence and so counters all trends to define and understand personal existence in purely individualistic terms. It forms the basis for what is known as the social view of the Trinity and has profound implications for understanding ourselves and the nature of the church and the world. It should, however, be stated that those who today advocate this line of reasoning based on the Cappadocians emphasize only some salient aspects of what is a complex, sophisticated view of the divine Trinity.

The emphasis on the *energeia* points to the being of God as known in the dynamics of his activity. God's being as triune is a being in action for us. This has immensely illumined our understanding and gives a more biblical conception of the living God. Two further tendencies sometimes come to the surface in this conception. One is that the external works of the Trinity are indivisible; this could imply that the distinction between the persons, so strongly emphasized otherwise, could be obscured. In later development this has led to the *energeia* pointing beyond themselves to an unknowable God who can be described only apophatically, while his being in personal relations is known and conceivable only in his activity. A wedge seems to be driven between God per se as utterly unknowable and God in his energies whom we know and can in some measure comprehend. Colin Gunton has rightly stated, "A breach between the being of God and his action in the economy of creation and redemption" is clearly manifest here.[13] The question inherent in the Cappadocian conception is this: Does not the strong emphasis on the hypostases combined with the unknowability of God in his essence tend to lessen the strong affirmation made about the ontological character and unity of God as three in one? All of which indicates that the Cappadocian and Eastern heritage, while helpful in many ways, is not to be adopted uncritically.

The Augustinian Heritage

There is little doubt that Augustine gained some of his views of the Trinity from Neo-Platonism, especially Plotinus, as well as spending a lifetime meditating on the mystery of the Trinity on the basis of Holy Scripture. It is these twin aspects that make his writings so complex and baffling, yet profound and influential. Augustine's view is that there is one being of God who is Father, Son, and Holy Spirit. He thus begins with the divine nature which is, as the Greeks also said, simple and immutable.[14] He accepted the reality and equality of the three "persons" since each, as divine, is identical with the others and with the divine essence.[15] While each contains the wholeness of the deity they are not three divine beings but one. Moreover, the Trinity has a single action and will. The persons work together indivisibly in their external operations. This, however, does not obliterate the distinctive individual roles of the persons. Rather, each has an action to perform which is appropriate to his subsistence—hence the later doctrine of *Appropriations*.[16]

The distinction of persons is grounded in their mutual relations within the Godhead.[17] Augustine was unhappy even about the use of the term "person," which to him smacked too much of individualism. Instead he opted for the term "relation," later stated in Western thought as "three real or subsistent relations." A relation, however, must have some concrete objective content, which Augustine's exposition largely lacks. He sought to overcome this by stating that they had real subsistence through relation to the divine being as including it in each and by way of what was later called a *relatio oppositorum*, that is, a relation contrasted to the other two. That means that the persons in the Trinity are related to each other in a negative way; for example, the Son is not the Father.

Augustine saw the Holy Spirit as the mutual love of Father and Son,[18] a view that seems to fail to give personal concreteness to the Spirit. The Holy Spirit comes from the Father but also from the Son and so is the gift of both, the *vinculum pacis*.[19] As such, while the Father is *principaliter* the source of the Godhead, he is, with the Son, the one source, *unum principium*, of the Spirit. Thus the Holy Spirit comes from both the Father and the Son—*Filioque*—a view the East rejected and still does today, believing that it points to two sources in God and not simply the Father, thus making the Father have two sons. Augustine used Saint John's Gospel to reply that the Father has given all things to the Son, which can include the power to be joint source of the life of the Spirit.[20]

A further controversial feature of Augustine's trinitarianism was his use of analogies or *vestigia trinitatis*.[21] We consider but two examples here. The first is the lover, the object loved, and love which unites. The second, and some would say the most important one, is the mind, which involves a triad of being, knowing, and willing. To be fair to Augustine, he seems to have intended these to be no more than distant images, like something seen in a mirror. They are by no means identical with the reality of the divine Trinity—the mystery of the Godhead. The three are personal entities in God; in us they cannot be. With the Eastern theologians Augustine also accepted the theory of perichoresis, the mutual indwelling of Father, Son, and Holy Spirit in one another.

However, the main criticism of Augustine must be that his beginning with Neo-Platonism and his failure fully to link the nature of God as triune with the economy of salvation gave him a framework which inhibited dynamic concreteness in thought and presentation, especially of the three persons. It is this, more than anything else, that made his positive biblical insights take a rather abstract form and made his views less concrete and dynamic than those of the East.

Colin Gunton has given one of the most recent and trenchant critiques of Augustine in four areas: his weakness in understanding the humanity of Christ and so the incarnation, the inadequacy of his interpretation of substance and persons, his use of analogy, and the nature of the Holy Spirit.[22] We deal here primarily with the second of these, briefly also touching on two others.

Gunton believes that Augustine failed to understand the distinction between *ousia* and *hypostasis*. Augustine accepts the traditional formula based on tradition which was formed by Scripture. He gives, however, the inadequate reason that we use these terms or their Latin equivalents so "that we might not be altogether silent when asked what three, while we confess that they are three."[23] It is therefore not "merely a matter of linguistic usage" that is involved here, but rather a matter of substance.[24] According to Gunton, the Greek Fathers, especially the Cappadocians, developed a new ontology of the Trinity which defined the three persons as "beings whose reality can only be understood in terms of their relations to each other, relations by virtue of which they together constitute the very being (ousia) of the one God. The persons are therefore not relations, but concrete particulars in relation to one another."[25]

Moreover, Augustine failed to give a proper definition of the "person," by understanding it simply as "relation." Here he subsumed the persons under an Aristotelian "substance-accidents" view based on a dualistic ontology. The relations take a secondary place to the unity and are understood logically and not ontologically. Thus "he is precluded from being able to make claims about the being of the *particular* persons, who, because they lack distinguishable identity tend to disappear into the all-embracing oneness of God."[26] The being of God underlies the persons and so tends toward modalism. By contrast, for the Cappadocians "the three persons are what they are in their relations, and therefore the relations qualify them ontologically, in terms of what they are."[27]

While this critique of Augustine is valid, two things should be added. First, Augustine did make an attempt to give the relations personal quali-

ties in the Godhead by seeing them as related to one another positively in
a variety of ways. The Son is begotten in relation to the Father and the Spirit
proceeds from the Father and the Son. While this is less concrete than the
Greeks view, it is not as abstract and lacking in particularity as Gunton indicates. Second, the Eastern perception needs to be expanded to show how
in fact the persons do as such and in their relationships constitute the unity
and the fullness of God. Is not an ontological conception bound to say how
more particularly "together" (if one can so speak) the persons constitute
the Trinity in unity and how in this conception each person can be rightly
spoken of as divine?

Gunton also argues that the famous trinitarian analogies go further than
merely pointing beyond themselves giving but a distant image of the nature
of God and exhibiting the limited nature of all analogies.[28] Rather, on the
basis of a platonic triad of memory, understanding, and will God is conceived as Supermind. Gunton is saying that basically what Augustine is
doing is substituting for the economy of salvation "the inner structure of
the human mind" as manifesting the immanent being of God.[29] Gunton
seeks to substantiate this "outrageous claim" on the basis that memory,
understanding, and will are used by Augustine not as producing analogies
but as "developing a doctrine of God with a stress on the unity."[30] This is
at least dubious and here one must accord Augustine the benefit of any doubt
that analogy is both meant and pursued. Gunton does not mention an
important point made by Collinge[31] that part of Augustine's purpose in all
this was by way of reflecting on the analogies to lead us closer to God and
so correspond in both life and thought to the divine nature. But as Karl
Barth has so successfully demonstrated, the *vestigia trinitatis* are not a help
but a hindrance to understanding since the basis of our knowledge of God
as triune is in the divine revelation in Holy Scripture. Barth incidentally also
shows how a limited Augustinianism can be helpful in some aspects of
trinitarian doctrine.[32]

Gunton admits that Augustine's view of the Holy Spirit as gift and love
has something in it.[33] What is lacking is that it is scarcely argued from the
perspective of the economy, and the eschatological note, so prominent in
the New Testament, is missing. This in turn means a lack of emphasis on
the Spirit creating community. The result, he concludes, is that Augustine
fails "to give personal distinctiveness to the being of the Spirit in the inner
trinity".[34]

A final question must be, "Is the basis of Augustine's deity personal?"[35]
Gunton writes, "The only conclusion can be that, in some sense or other,
it is the divine substance and not the Father that is the basis of the being
of God, and therefore, *a fortiori* of everything else."[36] This leaves an impersonal reality at the heart of the world. This may perhaps be so and Augustine
is not without blame in this regard. But is it not possible to begin with one
personal God who is at one and the same time personally Father, Son,
and Holy Spirit? Unity and threeness are both equally ultimate in the
Trinity.

Being and Person in God

As indicated previously, language and the meaning of terms have changed over the course of the centuries so that to speak of God as one being in three persons can be misleading. As a consequence, the word person as used in the Trinity has been closely examined and criticized in modern thinking. Walter Kasper shows that, while rationalism and the Enlightenment raised their own objections to the Trinity and its language, these are not our main concern. He writes, "One objection stands out as more important than the others: modern subjectivity and the modern concept of person which it has produced. In the modern period, person is no longer understood in ontological terms but is defined as a self-conscious, free centre of action and as an individual personality." He continues, "Once this new concept of person was accepted, the idea of three persons in one nature became impossible."[37] The reason is clear since it would lead automatically in a tritheistic direction. The modern concept of person as a distinct, separate individual, is therefore inappropriate for trinitarian use. Karl Barth and Karl Rahner have come to similar conclusions in seeking an alternative terminology.[38]

According to Barth, "'Person' as used in the Church doctrine of the Trinity bears no direct relation to personality" since one cannot speak of "three personalities in God. This would be the worst and most extreme expression of tritheism."[39] Personality is more applicable to the unity of God since in him there is equality of essence as Father, Son, and Holy Spirit. The same can be said against the view that there are three "consciousnesses" in God. Barth adopts the Cappadocian suggestion that we should use the phrase "three modes of being," meaning thereby three distinct ways in which the one God exists. Both East and West added to this the concept of "relation"—the East filling it out by giving it more personal content and the West by speaking of "subsistent relations," that is, the ways in which the three are related to one another in the divine being. In his early work Barth remains largely within the framework of Western thinking but later expands this in a way more related to the East. He defines God as being in action and in this way avoids the abstract nature of much Western thinking.[40] He develops his conception of the Trinity in the doctrines of God, creation, and reconciliation.[41] In his anthropology, in particular, Barth sees human beings related to God and to one another within the believing community and in society. The concept developed here as applied to the Trinity is close to that of the Easterners in that the three persons in relationship are constitutive of the being of God.

By contrast, the idea of relation in the West has a more impersonal connotation. The B.C.C. report therefore is correct in stating why Barth abandoned the word "person":

> Barth, believing that the word inevitably suggested "three centres of consciousness" individualistically conceived, suggested the abandonment of the word *person* in connection with God's threeness, and preferred to speak of

three mutually related modes (or ways) of being the one personal God. In so doing, he was attempting to mediate between Eastern and Western traditions, for the expression is borrowed from the Cappadocian Fathers who used both the term *person* and the term *modes of being* in an ontological and not a psychological sense.[42]

Barth himself writes, "Even in his inner divine being there is relationship. . . . [H]e [God] is not alone . . . in the simplicity of his essence he is threefold— the Father, the Son and the Holy Ghost" mutually related, loving one another eternally.[43] This is reflected in the community of God and man in Jesus Christ, in the believing community of faith and in the co-partnership of people in society and as male and female. The being of God is thus constituted in these inner relationships of Father, Son, and Holy Spirit. For this reason, one cannot agree with the B.C.C. report's criticism of Barth as in danger of underwriting individualism or of overemphasis on the unity.[44]

Karl Rahner also finds difficulties with the traditional language, which in turn affects our understanding of the content of the doctrine.[45] He prefers the traditional interpretation and definition of person given by Boethius rather than that of Richard of St. Victor. Boethius wrote that person means "that which subsists as distinct in a rational nature,"[46] whereas for Richard of St. Victor a more relational view of the persons is combined with a strong emphasis on the unity of God in his revelation as love. For him a person has being both in itself (as divine) and from another person (as relation). Rahner is critical of the term person being used in an individualistic, modern sense which he believes solves nothing. In trinitarian terms one must follow kerygmatic and salvation history and see the persons of the Trinity as "three distinct manners of subsisting."[47] Subsistence thus involves distinction, particularity, concreteness, and relationship. This includes a relation to the being of God which is left somewhat vague in Rahner's definition of the three persons. What he is seeking to do is obvious but it is done in a rather abstruse and abstract way. He wants to make quite clear that each "manner of subsisting" within the Trinity has a distinctive, concrete character while at the same time the three reveal to us the true being of God.

In a critique of Rahner, Kasper believes that this way of speaking may be technically correct theologically but is kerygmatically not meaningful—in fact, even unintelligible as a kind of code language.[48] Moreover, is "distinct manner of subsisting" usable in doxology, the language of praise and worship? Even Rahner's view can have at heart a trace of modalism—though this is untrue both of Rahner and of Barth. What is needed is not abandonment of the traditional language of person but its reinterpretation.[49] But this was in fact what Rahner was seeking to do, though neither he nor Barth can find a single word that can be a substitute for the rejected word "person." In turn, Kasper comments that the whole question is more one of content than of language but language is expressive of a certain content and both must go together.

Both Kasper and Moltmann follow a line of argument about the persons of the Trinity more in keeping with the East and opt for a view of God as "being in relationship." Their aim is approved by Regina Radlbeck but some of their use of terminology has been questioned in her thorough examination and critique.[50] She believes Richard of St. Victor's view comes nearest to an acceptable solution of the nature of the persons in the Trinity.[51] Kasper goes a long way with this but also wants to go back to Augustine and Thomas Aquinas and does not quite succeed. In Radlbeck's opinion he opts primarily and correctly for a modern relational view of person along lines similar to Martin Buber, Ferdinand Ebner and Franz Rosenzweig, whose philosophical views are personalistic.[52] At the same time, he combines this with an individualistic concept and sees the nature of the deity in the absolute person of God.[53] Radlbeck sees these latter concepts not as complementary to but as exclusive of and incompatible with Kasper's main thesis. She makes a plea for a primarily Eastern understanding of person as relational and for Richard of St. Victor's view as a possible synthesis of East and West.[54]

In what is a very relational view of the persons leading to the danger of overemphasis of their distinctions, Moltmann uses the two terms "person" and "divine subject" and largely equates them.[55] The latter is based on Theodor Adorno's view "that history arises out of the functional relationship of real, individual subjects whose action and suffering determine the course of history."[56] Here is a view similar to that of Hegel where the divine Subject or Spirit is manifest in history and as history. Here also "subject" applied to the persons of the Trinity acquires the meaning of "a centre of independent consciousness, will and act."[57] This applies to the real distinctions of persons in God in a questionable way. Moltmann clearly refers again to Hegel with his use of "subject" as both particular individuality and relational solidarity.[58] But the modern idea of "subject" has too great a degree of independence to refer properly to the persons of the Trinity. As in Kasper's case the two conceptions of persons as relational (ontological or eschatological) and as independent subjects are incompatible. Moreover, in Moltmann's case, one can never be certain that one is dealing with God in his wholeness or with persons in their completeness since his eschatological emphasis and trinitarian history of God mean that the triune God is fulfilled and completed only at the end.

The conclusion we draw briefly at this point is that the concept of person used for the three distinctive ways God exists must in both East and West be a relational one which sees the threeness and oneness in God as neither first nor second but sees each as equally real and ultimate in God. Their more precise relationship, and some kind of conclusion, we will look at in Chapter 8. Two questions—how being and person may be best brought together and, if possible, how the true insights in the two main traditions of East and West can be utilized and recognized—remain open.

Beyond Atheism and Theism

Karl Barth and Walter Kasper

There are, roughly speaking, two views put forward today in relation to the modern problem posed by atheism and theism in relation to the Trinity. The first is dependent largely on the theology of Karl Barth, who rejected all forms of theism and philosophical arguments for the existence of God and based his teaching exclusively on the Christian revelation. He saw theology as having an autonomous basis and as a science in its own right and also as giving us the clue in the divine revelation to the nature of the triune God. In turn, this revelation not only answers the needs of our human situation but undermines and exposes the false views of atheism and theism. In the first case it reveals the true God and his nature as love, and in the second it shows the weaknesses of a vague theism. Moreover, in Barth's view, it shows any other than the Christian conception of God as a projection of our sinful ideas upon the infinite. Barth has been followed in this, though in different ways, by Jüngel, Moltmann, and more recently by the Catholic theologian Walter Kasper.[59]

Barth's position has been admirably summarized by Eberhard Jüngel.[60] While it has a trinitarian dimension, it is based more specifically on Christology. Barth argues that since God has united humanity with himself in his Son by the Holy Spirit there is no human being who is apart from God. There may be godless people and those who do not believe in God but there is no absolute godlessness of man. By incarnation and atonement in Jesus Christ there is an ontological relationship established between God in Jesus and all humanity and creation. Barth writes, "We should be abandoning our starting point . . . if we were to ascribe to man an absolute and ontological godlessness. Man has not fallen lower than the depth to which God humbled himself in Jesus Christ."[61] This is, for Barth, the Christian, christological, trinitarian answer to atheism. The basis of the latter is unmasked as untrue and in its place we may know and believe in the true God of love.

The other half of Barth's argument is directed against theism, that is, against "the possibility that man by reason can reach, believe in and have knowledge of the supreme being whom one can identify as God."[62] Barth shows that there is no God whom we know except the one true God seen in the humanity of Jesus. There is no nonhuman God. Incarnation and atonement are based on God's purpose of election and show that, while as triune he is perfect in himself, at the same time, he chooses to be God with us and for us—*Logos Ensarkos* and not *Logos Asarkos*. Jüngel points out that the theistic or metaphysical view of the supreme being which dominated both Scholasticism and the Enlightenment cannot be the God of humanity with and for us. He is "above where we do not appear"[63] To posit and worship such a being is to fashion an idol.

Atheism ignores and seeks to undermine the true deity of God in Christ while theism does the same to the true humanity of God. By contrast, "Barth puts Jesus over against all traditional ideas of God *and* their denial in order precisely in this way to learn to *think* about God."[64] Jüngel continues, "Barth raised the same basic objection to both undertakings, that they do not think of God as *God* and therefore in their affirmation and denial have not affirmed and denied *God*."[65] They are two sides of the same coin, bypassing as atheism the true deity of God and as theism the true humanity known in Jesus Christ. But the God made known in Jesus by the Holy Spirit is the triune God.

A similar view has been put forward in the writings of Walter Kasper.[66] He argues that much of the cause of atheism can be traced to the Enlightenment. It formed a kind of belief structure based on rationality and progress. But in rejecting God it lost its direction and became largely discredited; rationalism became irrational, persons became cogs in a wheel, and there developed a sense of unease in modern culture.[67] Lack of a unified structure for living based on religion, as had been the case in the past, left humanity homeless and restless. In an almost incomprehensible way the Enlightenment fed on roots planted by Christianity and Western culture. When belief in God disappeared, atheism lost its inner vitality and credibility.

Theism was supposed to give meaning to life but its criticism by Kant and others has left it wounded if not dead. In fact it is argued by some that it was the nature of theism as a feeble argument for God that helped to give atheism its credibility for a time. It is not simply Christianity as traditionally understood but the tradition of metaphysical theism that the atheist rejects. One feeds on the other, though it must also be said that the atheist rejects Christianity as well. Reason, however, cannot take the place of God and without an Absolute undermines itself. Kasper quotes L. Kolakowski, who states, "The collapse of Christianity so largely awaited by the Enlightenment proved to be—to the extent that it came about—at almost exactly the same time the collapse of the Enlightenment." Kolakowski also writes that "the absence of God became the increasingly open wound of the European mind."[68]

This breakdown provides Christianity with its opportunity and challenge to rethink again the idea of God and to do so in a trinitarian way consistent with the idea of God as love having its own inherent rationality and truth claims. Kasper points out how in Catholic thought Vatican II has moved away from the traditional, rational arguments of Vatican I and a dualistic ontology of nature and grace. While not entirely displacing but rather transcending these, it has emphasized the divine revelation and proceeds "from the concrete, historic reality of revealed faith."[69] In this view a question mark is put against many efforts to define God as in theism. "God is not then a 'highest being', in the sense of Western metaphysics, but the living and liberating God of history, the God of hope (Romans 15:13), the God who is love. When such statements are not left simply hanging in the air, but are thought rigorously through to the end, they lead to a renewal of the doctrine of the trinity."[70] This argument is only a pointer to a program of positive interpretation and application of the doctrine and, negatively, a guard against possible false views. In a similar way Colin Gunton sees the Enlightenment as the alienation of humanity from its true source, claiming a false certainty for humankind and failing to provide authentic freedom and humanity. The God of Scripture is, on the other hand, the true and living God who gives the gift of freedom and is to be understood as triune from the perspective of the life, death, and resurrection of Jesus Christ.[71]

Similarly, Moltmann argues, from a center in the cross of Christ, that atheism is a protest against suffering and evil, feeding on a false theism which has little or no answer to our problem. It is

> a rebellion against . . . political, moral and philosophical theism [which] thinks of man at the expense of God. It is only in the trinitarian theology of the cross that we meet God who is one with us in our suffering and takes it to himself. The death of the Son on the cross is not "the death of God" but the beginning of that God event in which the life-giving Spirit of love emerges from the death of the Son and the grief of the Father."[72]

In these examples it has been shown that the God of love revealed as triune in the cross and resurrection of Jesus is the Christian answer to the problem of a rationalistic and protest atheism as well as its counterpart in a now seriously questioned theism.

Religion and Revelation: Wolfhart Pannenberg

Another view, while seeking to counter atheism, either retains a more philosophical approach, an acceptance of some form of Christian theism as an argument for a divine being, or works within a theological framework that has certain philosophical and supportive arguments. We look at one example, the theology of Wolfhart Pannenberg.

Pannenberg has largely summed up the views of his varied writings in the first volume of his *Systematische Theologie*.[73] In it he agrees with the previous writers to the extent that he believes the Christian revelation, which the doctrine of the Trinity expresses, is the answer to the question of the reality of God denied by atheism and affirmed by theism. However, his methodological approach and therefore his presuppositions are quite different from theirs. On the one hand he rejects the traditional theistic arguments based on natural theology and the "proofs" of God's existence as no longer providing evidence for theistic claims. At the same time he holds that there is a "natural" way of approaching the task of theology which follows a method that inexorably leads to the Christian conception of God as triune and at the same time answers the atheistic objection.[74]

This could be regarded as an attempt to marry the phenomenology of religion with Pannenberg's very particular view of the Christian revelation.

There are, roughly speaking, four steps in the movement toward this goal. Three of these are regarded not as proofs extrinsic to the Christian conception of God but as essential aspects intrinsic to it. To begin, therefore, as some do, with divine revelation based on Scripture alone is to isolate Christianity from the modern world, to make it irrelevant or a private, subjective, Christian, church concern. Each aspect of the argument in the first three sections is regarded by Pannenberg as necessary prolegomena to the fuller expression of the Christian revelation.[75] They may be briefly summarized as the intuitive, the rational (philosophy of religion), and the history of religions approaches.[76]

First, in place of the traditional view of the knowledge of God which can be acquired by every person, Pannenberg puts an intuitive feeling for the infinite in a way reminiscent of Schleiermacher. This indicates "an ontological structure of man's being that presupposes an infinity transcending man's nature."[77] This is similar to Rahner's transcendental metaphysic but is neither "empty transcendence" nor simply man's own ideas projected to infinity and therefore an idol. It derives from human experience, which has this religious element built into it and is closely related to universal history.

Second, Pannenberg favors the use of reason, a rational inquiry as a contribution to, as well as an arbiter of, truth including the claims of Christianity. This involves working out thematically what has been experienced intuitively. Stanley Grenz speaks of this as

> the movement from the implicit presence of the divine in the form of the infinite to its reflective thematicization. This movement opens the way for the rational element in theology. Pannenberg follows Karl Rahner in viewing God as the unspoken mystery present in human experience prior to the development of the religious life, which in turn explicates this mystery, giving rise to theology.[78]

Third, a more novel—if debatable—aspect in Pannenberg's view is that religion in general and the religions in particular are the place where the God-consciousness is most fully realized.[79] Here a bridge between philosophical theology and the religions leads to a critical reflection on religious traditions. The religions have a role to play in the revelatory process since they pose the question of God and the universality of the claims of the divine. Even the conflicts of the religious beliefs lead to choices between the true and the false. However, they cannot in their multiplicity and opposition to one another move from the many to the one, that is, to a universal concept of absolute deity. This comes to fruition only in Israel's monotheism and the fuller revelation in Jesus Christ.

The fourth and final stage in Pannenberg's argument is the Christian revelation.[80] Revelation for him is conceived eschatologically, being proleptically manifest in the resurrection of Jesus, which has retroactive significance by affirming his oneness with God. The historical character and universal nature of this revelatory event can be finally confirmed and fully experienced only at the end. This anticipatory character of the revelation of the triune God makes all truth claims, however valid, contestable in the present and therefore essentially provisional.

What Pannenberg is seeking to demonstrate is that various forms of "knowledge" in humanity and history which have a religious character are an entrée into the fuller truth of God's eschatological revelation in word and history in Jesus Christ. He sees all four aspects as one, however varied in importance each may be. While it is true that the first three stages do not, according to Pannenberg, offer rational proofs of the existence of God, they do, nonetheless, pose the God question—the truth of which is more fully given in the revelation of the triune God. In this way Pannenberg seeks to combine an openness to the world, to the whole of humanity, and to history (especially religious history) with the Christian conception of God. Indeed, in one sense they are all varied aspects of this one all-embracing unity or holistic vision.

The legitimacy of such a procedure is, however, to be queried in several ways. Does our supposed intuitive feeling of the infinite correspond to any reality and is it not too anthropocentric? Could it not be interpreted, as Barth interprets it in the light of our sinful humanity, as a projection of our own ideas and therefore as fashioning an idol? Does the reflective view pursuant on the initial intuition lead us any further if the unreflective is itself dubious? Is, indeed, Pannenberg's conception of the Infinite to be equated in any sense with the triune God? Further, to say that religion is the sphere of the appearances of the divine may have some truth claims but, in the light of Pannenberg's recognition of the rivalries of the religions, by what criterion does one judge the true from the false? Has one not already surreptitiously introduced the final revelation in Christ as arbiter? Why then should this not be done, as some theologians do today, at the beginning?[81]

Moreover, Pannenberg's view of revelation has been rightly criticized as being too future-oriented and, while being properly bound to history, failing to give an adequate view of the exclusivity of God manifest in Christ.[82] Finally, Pannenberg's way of relating religious history to Christian revelation is a highly problematic one. There may be "truths" and "lights" in the world that God uses to make himself known especially in other religions than the Christian. But such truths and lights are to be measured by the one truth and light of God in Jesus Christ rather than being seen as contributory phases necessarily leading to its fullness. To make these provisional aspects essential factors of theological prolegomena is not to enhance but to diminish the uniqueness of the Christ event and so the true universality of the Christian message of the triune God. Nor is it likely that either atheists or theists will be particularly influenced by this approach. Too much of it comes close to what they have already examined and denied and indeed is quite simply a different form of the older arguments, though less rationalistic in form.

It is my belief, with Barth and Kasper, that the Christian revelation of God as triune gives us the true understanding of his reality and of his relationship to the world and humanity. It is this which also exposes the falsity of many ancient and modern alternatives while not denying the reality of "reflections" and "signs" of his activities in nature and in the world.

Notes

1. Walter Kasper, *The God of Jesus Christ*, tr. Matthew J. O'Connell (New York: Crossroad, 1989), pp. 285–86.

2. R. P. C. Hanson, *The Search for the Christian Doctrine of God* (Edinburgh: T. & T. Clark, 1988), p. 873.

3. Yves Congar, *I Believe in the Holy Spirit*, vol. 3, The River of Life Flows in the East and in the West, tr. David Smith (London: Geoffrey Chapman, 1983), p. 81.

4. John D. Zizioulas, *Being as Communion: Studies in Personhood and the Church* (Crestwood, N.Y.: St. Vladimir's Seminary Press, 1985), p. 39.

5. J. N. D. Kelly, *Early Christian Doctrines*, 5th ed. (London: Adam & Charles Black, 1977), p. 254.

6. G. L. Prestige, *God in Patristic Thought* (London: William Heinemann, 1936), p. 235.

7. Congar, p. 8f.

8. Ibid., p. 8.

9. *The Forgotten Trinity. The Report of the B.C.C. Study Commission on Trinitarian Doctrine Today* (London: British Council of Churches, Inter-Church House, 1989), vol. 1, p. 21 (hereafter cited as *B.C.C. Report*).

10. Basil of Caesarea, *Adversus Eunomium*, P.G. 29(497–669); *De Spiritu Sancto*, p. 45; *Letters*, P.G. 32 (220–1112). Gregory of Nazianzen, *Orations*, P.G. 35–36, 40–41; *Letters*, P.G. 37. Gregory of Nyssa, *Adversus Eunomium*, P.G. 45 (237–1112); *Epistles*, 189; *Quod Non Sint Tres Dei, Ad Eustathium de Sancta Trinitate*. See Hanson, pp. 313–26; Prestige, passim; T. F. Torrance, *The Trinitarian Faith: The Evangelical Theology of the Ancient Catholic Church* (Edinburgh: T. & T. Clark, 1988), pp. 263–69.

11. Torrance, p. 319.

12. B.C.C. Report, vol. 1, p. 22.

13. Colin Gunton, *The Promise of Trinitarian Theology* (Edinburgh: T. & T. Clark, 1991), p. viii.

14. Augustine, *De Trinitate*, bks. 1–4; 5:13, 7:10.

15. Ibid., 5:9.

16. Ibid., 2:9, 2:18.

17. Ibid., 5:6, 5:8, 5:15.

18. Ibid., 15:27.

19. Ibid., 15:27, 5D.

20. Ibid., 15:47.

21. Ibid., chaps. 9–14.

22. Gunton, pp. 31ff.

23. Augustine, *De Trinitate*, 5:10; Gunton, p. 44.

24. Gunton, p. 40.

25. Ibid., p. 39.

26. Ibid., p. 42.

27. Ibid., p. 41.

28. Ibid., p. 44.

29. Ibid., p. 45.

30. Ibid. p. 47.

31. William F. Collinge, "*De Trinitate* and the Understanding of Religious Language," *Augustinian Studies*, vol. 18, 1989, p. 147 n.19.

32. Karl Barth, *Church Dogmatics*, I/1, pp. 487ff. (hereafter cited as *C.D.*). Barth sees this in relation to the Holy Spirit as gift (ibid., p. 489).

33. Gunton, p. 48.

34. Ibid., p. 51.

35. Ibid., p. 53.

36. Ibid., p. 54.

37. Kasper, p. 285.

38. *C.D.*, 1/1, pp. 351ff. Karl Rahner, *The Trinity*, tr. Joseph Donceel (London: Burns and Oates, 1970), pp. 103ff.

39. *C.D.*, 1/1, p. 351.

40. *C.D.*, II/1, pp. 251ff.

41. *C.D.*, II/1, III/1, III/2, IV/1–4.

42. *B.C.C. Report*, vol. 1, p. 21; cf. Donald Baillie *God Was in Christ: An Essay on Incarnation and Atonement* (London: Faber & Faber, 1956), p. 136 n. 8, for a similar view.

43. *C.D.*, III/2, p. 218.

44. *B.C.C. Report*, vol. 1, p. 21.

45. Rahner, pp. 103ff.

46. Ibid., p. 104 n.25.

47. Ibid., p. 109.

48. Kasper, p. 288.

49. Ibid.

50. Regina Radlbeck, *Der Personbegriff in der Trinitäts theologie der Gegenwart: Untersucht am Beispiel der Entwürfe Jürgen Moltmanns und Walter Kaspers* (Regensberg: Verlag Friedrich Pustet, 1989), pp. 205ff.

51. Ibid., pp. 188–89.

52. Ibid., p. 146; see Kasper, p. 289; cf. the similar views of the Scottish philosopher John Macmurray; Gunton, pp. 90–93.

53. Radlbeck, pp. 179ff., 210–11.

54. Ibid., pp. 202–3.

55. Ibid., pp. 94ff; see Jürgen Moltmann, *The Trinity and the Kingdom of God*, tr. Margaret Kohl (London: S.C.M. Press, 1981), pp. 125ff.

56. Radlbeck, p. 94.

57. Ibid., pp. 210, 95.

58. Ibid.

59. Eberhard Jüngel, *God as the Mystery of the World*, tr. Darrell L. Guder (Edinburgh: T. & T. Clark, 1983), passim. Jürgen Moltmann, *The Crucified God*, tr. R. A. Wilson and John Bowden (London: S. C. M. Press, 1976), pp. 249ff. Kasper, pp. 16ff.

60. E. Jüngel, "'Keine Menschenlosigkeit Gottes': Zur Theologie Karl Barths zwischen Theismus und Atheismus," *Evangelische Theologie*, vol. 31, no. 7, 1971, pp. 376–90. John Thompson, *Christ in Perspective in the Theology of Karl Barth* (Edinburgh: Saint Andrew Press, 1978), pp. 98ff.

61. *C.D.*, IV/1, pp. 480–81.

62. Thompson, p. 106.

63. Jüngel, "'Keine Menschenlosigkeit Gottes,'" p. 378.

64. Ibid., p. 380.

65. Ibid., p. 381.

66. Kasper, *The God of Jesus Christ*, pp. 16ff.; "Is God Obsolete?" *Irish Theological Quarterly*, vol. 55, no. 2, 1989, pp. 85ff.

67. Kasper, "Is God Obsolete," p. 86.

68. Ibid., p. 92.

69. Ibid., p. 93.

70. Ibid., p. 96.

71. Colin Gunton, *Enlightenment and Alienation: An Essay Towards a Trinitarian Theology* (London: Marshall Morgan and Scott, 1985), p. 142.

72. Moltmann, *The Crucified God*, p. 252.

73. Wolfhart Pannenberg, *Systematische Theologie* (Göttingen: Vandenhoeck and Ruprecht, 1988), vol. 1. Cf. Christoph Schwöbel, "Wolfhart Pannenberg," in *The Modern Theologians: An Introduction to Christian Theology in the Twentieth Century*, David Ford, ed. (Oxford: Basil Blackwell, 1989), vol. 1, pp. 248–92.

74. Pannenberg, pp. 121ff.

75. Ibid., pp. 133ff.

76. Ibid., pp. 121–207.

77. William J. Hill, *The Three-Personed God: The Trinity as a Mystery of Salvation* (Washington: Catholic University of America Press, 1982), p. 156.

78. Stanley Grenz, *Reason for Hope: The Systematic Theology of Wolfhart Pannenberg* (New York: Oxford University Press, 1990), pp. 32–33.

79. Pannenberg, pp. 133ff.

80. Ibid., pp. 207ff.

81. Schwöbel offers a similar criticism (p. 287).

82. Grenz, pp. 73–74.

8

Conclusion

In the previous chapter, some of the main issues that are involved in the modern debate on the Trinity were outlined. In this light then what can we say about the being of the triune God? In this concluding chapter, we look at several issues involved in such a reassessment, especially the meaning of unity in Trinity and Trinity in unity. Each issue raises the further question of the validity of the Eastern and Western views, and how far each is right or needs correction. It also leads into ecumenical perspectives. I look first at the unity of the triune God.

Unity in Trinity

Trinity means the reality of one God who is three persons. There are not three Gods somehow joined together, which would be explicit tritheism, nor can one envisage the three persons as "together" making up the Deity. This would reduce the "persons" to partial gods and mean that the Trinity was some kind of mathematical conundrum. Nor can the unity in Trinity be seen as simply a variety of attributes or perfections which constitute the being of God. Rather, the Trinity affirms that while each person is wholly divine both per se and in relation to the others, there is only one God. God's being is a unity in Trinity and not otherwise. This naturally excludes the view that one can begin with a different conception of unity to which the Trinity must in some measure conform. It also indicates that the being of God as one can only be known as mystery in the actions of his grace and salvation in Jesus Christ by the Holy Spirit or, to put it otherwise, in revelation and reconciliation. But if God is the one God as the Father sending the Son by the Holy Spirit, how do these three persons or ways of God's being in action express his unity? That is *the* question. Two main answers have been given but elaborated in various ways. The first favored by the Orthodox East and by many Western theologians today is summarized cryptically as "being in relationship" or "being as communion"[1] or "onto-relational unity."[2] The second traditional Western view sees the persons as inhering in the being of God as the focus of unity.

Being as Communion

This statement implies a certain logical priority given to the persons who are seen not as centers of individual consciousness but as relational. They exist only in relation to each other and as such constitute the Godhead and so are the basis of unity in Trinity. According to the modern Eastern view going back to the Cappadocian Fathers, the being and so the unity of God "was identified with the person."[3] In this view God is not first one being "and then exists as trinity, that is as persons."[4] Rather the unity is in the persons in relationship. To this was added that "among the Greek Fathers, the unity of God, the one God, and the ontological 'principle' or 'cause' of the being and life of God does not consist in the one substance of God but in the *hypostasis*, that is, the *person of the Father*."[5] In other words, the Father is, and indeed must be, the principle of the unity of being in the Trinity. The Son and Spirit receive their divine being from him. Each is therefore fully divine and indwells the others in mutual relationships. Their unity has one principle, the Father, but this expresses itself in ontic relationships, communion, and reciprocity. T. F. Torrance states what he believes Gregory of Nazianzen meant in this regard:

> As he understood them the relations between the divine persons are not just modes of existence but substantial relations which belong intrinsically to what Father, Son and Holy Spirit are in themselves as distinct hypostatic realities as well as in their objective, reciprocal relations with one another. The relations between them are just as substantial as what they are in themselves or by themselves. Thus the Father *is* Father in his indivisible ontic relation to the Son and the Spirit, and the Son and the Spirit *are* what they are as Son and Spirit precisely in their indivisible ontic relations to the Father and to one another.[6]

This comprehensive statement has the advantage of drawing out in a way often omitted what is meant by being in communion or relationship. Torrance believes we have here "a rather more satisfactory view of the triunity of God than that of the other Cappadocians, for the *monarchia* is not limited to one person: it is a unity constituted by and in the trinity."[7] This fine statement goes further than most Easterners (including Zizioulas) do today, for the Father remains the source of the Trinity for them. It also goes further than Moltmann[8] and Pannenberg,[9] whose perspectives are primarily eschatological yet who also favor an Eastern view. That persons in relationship and communion are in a real measure constitutive of the unity and being of the triune God is highly significant for our view of God and of his actions in the economy of salvation. It is this view which, in various forms of expression, is gaining considerable support today.

One must ask, however, if it is not also legitimate to start, as some Western theologians do today, with the baptismal formula in the New Testament.[10] There baptism is in the one name of Father, Son, and Holy Spirit—one God, or, as others put it, God reveals himself as the one God in Christ by the Holy Spirit. Revelation of the one God reveals him as three persons in one.[11] There is a unity here which is not inconsistent with beginning with God as he speaks, acts, and comes and so makes known how and who he is. This does not necessarily posit an underlying essence in which the persons inhere but rather says that the unity of being is given in and with the revelation of the knowledge that he is Father, Son, and Holy Spirit. In this view what is stated is that unity in threeness is the very nature of God. The divine being and the trinitarian persons are one and equally ultimate in God. This beginning with salvation history brings Eastern and Western views closer together at this point.

The Western tradition stemming from Augustine sees the unity more in the essence of God than in the persons. In this tradition the distinctive aspects of the persons were seen as subsistent relations. This was no doubt intended to indicate what the East said more explicitly and concretely; that is, a person is not a bare relation but has personal distinctness in relation to the other persons. Nonetheless, the persons here are given a less prominent ontological, relational character than in the East. However, even within this tradition there are signs today of movement toward a more relational view. E. L. Mascall points out that Jean Galot goes as far as to say that the one being of God can be interpreted as "relational being."[12] In other words, it could be conceived in much the same way as the East, as giving ontological content to the relationships of the persons with one another as divine. It is seen as denoting "being whose status is constituted solely by its relatedness. . . . What distinguishes them is simply their *relations* to one another. . . . Like everything else in God, these relations are not static but dynamic, and not schematic but constitutive."[13] In other words, the unity of the Trinity is basically related to the being in communion of the three persons. The unity of God is thus neither in being nor in persons as such but in the being of God as expressed in the persons who in themselves and in their interrelatedness constitute the divine Trinity.

We can draw all this together by saying that the three persons are ontologically one in their being and relationships and as such constitute the divine unity. Moreover, each shares in the divine being, in the distinctive work of the others, and in these ways also exhibits God's unity. Further, each indwells the others as distinct, divine persons and in this perichoretic way God is one.

It is therefore important not only that we speak of being as communion and of the persons as constitutive of the deity but draw out, as we attempt to do here, some of the other ways in which this unity can be understood.

It is when we look at the persons in these different forms of unity that one has a true glimpse of something of the richness and the fullness of the triune God.

One must also affirm, in opposition to certain views, that the triune God has this fullness of deity in himself. He is not incomplete without the world and its action on him, however related to or involved with history, its sin, contradiction, and life he may be and is. It is good to be reminded of doxology,[14] of our worship and glorification of God, Father, Son, and Holy Spirit, who is one in himself, and of the way each person relates to this and exhibits this glory. It is, however, illegitimate to go on to say that our worship and doxology belong essentially to that glory as factors that contribute to the fullness of the divine being. That would make the world and our response to God an aspect of the very being of God himself which confuses the creator and the creature and both obscures and misrepresents his true unity.

Trinity in Unity

The Persons in Relationship

I now examine several aspects of the persons in relationship. We have indicated the danger of giving too great a priority to the Father. Yet priority there is and must be. In our worship and prayers we come to the Father through Jesus the Son and by the Holy Spirit. God is the Father of our Lord Jesus Christ and so by the Holy Spirit our Father too. Both East and West give priority to the Father but in different ways, the East by seeing him as the source of the deity of the Son and through the Son of the Spirit; the West by seeing the Father with the Son as *principaliter*, the source of the Holy Spirit.

Further, traditional formulas have all rightly seen a *taxis*, or order, in God as Father, Son, and Holy Spirit, one God and not otherwise. This is not speculation but a theological necessity as the consequence of the way God has revealed himself to us. In the immanent being of God, the Father is the ultimate source as unbegotten, the Son is with and comes from the Father by way of generation, and the Spirit proceeds from the Father and the Son (Western view) or through the Son (Eastern view). Yet this is not to be seen as simply a linear form of order. While necessarily retaining this trinitarian order, modern trinitarian perspectives see a greater movement of interrelationships between the persons than many of the traditional formulas. The Father gives being to the Son, but in this the Son is not simply passive; he responds in receiving and accepting in obedience. Likewise Son and Spirit are bound together in mutually receiving from the Father. From a Western perspective, Mascall states well what this means:

> It means that all that distinguishes the Father and the Son from each other is that the Father possesses Godhead paternally and the Son filially, and that

this involves eternal and complete self-giving by the Father and eternal and complete self-response by the Son. It must be emphasised that it is precisely because the self-giving of the Father is complete that it is the begetting of a co-equal Son and not the creation of an inferior creature; and it carries the implication that the glory of the Godhead consists not in an eternal self-possession but in an eternal self-giving.[15]

Yet this reciprocity has its limitations in the very being of God known in the reality of revelation. To go outside these boundaries is to speculate and create all kinds of interrelationships which exceed the possible. This is the temptation in writings like Moltmann's[16] and his followers', who speculatively derive a great variety of reciprocal relationships from an open and free Trinity somewhat loosed from the moorings of Holy Scripture.

These relationships of giving and receiving are not meant to imply any kind of inferiority of the persons of the Son and the Spirit to the Father. There is and must be total equality; this was guaranteed in the patristic era by the success of the *homoousion*, which means that each person is fully divine. At the same time, since Son and Spirit have their source in and come from the Father, owing their being to him, there inevitably arises a form of subordination. Karl Barth points out that there is an "above" and a "below" in God—a subordination that is not subordinationism or any inequality of being in God.[17] It is, he argues, this downward thrust in God, from Father to Son by the Holy Spirit, that is the basis of and makes possible the incarnation and reconciliation. God is seen as no solitary, lonely being but has this fellowship in these relationships in himself. The very nature of these differentiated relationships is, in the freedom and election of God, the basis for his actions *ad extra* and makes possible the creation as well as the redemption of the world.

Traditional theology also spoke of appropriations corresponding in the economy to God's inner relationships. As the Father is the source of the life of the Son, so he gives life to all that is other than himself, that is, to creation. As the Son humbly obeys the Father in heaven it is he who is sent down in humiliation by the Father in the power of the Spirit and accepts this role in obedience. By this he comes and acts in the flesh for our salvation. And as the Spirit proceeds from and is the fellowship of Father and Son, so likewise he is the source of fellowship in the church, in society, and between peoples on earth. At the same time no person in the Trinity acts alone, for that would deny God properly as triune. The Father creates by the Son who is the source, goal, and sustainer of the universe. The Son comes from the Father by the power of the Holy Spirit and is accompanied in his work by the Father and the same Spirit. The Holy Spirit sanctifies and creates communion in concert with the Father and the Son.

A further way in which the distinctions of the persons are described in modern theology is by the term "space." This is not meant to be understood univocally in creaturely terms but indicates those relationships in God which clarify their significance and distinctiveness as persons and at the same time make possible and interpret his relationship to the world. In a novel section on how the Holy Spirit communicates the life of God to us, Barth speaks of his work as mediation and transition.[18] The Spirit mediates to us the love, grace, and salvation of the Son from the Father. This in turn reflects the Holy Spirit's place in the Trinity as One who is the unity and fellowship of Father and Son—indeed of the three in one. But just as there is "space," or "distance," between the grace of Jesus Christ and what the Holy Spirit brings as fellowship, so this reflects "in the first instance distance and confrontation, encounter and partnership . . . in [God] himself."[19] Here Barth is emphasizing primarily the unifying presence of the Holy Spirit in God and in us. This, however, points also to what can be described as distance or space and indicates the clearest possible distinction between the persons of the Trinity. One could not, however, so speak had one not the equally, if not more important basic conception of the unity of the persons in their distinctions. Another way in which this aspect of the relationships of the persons can be stated is by pointing to their "otherness" in their unity. This again is related to the freedom of God in his personal relationships since he is free in himself to have otherness as his own relational being. He is at the same time free to be for us, with us, and in us in the economy of salvation. Thereby he creates space for us to have free relationships with himself by the Holy Spirit and fellowship with one another.[20]

Hans Urs von Balthasar has taken up this view and expounded it, going, if anything, beyond Barth's interpretation. He also speaks of a distance in God in the relations between the persons. It is related dynamically to the self-giving of the persons to one another, or, in O'Hanlon's phrase, it is a "mutual exchange of love."[21] The same writer states, "The selfless love which unites the infinite distance between the persons and the trinity is so real that it can contain within it all inner worldly distances, events and pain."[22] This in no way confuses creator and creation but is the basis and the possibility of God being able to have a world other than himself where pain, suffering, and sin exist but can be dealt with redemptively through the action of the Father and the Son by the Holy Spirit. By a real distinction, otherness, and self-giving love between the persons made known and given to us in Jesus Christ, God can overcome all that opposes him and transform it to his own glory and the creatures' eternal good and salvation. This is seen most particularly and paradoxically in the cross, with its trinitarian presuppositions, background, and content. "These allow us to point at least in the direction of our understanding of the crucified Christ in his obedience as the supreme revelation of God's love in which the positive difference between the Father and the Son takes on such an extreme form without detriment to their unity in the Holy Spirit."[23] It is from this perspective that distance, otherness, self-giving, and mutual love may all be positively and fruitfully integrated into a relational and communal view of the persons of the Trinity which gives us a true revelation of the being of God as well as a living experience of his salvation. God manifests himself in the supreme contradiction of the cross in our sinful humanity and so is known to us as the God of love.

Another aspect to be considered is how one relates each person as distinct to the others as forms of consciousness. As we saw in the last chapter, to allow each person a distinct, individual selfhood or separate center of consciousness as in humans would be tantamount to tritheism. Yet the New Testament language and thought are fairly explicit: while each person shares a common essence or deity, each relates to the others in a way somewhat analogous to human persons. T. F. Torrance pushes this conception to its limit in two ways.[24] In the first place, he believes some form of consciousness should be given to each person distinct from each one's unitary consciousness of deity. He writes,

> The concrete personalization of God's self communication to us in Jesus Christ and in the distinct identity of the Holy Spirit requires us to give *consciousness* some real place in the notion of person as applied to the three persons in God. Not only is the divine consciousness proper to the nature of the one God, common to Father, Son and Holy Spirit alike, but each divine person in virtue of his distinctiveness shares in it differently and appropriately, so that we would have to say that while Father, Son and Holy Spirit constitute one indivisible God they do so as three conscious subjects in mutual love, life and activity. That is to say, *co-inherence* applies fully to the three divine persons as conscious of one another in their distinctive otherness and oneness.[25]

If one must go in this direction with all the paradoxes and dangers implicit in it, it is, I believe, with the proviso that "consciousness" here means something different from that of the one divine being constituted by these three. Torrance goes on to make the more difficult, even dubious, suggestion that we must apply the term "person" to God *simpliciter* as well as to each of the three.[26] This may be accepted in the sense stated that God has in himself "a fullness and communion of personal being" and is at the same time "creatively personalising or person-constituting, in his activity toward us through the Son and in the Spirit."[27] Here as always in trinitarian doctrine language is being strained to the uttermost.

This leads Torrance on to his second argument in favor of some form of consciousness which each person has of the others. He believes a deeper ontology of personal being is required where the "person is free to go outside of himself while remaining in himself in relation to others what he distinctively is. In other words, it helps to build into the basic concept of the person inter-personal relations and making the person an onto-relational concept."[28] This excludes person as meaning an individual, separate center of consciousness apart from the others but rather involves one which is personal only in relationship and communion, which at the same time constitutes and defines the being of God. There can be little doubt that this is a logically paradoxical truth but does conceptually point in the right direction and leads us to contemplate more fully the mystery of the triune God.

Walter Kasper points out that "from the standpoint of the traditional doctrine of the trinity it is clear that the unity of being in God entails unity of consciousness. It is impossible to accept three consciousnesses in God."[29]

This is the Western tradition which Karl Rahner accepts. On the other hand, Bernard Lonergan goes somewhat further and suggests that it is possible to speak of three subjects in God who cannot simply be unconscious either of themselves or of the one consciousness of God. The conclusion from this Kasper states as follows: "We have no choice, then, but to say that in the trinity we are dealing with three subjects who are reciprocally conscious of each other by reason of one and the same consciousness which the three subjects 'possess', each in his own proper way."[30] This means that Father, Son, and Holy Spirit are conscious of one another through their united consciousness and possession of the one divine essence and therein lies the unity of God. This does not go as far as either the Eastern tradition or the statement of Torrance.

Kasper, however, does opt for a view similar to the East and analogous to modern personalism, though he recognizes that all human analogies have their dissimilarity to the divine. He speaks in terms of a dialogical relationship between the persons similar to our human communion with and relation to one another in mutual awareness. He writes, "The divine persons are not less dialogical but infinitely more dialogical than human persons are. The divine persons are not only in dialogue, they *are* dialogue."[31] He writes further, "The Father is a pure self-enunciation and address to the Son as his Word; the Son is a pure hearing and heeding of the Father and therefore pure fulfilment of his mission; the Holy Spirit is pure reception, pure gift. These personal relations are reciprocal but they are not interchangeable."[32] These quotations from Kasper indicate some form of conscious relationships between the persons. They also show a great variety of ways in which the relations between the persons of the Trinity may be spoken of though at the same time affirming the fact that they must be related to the unity and order of the divine life as well as its dynamic and activity. What they are in fact saying is that the persons have a three-way relationship and consciousness—a self-consciousness as divine, a consciousness of the other persons as of one divine being with them, and a consciousness of the others as persons in relation to them. It is this varied yet relational being in community that constitutes God as triune.

The Holy Spirit and the Trinity

Much modern theology of the Trinity, including the Western writings, is highly critical of the neglect of the nature and place of the Holy Spirit in past statements. These criticisms range over a wide area. There is, it is said, scant attention paid to the role of the Spirit in the earthly life of Jesus and a predominance of the role in the *applicatio salutis.* In other words, there is a subordination of pneumatology to Christology or an inadequate view of the relationship of these to each other.[33] In the West the relation of the Spirit to Father and Son is seen as a mutual communion of both, a view which, it is argued, tends to depersonalize the Spirit and make him less than Father and Son.[34] Finally, the West has unilaterally added the *Filioque* to the Nicene creed and given a dubious theological undergirding to this. Much modern writing in both East and West sees itself as seeking to address and correct these "mistakes" and, if possible, provide a better pneumatology, one more theologically valid and more fully integrated with the rest of Christian doctrine. It is hoped that this may provide some advance in ecumenical relations leading to a measure of consensus in trinitarian thought. We look at these objections in turn, particularly the subordination of pneumatology to Christology.

The Spirit and Christology

The hesitancy with regard to the Spirit's person and work rests theologically on the fact that a predominant strain in the New Testament teaching on the Holy Spirit is his self-effacing quality. The Spirit does not speak about himself but about Christ and leads us to the truth as it is in Jesus. Historically, too, the deity of the Spirit came to be expressed fully only after the affirmation of the *homoousion* of the Father and the Son. There is, therefore, some ground for seeing the Spirit as taking a secondary place, as there is also ground for seeing the Spirit serving the person and work of the Son in the divine economy. This in no sense means any inferiority of the Spirit to the Son or the Father since he is of one essence with them.

It is, however, argued that to stress this aspect alone, however true, is one-sided.[35] One must see the Spirit also as the One who is the agent of the Virgin Birth of Jesus and the incarnation, the One who inspires his earthly life, sanctifies him, enables his works and his sacrifice on the cross, and is also the agent with the Father in raising Jesus from the dead. Lukas Vischer states this clearly and cogently and goes on to say that "the Spirit thus appears in the New Testament as he who rests upon Jesus and fills him in his humanity."[36] This is precisely the point that often seems to be forgotten. In the earthly life of Jesus, the Spirit is related to the one Lord Jesus Christ, is given to him, but is given specifically to his humanity. This point is made massively and tellingly by Karl Barth.[37] P. T. Forsyth[38] points out that the Spirit spoken of in the Synoptics and given to Jesus, while given to the whole person, comes in an incomplete situation. One must see the person of Christ as a whole, what Forsyth called "the whole New Testament Christ," and not isolate the first three Gospels from their context in the later New Testament writings and the completed work of Christ. There it is clear that the Holy Spirit is sent from the Father and by the Son to create a new community of people. This is made particularly evident in John's Gospel and in the rest of the New Testament writings, which draw out theologically the deeper, ultimate significance of the person and work of Christ and of the Holy Spirit's role in this as well as their interrelationship. There Jesus Christ is seen as the One who gives and sends the Holy Spirit. In John's Gospel the work of Christ is seen as incomplete until the cross. The Spirit is not yet given, in the full sense, during his earthly life, since Jesus is not yet glorified (John 7:39). This means that he is not yet exalted on the cross and to the Father and indicates that the Synoptic view points forward to this later fulfillment, which is ultimately determinative.

It is therefore dubious exegesis of the New Testament to coordinate and almost equate the coming of the Spirit in fullness on Jesus and the sending of the Spirit at Pentecost by the risen and exalted Christ. Vischer does not seem to see the incongruence of on the one hand stating that the Spirit fills Jesus in his humanity and on the other speaking of "the Spirit-giving being of Jesus" as if the two were simply coordinates.[39] He goes on then on this basis to argue for a reciprocity, mutuality, and interaction between the Son and the Holy Spirit by which one can state that the Spirit in one sense can be spoken of as with the Father the source of the Son. The fact of reciprocity and mutuality may be capable of being argued and demonstrated but scarcely on this basis, since it destroys the order of the Trinity.

Another way in which the same objection is put is by saying that the Spirit is scarcely "more than an appendage of Christ,"[40] the One who applies to us what Christ has done for us and therefore his distinctive personal existence is underplayed. This fact of the Spirit's work is, of course, a reality since he comes from Jesus and gives us the knowledge of his person and work. At the same time this in no way makes the Spirit simply a necessary extra. It is precisely in being the One who unites us with Christ that the Spirit is Lord, that we know his deity and experience him as the power of God in person. There may be, as the B.C.C. Report states, pressure operating in the tradition which prevents it from giving adequate personal weight to the Spirit.[41] This can, however, be corrected by a more adequate statement of the Spirit's activity and person in relation to the Father and the Son.

The inadequate treatment of the Spirit is said to be seen also in ecclesiology.[42] Too close adherence to Christology leads, it is argued, to stress on the past and on the institutional aspects of the church. Even Vatican II is suspect here. Christology, it is said, determines its ecclesiology in the first instance and the Holy Spirit is introduced later to animate the structure. Catholic theologians like Yves Congar argue strongly against this interpretation of what is sometimes called Christomonism and believe that Vatican II does in fact give a relatively balanced view of the relationship between Word and Spirit.[43] It is of course true to say that many people today do suspect institutions and institutional religion. Hence a proper trinitarian pattern, with a prime emphasis on communion, which is par excellence the Spirit's work, can help to redress any imbalance there may be between community and institution. If the action of the Spirit is stressed as equally important with that of the Son, this again would help to give a more coherent, practical, and theologically satisfying trinitarian form to the church. This form, which is primarily a matter of fellowship, cannot and does not, however, exist without institutional aspects, those of ministry, word, and sacraments—the traditional means of grace.

The role of the Spirit in the Trinity is again a subordinate one if he is seen, as in much Western Augustinianism, as simply the mutual relation of

Father and Son.[44] This, it is argued with a considerable degree of truth, has two errors built into it. On the one hand, it conceives the Spirit in bare terms as simply a "relation"; on the other, it tends, as above, to blur the personal distinctive character of the Spirit. It thus puts a question mark opposite the whole Trinity, for how can God be three persons in one and one in three if obscurity reigns in the nature and work of the third person?

This difficulty can be overcome if we look at the economy of salvation and move from there to the immanent Trinity. In the economy the Holy Spirit is the One who brings a community, the church, into being. In this way, he acts as Lord and is known as the personal presence of God with and in us. This view gives a distinct personal existence to the Holy Spirit. As such, he is the One who is the union, communion, and goal of all three persons of the Trinity. Without the Spirit as fully personal and divine, God would be neither God nor triune. This *opus ad extra* of the Spirit mirrors his place, being, and function in the divine life of the Trinity and his personal relationship to the Father and the Son.

The Filioque

The most notable and debated area of disagreement between East and West is the *Filioque*—the statement that the Spirit in the immanent Trinity is from the Father and the Son. This is based on the correspondence between the economic and immanent Trinity and means that since the Spirit in the economy comes from both Father and Son, this is how God is as triune eternally, "antecedently in himself."[45] The *Filioque* is rejected by the East, not only because it is regarded as improper theologically but also because it was not part of the original ecumenical creed, being imposed instead by papal authority, and so is regarded by some as a threat from the West to Eastern autonomy. This latter is more an ecclesiopolitical than a theological issue.

I now set out briefly the differences between East and West as traditionally stated and then go on to see if, in modern trinitarian perspectives, there is any possibility of a closer approximation of the two views than in the past.

The Eastern view affirms the monarchy of the Father (sometimes his sole monarchy, known as monopatrism), which means that he is the source of the deity both of himself and of the Son and the Spirit. The Spirit does not come from Father and Son as one principle but from the Father through the Son. Hence the Son cannot be a second or joint source of the Spirit. On these premises, "the Filioque compromises the individual property of the Father as the unbegotten and only cause within the trinity"; at the same time, "it confuses the individual properties of the persons of the trinity."[46] The Eastern position is that at the economic level the *Filioque* is acceptable, since it "becomes a matter of the truth of God as revealed to us and about our relations with him—a matter of salvation."[47] But is our salvation in God's activity (*energeia ad extra*) not the clue to who he is in himself? And on that basis, is not a view on the *Filioque* in the immanent Trinity possible and even necessary?

There is a danger here of too great a distinction being made between the hiddenness of God in his immanent being and his revealed nature in the economy—a view which goes, incidentally, in exactly the opposite direction from that which Rahner points in seeing economic and immanent Trinity as one and vice versa.

The West followed the Augustinian tradition which, on the basis of Scripture, saw the Spirit as coming from both Father and Son. Augustine added a further, more philosophical reason based on analogy: just as will comes from knowledge or intellect, so the Spirit comes from the Son. For those, like Barth, who reject the latter view, one bases one's doctrine on the biblical revelation. Barth writes, "The reality of God which encounters us in revelation is his reality in all the depth of eternity. . . . In connexion with the specific doctrine of the Holy Spirit this means that he is the Spirit of the Father and the Son not just in his work *ad extra* and upon us but . . . to all eternity."[48] Mascall follows a similar line in arguing that since the Father not only breathes the Spirit but also generates the Son, one cannot isolate the Spirit from the Son but must inevitably include the Son in the Father's action toward and relation to the Spirit.[49] Mascall goes on to suggest an ingenious logical solution that leans toward the Western tradition. Since Son and Spirit both derive their existence from the Father by generation and procession, "this very fact involves a relation between them."[50] But, asks Mascall, may it not be possible to hold that both procession and manifestation "are included in the one procession of the Spirit which the West ascribes without differentiation to 'the Father and the Son'? Does it really make sense to dispute whether there are two acts or two elements in one act?"[51] This looks like a neat way of using logic to argue from the Eastern to the Western *Filioque* or to combine them, but it is not entirely convincing. For the East the dispute does make sense, however, because the "two elements in one act" do query the sole, distinct monarchy of the Father and the subordinate role here ascribed to the equally divine Son. The *Filioque* must be argued on a less logical, more theological basis in revelation.

Critique of the Filioque by Western Theologians

There are several constituents that usually (although not always all together) determine a critique of the Western tradition of the *Filioque* from within its own ranks. They are a Christology from below, which sees the Son as "the prime receiver of the Spirit from the Father,"[52] and a view of eschatology with the glorification of the Father by the Son on the basis of the same Holy Spirit. Hence the Spirit does not come simply from the Father and the Son but is seen as a gift to the Son enabling the mutual union of Father and Son. The Spirit's place with the Father and the Son in the Trinity is not to be seen as in the West, and to a large extent in the East, as relations of origin but by perichoresis, as reciprocally and mutually conditioning one another. These Western theologians make several suggestions for alternative statements. Moltmann, for example, argues that the Spirit proceeds from the Father and receives from the Son. This is in line with the Eastern view which distinguishes between procession from the Father and manifestation through the Son. The Son is not just passive but actively responsive to the Father as the recipient of his love and must therefore in some measure be the agent of the Spirit. Moltmann, however, adds a speculative distinction at this point by speaking of "existence" and "form." He puts forward a formula for consideration as follows: "The Holy Spirit who proceeds from the Father of the Son and receives his 'form' from the Father and the Son."[53] This seems to mean that the being of the Spirit (his divinity) is from the Father alone, whereas his 'person' is from the Father and the Son—a modified view of the *Filioque*. This is dubious theologically and unlikely to gain much acceptance since it introduces a further speculative suggestion as a possible solution. The distinction between existence and form is difficult to maintain. Moltmann's view must be argued on better exegesis of the text and a more adequate Christology. This will not in the end deny mutuality but lead to a more limited application within the parameters of the nature of revelation. Pannenberg's view is more biblically oriented than Moltmann's; indeed he criticizes Moltmann's position as well as those of both East and West.[54] The result of the more speculative views of Moltmann leads to a plethora of possibilities which the limitations of revelation forbid.

If, however, one follows the East and says that the Spirit comes from the Father through the Son, this is regarded by many Westerners as correct as far as it goes, but it does not go far enough. Thomas Smail argues on the basis of the Spirit given to Jesus that he shares in the generation of the Son with the Father and suggests we add to the Eastern statement that the Son is "eternally begotten of the Father *through the Spirit*."[55] But, as I have tried to show, the Spirit given to Jesus pertains in the first instance to his humanity. To transfer this directly to the eternal Son and then say he was begotten of the Father through the Spirit is exegetically problematic and theologically speculative. It moves away, in an unhelpful way, from the main thrust of the biblical revelation and our experience of salvation.

It is my considered opinion and conclusion that the inclusion of the *Filioque* in the original Nicene Creed at a later date was and is undesirable and unnecessary as well as harmful ecumenically. Nonetheless, it expresses the reality of the relationship of the persons in God more adequately than some alternatives and as a theologoumenon should be accepted.

The B.C.C. report reaches a similar conclusion even though, with me, it accepts much Eastern criticism of Western views:

> The [Eastern] teaching that the Spirit proceeds from the Father alone on the immanent level can easily lead to a bypassing of the Son on the economic level and to a Spirit-centred mysticism, to which the person of Christ can

easily become peripheral. This allusion to Barth's defense of the *Filioque* takes us to the strength of the Western position which is that the New Testament does assert a close connection between the Son and the Spirit on the economic level. If, then, the doctrine of the immanent trinity is to be true to Scripture, it is reasonable to conclude that any teaching about the immanent trinity should take due account of the connectedness of Son and Spirit in the economy. The Western position, that is to say, can be taken to serve as a safeguard against speculation about the being of God which is unrelated to the way in which he is made known in Scripture.[56]

This can only be taken as a virtual endorsement of the *Filioque* as a correct interpretation of Scripture but not as absolutely necessary explicitly to include in a creed.

Ecumenical Perspectives

There are several aspects of the Holy Spirit's place in the immanent Trinity where East and West still differ, though the differences focus on the *Filioque*. At the same time, the mutual critique has revealed weaknesses in each view—the West being chiefly and rightly accused of a form of Scholasticism and abstraction, the East failing to connect adequately the immanent and economic aspects of the Trinity. Further, it is not always sufficiently realized that the interpretations of East and West, of necessity, involve a complex variety of aspects because of the nature of the Trinity as a divine mystery and also because these two main traditions start with different presuppositions. It may be true, as La Cugna and McDonnell state, that later interpretations of the Trinity go into a "far country" greatly removed from the worship of the church and the New Testament revelation.[57] Yet in some sense this must always be so, since the Trinity is a matter of great mystery and hence attempts must be devoted to a fuller understanding of its significance. This inevitably requires considerable refinements of thought, conceptuality, and language. It is clearly also equally dubious to seek, as is sometimes done in modern theology, to encapsulate the Trinity in a brief formula like being in relation, however correct this may be, in an attempt to provide a simple basis for a social analogy.

One positive result of modern thought has been the grounding of the Trinity in the economy of salvation, or what T. F. Torrance calls a "rapprochement between the systematic theology of the trinity and biblical teaching."[58] This involves, as so many present-day theologians point out, a centering of the Trinity on the cross and resurrection. Torrance also sees two other areas of ecumenical advance—in an approximation of Latins and Greeks and in a move from a more abstractive or scholastic framework of thought to one more related to piety, worship, and the experience of the church. He also notes that Evangelical and Roman Catholic trinitarian theology draws closer together through Karl Barth's and Karl Rahner's emphasis on God's revelation and self-giving as the root of the doctrine of the Trinity and its place at the forefront of one's doctrine of God. Torrance is particularly appreciative of the fact that, like Lossky[59] and the Eastern-ers, Barth seeks to exclude all philosophical or other bases for the Trinity and to establish it firmly on revelation. He writes, "Karl Barth approached the doctrine of the Holy Trinity entirely on the ground of God's self-rev-elation and self-giving in Christ and in the Holy Spirit interpreted through the *homoousion*."[60] As a result, Barth gave it a primary place in church doc-trine and a determinative role in the structure of the *Church Dogmatics*. To that extent, he "represents a decided departure from the Western theo-logical tradition and a distinct rapprochement to the Eastern theological tradition shaped through the great Greek Fathers."[61] He thus rejected a basis in a distinction between *De Deo Uno* and *De Deo Trino*. Yet it is also clear that Barth takes much from Augustine, including the *Filioque* and the role of the Holy Spirit as a mutual union and communion of Father and Son.

Further, the event character of revelation and the consequent dynamic character of Barth's thought with his linking of the being of the triune God with his action has strong resonance of "Athanasius' discussion of the one activity (mia energeia) of God Father, Son and Holy Spirit intrinsic to his being and of the one being (mia ousia) of God in his saving acts as Father, Son and Holy Spirit."[62] Here Athanasius and Barth are more comprehen-sive than the Cappadocians. Barth's view of the being of God who repeats himself three times—a oneness in threeness and a threeness in oneness—gives a more balanced view than simply beginning with the persons or with the one essence. If the West can rightly be accused of overemphasizing the unity, the East is equally open to the charge of giving priority, logically at any rate, to the threeness.[63] However, each aspect of the mystery of God needs to be thought through and understood together. The triune God is to and from all eternity one in three and three in one—a sharp reminder to both East and West of the richness and fullness of God and the great difficulty of reaching a view that comprehends and includes all aspects.

As I have tried to show, much has happened since Barth's seminal writ-ing helped to bring back the Trinity to the forefront of theological think-ing. The B.C.C. report may be taken as a general summary of much cur-rent thought when it states,

> Ecumenically, we believe the doctrine of the trinity has much to contribute to the process in which the divided churches of Christendom are drawing nearer to one another. The unity of Christians will be achieved as we gather in worship in the communion of the Holy Spirit. Attention to formulations is secondary, but is nonetheless important, partly because it is often formu-lations which have divided us.[64]

While this is true, it is also sobering to realize that considerable agree-ment on the Trinity can and does coexist with varied and often competing views on ecclesiology and ministry. There may be and are many areas of agreement on the Trinity, but these can be used to form a basis for such diverse views as hierarchical structures of ministry as in Orthodoxy and

Roman Catholicism on the one hand and a virtually congregationalist polity on the other. For further ecumenical advance and agreement to take place it must do so in these areas as well and cannot be confined simply to trinitarian doctrines.

Notes

1. John D. Zizioulas, *Being as Communion: Studies in Personhood and the Church* (Crestwood, N.Y.: St Vladimir's Seminary Press, 1985).

2. T. F. Torrance, "Towards an Ecumenical Consensus on the Trinity," *Theologische Zeitschrift*, vol. 31, no. 6, 1975, p. 348.

3. Zizioulas, p. 40.

4 Ibid.

5. Ibid.

6. T. F. Torrance, *The Trinitarian Faith* (Edinburgh: T. & T. Clark, 1988), p. 231. Cf. G. L. Prestige, *God in Patristic Thought* (London: William Heinemann, 1936), pp. 260–61, for a verdict on Gregory Nazianzen similar to that of Torrance.

7. Torrance, *The Trinitarian Faith*, p. 231.

8. Jürgen Moltmann, *The Trinity and the Kingdom of God*, tr. Margaret Kohl (London: S.C.M. Press, 1981), p. 177f.

9. Wolfhart Pannenberg, *Systematische Theologie* (Göttingen: Vanderhoeck and Ruprecht, 1988), vol. 1, p. 326.

10. Walter Kasper, *The God of Jesus Christ*, tr. Matthew J. O'Connell (New York: Crossroad, 1989), pp. 245ff.

11. Karl Barth, *Church Dogmatics*, I/1, pp. 295ff. (herafter cited as *C.D.*).

12. E. L. Mascall, *The Triune God: An Ecumenical Study* (Worthing: Churchman Publishing, 1986), p. 26.

13. Ibid.

14. Moltmann, pp. 151ff.

15. Mascall, p. 18.

16. Jürgen Moltmann, *The Church in the Power of the Spirit*, tr. Margaret Kohl (London: S.C.M. Press, 1977), pp. 50ff.

17. *C.D.*, IV/1, p. 201f.

18. Ibid., IV/2, p. 342.

19. Ibid., pp. 342–43.

20. Ibid., p. 346. Cf. Colin Gunton, *The Promise of Trinitarian Theology* (Edinburgh: T. & T. Clark, 1991) pp. 131–176.

21. Hans Urs von Balthasar, *Theodramatik*, II/1 (Einsiedeln: Johannes Verlag, 1976), pp. 233ff; G. F. O'Hanlon, *The Immutability of God in the Theology of Hans Urs von Balthasar* (London: Cambridge University Press, 1990), p. 55.

22. O'Hanlon, p. 72. This view, which claims to distinguish Creator and creature, could easily be interpreted as leaning toward a form of panentheism.

23. Ibid., p. 139 (p. 131 in the original thesis of the same title).

24. Torrance, "Towards an Ecumenical Consensus on the Trinity," p. 345f.

25. Ibid., p. 347.

26. Ibid.

27. Ibid.

28. Ibid., p. 348.

29. Kasper, pp. 288–89.

30. Ibid., p. 289.

31. Ibid., p. 290.

32. Ibid. Von Balthasar speaks of these as "dramatic acts" and Barth as "history."

33. *The Forgotten Trinity. The Report of the B.C.C. Study Commission on Trinitarian Doctrine Today* (London: British Council of Churches, Inter-Church House, 1989), vol. 1, p. 31 (hereafter cited as *B.C.C. Report*).

34. Ibid., p. 32., Lukas Vischer, ed., *Spirit of God, Spirit of Christ: Ecumenical Reflections on the Filioque Controversy* (London: S.P.C.K., 1981), p. 17.

35. Vischer, p. 8.; Gunton, p. 75.

36. Vischer, p. 8.

37. *C.D.*, I/1, pp. 485–86. Barth points out that to accept a relationship of origin between the Spirit and the Son contradicts the order of the triune God and the perichoresis is not one of origins or a circle of such. Of the more difficult exegetical question, Barth writes, "It is this man Jesus of Nazareth, not the Son of God, who becomes the Son of God by the descent of the Spirit" (p. 485); "What the Son 'owes' to the Spirit in revelation is his being as man" (p. 486).

38. P. T. Forsyth, *The Person and Place of Jesus Christ* (1909: reprint, London: Independent Press, 1946), pp. 123ff.

39. Vischer, p. 9.

40. *B.C.C. Report*, vol. 1, p. 31.

41. Ibid.

42. Ibid., p. 29.

43. Yves Congar, *The Word and the Spirit*, tr. David Smith (London: Geoffrey Chapman, 1986), pp. 113ff., seeks to answer the Orthodox Nikos Nissiotis and Vladimir Lossky, who make the accusation of "Christomonism" against Vatican II, meaning thereby a relative neglect of the Holy Spirit and too great an emphasis on Christ.

44. Gunton, pp. 40ff.

45. *C.D.*, I/1, pp. 384ff.

46. Theodore Stylianopoulos, "The Orthodox Position: Conflicts about the Holy Spirit," in *Concilium*, Hans Küng and Jürgen Moltmann, eds., (Edinburgh: T. & T. Clark, 1979), p. 26.

47. Ibid., p. 29.

48. *C.D.*, I/1, p. 479.

49. Mascall, pp. 66–68.

50. Ibid., p. 66.

51. Ibid., pp. 67–68.

52. Pannenberg, p. 346 n. 184 and contra Barth.

53. Jürgen Moltmann, "Theological Proposals towards the Resolution of the *Flioque* Controversy," in Vischer, *Spirit of God, Spirit of Christ*, p. 169.

54. Pannenberg, p. 346 n.184, where he accuses Moltmann, with the Western tradition, of failing to see that the Son receives the Spirit from the Father and thereby is the medium of the obedience of the Son to the Father. See, however, a critique of this position above.

55. Gunton, p. 169, quotes Thomas Smail, "The Holy Trinity and the Resurrection of Jesus," in *Different Gospels*, Andrew Walker, ed. (London: Hodder and Stoughton, 1988), pp. 76–78.

56. *B.C.C. Report*, vol. 1, pp. 33–34.

57. C. M. La Cugna and K. McDonnell, "Returning from 'The Far Country': Theses for a Contemporary Trinitarian Theology," *Scottish Journal of Theology*, vol. 41, no. 2, 1988, pp. 191–215.

58. Torrance, "Towards an Ecumenical Consensus on the Trinity," p. 337.

59. Vladimir Lossky, "The Procession of the Holy Spirit in Orthodox Trinitarian Doctrine," in *In the Image and Likeness of God*, John H. Erickson and Thomas E. Reid, eds. (Crestwood, N.Y.: St. Vladimir's Seminary Press, 1974), p. 88, takes the extreme view of seeing the *Filioque* as contra revelation and coming from the God of the philosophers and natural theology. He claims his view represents "an understanding open to the full reception of Revelation."

60. Torrance, "Karl Barth and Patristic Theology," in *Theology beyond Christendom*, John Thompson, ed., (Allison Park, Pa: Pickwick Publications, 1986), p. 223.

61. Ibid.

62. Ibid., p. 224.

63. Yves Congar points out that there was and is a tendency to simplify the differences in this way. While true up to a point, taken by themselves they are misleading since other equally important areas of disagreement remain. Nonetheless, he rightly believes that future advance can take place only if both recognize a common community of faith and seek, on that basis, to move toward greater agreement. *I Believe in the Holy Spirit*, vol. 3, *The River of Life Flows in the East and in the West*, tr. David Smith (London: Geoffrey Chapman, 1983), p. xvi.

64. *B.C.C. Report*, vol. 1, p. 43.

Author Index

Abraham, W., 77, 91
Adorno, T., 133
Anselm of Canterbury, 5, 125
Aquinas, T., 5, 17, 28, 64, 133
Arius, 15
Athanasius, 15, 16, 28, 117, 156
Augustine, 5, 6, 28, 110, 126, 128–30,
 133, 139, 144, 153, 156

Baillie, D., 91
Barth, Karl, 1, 3, 4, 6, 7, 8, 9, 13, 14,
 17, 18, 20, 23, 24, 29, 30, 31, 32,
 34, 36–38, 39, 40, 45, 47, 48, 49,
 52–53, 55–57, 58, 59, 60, 61, 63,
 64, 65, 66, 70, 71, 74, 75, 76, 77,
 79, 80, 85–86, 89, 90, 91, 92, 93,
 109–110, 111, 112, 113, 118, 122,
 124, 130, 131, 132, 134–36, 138,
 140, 146, 147, 150, 153, 155, 156,
 157, 158
Basil of Caesarea, 126, 139
Bauckham, R., 33, 34, 42, 50, 62, 64, 65,
 67, 83, 92
Berkhof, H., 41, 90, 92
Berkouwer, G. C., 64
Bernhardt, R., 91
Bøckmann, P. W., 93
Boethius, 132
Boff, L., 107, 108, 120, 121, 122, 123
Breuning, W., 29, 41
Brown, D., 17, 119, 123
Buber, M., 133
Bultmann, R., 16

Calvin, J., 70, 81, 92, 121
Clement of Alexandria, 80
Clement of Rome, 80
Colinge, W. F., 140
Congar, Y., 6, 27, 28, 41, 110, 116, 122,
 125, 126, 139, 151, 158, 159
Courth, F., 11, 18
Cyprian of Carthage, 80

Di Noia, J. L., 28, 41
Dodd, C. H., 96, 104
Dorner, I., 118

Ebner, F., 133

Fedorov, N., 106
Fiddes, P., 45, 63
Ford, D., 69, 89, 104
Forsyth, P. T., 48, 49, 64, 70, 74, 90, 93,
 150, 158

Gregory of Nazianzen, 126, 139, 157
Gregory of Nyssa, 126, 139
Grenz, S., 137, 141
Grillmeier, A., 64
Gruntvig, N., 106
Gunton, C., 1, 9, 10, 17, 18, 68, 89, 112,
 113, 117, 122, 123, 129, 130, 136,
 139, 140, 141, 152, 158

Hanson, A. T., 6, 12, 13, 18, 19
Hanson, R. P. C., vi, 7, 15, 16, 17, 18,
 124, 139

Subject Index

Analogy, 38, 57, 61, 65, 68, 78, 84, 109
  analogia entis, 113
  analogia fidei, 113
  analogia relationis, 113
Anthropology, 23, 111–14. *See also* Society
Apatheia (*patripassians*), 54, 56, 58, 61, 62
  passio Dei, 62
  pathos, 62
Apocalyptic writings, 34
Arianism, 34, 70, 118
Atheism, 124, 134, 135, 136. *See also* Modern thought
Atonement. *See* Reconciliation

Baptism, 144

Capitalism, 107
Catholic theology, 21, 26
Christology, 34, 60, 81, 84, 85, 120
  christological concentration, 74
  Christomonism, 151, 158
Church
  being and community, 9, 80, 85–86, 92, 108
  and the churches, 87–88
  community and institution. *See* Church: being and community; Trinity
  ecumenical, 29–30, 76, 85, 88–90, 109, 142, 155–57
  ministry and episcopacy, 81–82, 85
  Orthodox perspectives
    community and hierarchy, 83–85
    Spirit Christology, 83–85

Roman Catholic perspectives
  apostolic succession, 86–87
  ecclesial communities, 86–87
  hierarchy, 86–87
  irreformable dogma, 86–87
  Lumen Gentium, 86–87
  Petrine authority, 86–87
  Vatican II, 86–87
  unity, 73, 76, 80, 88–89
Corpus Christianum, 68
Cosmos, 70, 71, 73
Creation, 2, 32, 62, 69, 70, 71, 76, 79, 99, 115–16, 121
  and suffering, 62

Denominations, 76

Election, 55, 109
Enlightenment, 4, 10, 124, 131, 135, 136
Evangelical, 77, 89

Feminism, 3, 114–17
  Holy Spirit as mother, 116–17
  Jesus as brother, 116–17

Glory, 33, 34, 35, 48, 53, 71, 72, 79, 101–4, 145. *See also* Worship: doxology
God
  "becoming" in God, 32–34
  as creator, 21
  change in, 61
  death of, 59
  dialectical-dialogical, 115, 149

163